AMERICAN CONSERVATIVE

AMERICAN CONSERVATIVE

RECLAIMING CONSERVATISM FROM THE RIGHT

AUGUSTUS P. LOWELL

Algora Publishing
New York

Library of Congress Cataloging-in-Publication Data —

Names: Lowell, Augustus P., 1961- author.
Title: American conservative: reclaiming conservatism from the right /
    Augustus P. Lowell.
Description: New York: Algora Publishing, 2016. | Includes bibliographical
    references and index.
Identifiers: LCCN 2016032023 (print) | LCCN 2016033044 (ebook) | ISBN
    9781628942439 (soft cover: alk. paper) | ISBN 9781628942446 (hard cover:
    alk. paper) | ISBN 9781628942453 (pdf)
Subjects: LCSH: Conservatism—United States. | Right and left (Political
    science)—United States.
Classification: LCC JC573.2.U6 L68 2016 (print) | LCC JC573.2.U6 (ebook) |
    DDC 320.520973—dc23
LC record available at https://lccn.loc.gov/2016032023

Author's photo, back cover: Courtesy of Allison Beuker Photography

Printed in the United States

For Lisa (my) Love

who endured all of this as rants before ever having to read (and edit) it as a tract,

and

For Robert Kalman

who gave me some of my first real lessons in how to observe the world around me, in how to think, and in how to write; and who nudged me into the educational pathways that led me here, pathways that might, otherwise, have been beyond the bounds of my small town imagination.

Table of Contents

Preface

Decades ago, a gay friend of mine remarked, upon observing some self-proclaimed spokesman for the "gay community" and "gay issues" — a spokesman who embodied many of the classic stereotypical characteristics of male homosexuality, including a flamboyance bordering on exhibitionism and a libertine view of sexual propriety — that he really despised such "pansies" and wished they would just shut up; that "they make the rest of us look bad!" His bitter rebuke of someone "like him," of someone ostensibly working to further his interest, was both unexpected and enlightening. We are all familiar with the old prayer that we be granted the wisdom to see ourselves as others see us, but few actually manage to achieve such a state of Grace.

I've often thought, in the years since, that much of what appears as anti-gay bias in modern American society is not as much about *homo*sexuality as it is about *public* sexuality, coupled to a more general and radical disrespect for all social convention, sexual or otherwise. Although in recent years it has changed for the better, and the better to reflect the reality represented by those like my friend, the pervasive public image of homosexuality historically projected by such "spokesmen" was more akin to Hugh Hefner than to Hugh Grant. And if, in that context, we were uncomfortable offering homosexuals a place in polite society it was, perhaps, for the same reason that we would be uncomfortable offering a place in polite society to *Playboy* centerfold models.

The problem, for my friend and for the rest of us, is that the prevailing American model for conversations about cultural or political ideas presumes each of us is defined by some sort of monolithic cultural and political identity, an identity assigned primarily based on what group we belong to and represented to others by a self-selected coterie of advocates and spokesmen who agitate on its behalf.

And it demands that our perception of what group we belong to derive from a peculiarly narrow and similarly monolithic hierarchy of interests in skin color, sexual orientation, ethnicity, gender, and economic class. My friend is gay, so he must agree with whatever some "gay advocate" says, no matter how nonsensical, and be comfortable with the way some "gay spokesman" behaves, no matter how disagreeable. Thomas Frank famously lamented, "What's the matter with Kansas?" based on a presumption that the people of Kansas, being disproportionately poorer than the rest of the country, must ipso facto have a compelling interest in a government that gives them things. The only explanation Frank could think of for why they would vote against such a government is bamboozlement: what other interest could possibly trump that raw and immediate economic one?

Unless, of course, they were gay Kansans, or Latino Kansans, or African American Kansans who must, by definition, be less interested in economics than in sexuality or in ethnic heritage or in skin color.

In pondering the general tenor and particular content of political debate over the last ten or fifteen years, and in trying to decide what to do with my vote in the most recent elections, I realized that the way my friend felt about those self-proclaimed gay spokesmen is precisely the way I feel about so-called conservative ones: *I wish they would just shut up. They make the rest of us look bad!*

For many of the cultural leaders and analysts and politicians who would hold themselves up as the very embodiment of modern American conservatism have, in reality, become caricatures of the worst stereotypes of conservative excess:

- They have replaced the traditional conservative defense of social and cultural stability as intrinsic social goods with a dogmatic exaltation of one particular cultural (and religious) paradigm; and, in their narrow-mindedness and stridency, they transform a reasonable and healthy defense of western culture and tradition into theocracy and xenophobia.
- They have made the *ideal* of small and unobtrusive government an end unto itself rather than a precaution in defense of liberty and against inefficiency and corruption; and, conversely, they have abandoned entirely the *practice* of small and unobtrusive government both to advance their own social vision and to purchase the votes required for that project.
- They have invoked the principle of *laissez faire* to excuse a general degeneration in both ethics and accountability, while in the name

of "capitalism" they have appropriated the political process to the benefit of their most supportive constituents.

- They invoke patriotism both casually and inaptly until the distinction between patriotism and blind, obedient nationalism begins to blur.
- They have transformed a prudent and principled resistance to the use of political power as an instrument of social and economic leveling into a doctrinaire policy of social and economic Darwinism; and in the process they have undermined indispensable traditions of civic responsibility and personal charity.

Further, they compound those policy foibles with character traits anathematic to governance: hubris, hypocrisy, a close-minded anti-intellectualism and rigidity, political cowardice, incompetence, and corruption.

And, worst, they have strayed so far from the roots of conservatism that they now occupy the traditionally leftist territory of self-righteousness and self-justification, convinced that their master plan for the world is so indisputably correct and so manifestly beneficial that they have a moral duty to impose it on the rest of us — and a duty, therefore, to maintain, at all costs and by any means, the grip on power that makes that imposition possible.

Yet, my alienation from these "conservatives" does not imply an attendant alienation from *conservatism* and implies even less a reflexive embrace of American liberalism in its modern guise. Despite conclusions the arbiters of public opinion draw from the last few election results and from the current state of the Union, rejecting this dismal cohort of modern "conservatives" does not lead inexorably to an impetuous amity with a similarly dismal — and, perhaps, similarly unrepresentative — cohort of modern "liberals" and their paradoxical penchants for communalism, paternalism, authoritarianism, ethnic and gender and economic balkanization, social anarchy, moral and cultural relativism, elitist egalitarianism, credulous pacifism, autotelic diplomacy, environmental spiritualism, spoils-to-the-victor populism, Marxist economics, self-congratulatory claims to singular compassion and decency; and their reflexive antipathy toward the cultural and political legacies of the Enlightenment, toward economic liberty, toward individual striving, reward, and responsibility, toward American institutions and the American nation, and toward any cooperative endeavor not "guided" by the coercive hand of government.

Where, then, does that leave me or anyone who, like me, fancies themselves conservative in an era when conservatism is in disrepute?

It leaves us constantly telling people, "That's not me!" and then trying to explain why. It leaves us constantly frustrated that genuine conservative ideas are no longer recognizable within the shallow and insular nonsense that has become the popular language of "conservatism."

That is the root and the purpose of this book: to recognize and, hopefully, to promote the genuine and foundational ideas of American conservatism; to separate them from superficial and goal-oriented claims to conservative principle that have more to do with a particular and narrow cultural or economic or political agenda than with traditional conservative philosophies.

If someone were to ask me why I wrote this, I would say I hope to start a conversation between those on the right and those on the left about what they might have in common. If someone were to ask me who I wrote it for, I would say for those who read only the *New York Times* and for those who read only the *Wall Street Journal*, for those who read only the *Atlantic* and those who read only the *National Review* — for people who are intelligent and thoughtful, who honestly try to inform themselves and to think deeply about things, who are generally fair and tolerant and caring — and yet who can be, at times, closed-minded, parochial, and condescending toward those who don't believe everything they believe and want everything they want.

And, if someone were to ask me what I hope for from having written this, I would say I hope to open a few closed minds on the right and on the left so they could talk to each other without bitterness, as peers rather than as adversaries.

To that end, my primary goal is education, not persuasion. I would, naturally, be pleased if I convinced a few people to change their minds, convinced a few liberals (and even a few conservatives) that these conservative principles form a better basis for a political philosophy than whatever it is they believed before. But my aim is narrower: to induce reflexive conservatives to think about, rather than merely to feel, what they believe — and, as important, what they do *not* believe — and why; and to persuade skeptical liberals that conservatism is not a mere muddle of crackpot beliefs shouted by narrow-minded bigots but a reasoned, reasonable, coherent and, most importantly, legitimate way of understanding political society.

My intent in writing this book was to discuss conservatism as it is understood and practiced now, in modern America, not conservatism around the world or as a broad historical movement. That doesn't mean I've presented some idiosyncratic view of conservatism completely disconnected from its historical antecedents or its philosophical roots. It merely means that I'm more interested in describing what we've ended up with than in describing how we got here.

I've provided some footnotes in the text to point you to a variety of primary sources for conservative philosophies, should you find your curiosity piqued, and all the principles and assumptions I discuss, and the arguments I make on their behalf, have their roots either in those or in related works. And I've tried to do justice to those arguments, to put American conservatism into an intellectual context if not into a historical and genealogical one. But I've chosen not to encumber the text — and myself — with trying to create a map of the evolution of conservative thought. Although all my arguments are derived from earlier work, I don't argue from authority by pointing to that earlier work as a justification for their validity. The risk I've taken by choosing that approach is that the arguments I present must stand or fall on their own merits, without the supporting crutch of some intellectual or historical pedigree. It is my goal, therefore — and my burden and my conceit — to convince you to take them seriously because they make sense, not because they have been crafted and blessed by eminent scholars of the past.

Although the ideal might be to describe conservative principles and policies on their own terms, without reference to a particular political context or to alternative principles and policies, in practice conservatism is so much a reaction to liberalism, and therefore so specific to the political context in which it operates, that a description without such references would often be too abstract to be useful. Hence, the text also includes various depictions of modern 'liberalism' and of modern 'liberals.' In that regard, the view of liberalism I present is similarly narrow and focused on contemporary practice, the 'liberalism' of Barack Obama and of MoveOn.org and of the Occupy movement, not necessarily the liberalism of John Stuart Mill.

I freely acknowledge that my characterizations of liberalism and conservatism will, in many ways, differ from what you would read if you looked up "liberalism" and "conservatism" in the encyclopedia. I contend that is because a preponderance of self-described liberals and self-described conservatives in America don't seem to have read those articles; and that those articles tend to be heavy on the philosophical history and intellectual genealogy of the liberal and conservative movements generally but not much interested in what's become of them recently and in the specific American context; and, perhaps most pertinent, that the American electoral system, which awards exclusive control of the executive branch to the winner of the last election, regardless of how narrow the margin of victory, almost demands that various interrelated but divergent political and philosophical movements, which might remain distinct and individually identifiable in some other places, here subsume themselves under the monolithic marques of 'liberalism' and 'conservatism' in order to build and sustain the coalitions-of-interest that define our two dominant political parties as they strive for electoral majorities. Contemporary American 'liberalism' and 'conservatism' are thus both narrower and broader than the philosophical traditions from which they derive their labels.

Using examples of modern liberalism as a contrast to conservatism presents its own problems: I have not attempted to — nor am I particularly qualified to — define what modern 'liberalism' is in any detail, and a resort to descriptions of 'liberal' policy and principle must, therefore, be ad hoc and open to criticism. If someone else were to write a volume, similar to this one, outlining modern 'liberal' principles and assumptions, I would welcome it and read it eagerly and, perhaps, update my depictions of what 'liberalism' is and says accordingly.

In the meantime, although I may describe 'liberal' policies and/or expressions of principle, I make no claim to portraying accurately either liberalism as a whole or the place those policies and principles may or may not occupy within a broad liberal ideological and philosophical framework. I claim only to convey a legitimate conservative understanding of particular policies and principles advanced by some significant and vocal subset of contemporary Americans who, accurately or inaccurately, wrap themselves in the banner of "liberalism."

This is not an academic work. It does not adhere to academic standards of attribution and bibliography, and it was my intent, though perhaps not my achievement, to write it in plain and straightforward language accessible to the non-academic reader. Parts of it are pedantic because they are trying to render a chain of logical argument, rather than merely presenting disconnected pieces of a puzzle or a personal narrative, but I have tried to avoid the impersonal and formalized academic tone that those kinds of arguments sometimes encourage. There are places where things get a bit abstract and I, as the author, disappear; but, in general, I have tried to make this at least partly a personal journey.

It is, I suppose, a polemic inasmuch as it strives to overturn the conventional contemporary assumptions about what conservatism is. It arose from years of reading and thinking about politics and about philosophy and about human nature, both on my own and in (sometimes vehement) conversation with others.

At this point I could not honestly tell you where all the pieces and arguments came from. My explorations were always a personal attempt to understand the way things work and the way people and institutions behave. They were never a research project and were never conducted as such. I took no notes. I have no record and no reliable memory of which ideas I read in textbooks or in political tomes or in newspaper and magazine commentary or in novels or in grocery lists and repair bills (never mind in which particular place and time), which ones were handed to me by my conversational partners and which ones may be truly my own inspiration. I don't remember which came to me fully-formed and which ones are my own expansions or generalizations or leaps of imagination.

I have tried to add some smattering of footnotes for curious people to follow or to show that some claim I make actually has a factual basis, but these were in the nature of post-hoc research, matching source materials to things I knew I had seen somewhere and had already written down. I have certainly not been rigorous or thorough about it.

For all I know some of this may, indeed, be novel. There may be insights that I am bringing to the world for the first time. But I tend to doubt it and I have neither the time nor the resources to track down, in hindsight, where each idea may or may not have come from and, from that, to identify what may or may not be new.

In short, I make no claims that anything here is of my own invention, no claim that I am doing anything more than collecting and summarizing the work of others.

I will, however, take credit (or blame) for the way the material is organized and the way the ideas are stated. Though I did, occasionally, check a fact or refresh my memory with a little bit of contemporary research, I had no books in front of me as I wrote this from which to copy phrases or structure. I willingly accept responsibility for the faults in the text; I would also appreciate acclaim for what, if anything, I did well.

I would also like to acknowledge that what I did well is due, in large measure, to the few trial readers who, though they may not agree with me, nonetheless, plowed through the first drafts and gave me constructive criticism. Thank you, then, in no particular order, to Paul Kahn, Brian Wilfley, Joanna Ellis-Monaghan, Lige Gould, Austin Lowell, and especially to Lisa Taylor, who both read and edited it — multiple times.

Augustus P. Lowell
August 2016

What Is A "Conservative"?

An article some time ago by Noemie Emery in *The Weekly Standard* disputed what she called "a cartoonish view of Republicans" promulgated by the Democratic establishment to help them win elections. Recent campaigns for the Democratic presidential nominations, for the Presidency itself, for the most recent Congresses, and for a wide range of state and local offices, have reinforced her premise — with, to be fair, some significant assistance from a vocal subset of Republicans who have behaved in particularly cartoonish ways.

The article itself was primarily a rebuttal of the perennial charge — accentuated at the time by the political assisted suicide of Trent Lott, later by fears of a "Bradley Effect" that would overwhelm Barack Obama's candidacy, and currently by presumptions about what motivates the "Tea Party" movement — that Republicans and, by extension, all conservatives are latent racists. But the broader point, that American conservatism is often portrayed by its opponents, by the major media, and even by its own advocates as a caricature of itself, has resonance for many conservatives who are tired of having to defend their beliefs primarily by reference to what they are not.

In political contests we expect opponents to try to define each other to the electorate in unflattering terms. Both Republicans and Democrats indulge that expectation beyond the borders of honesty. Thus, supporters of an economic safety net are "socialists," while those concerned about excesses and pathologies of the welfare state (including the ballooning federal debt) are cold-hearted villains who want to "turn children out into the street." Those who question the wisdom and justice of the excesses of affirmative action are "racists," while those who want to level the field for victims of discrimination favor a "racial spoils system." Those who think conserving the ecosphere has a value on a par with economic development are "Luddites," while those who think both benefits and costs should be considered when evaluating ecological regulation want to "lay waste to the planet." And on and on and on.

But we hope these excesses are transparent to most people. We hope that the debate turns on substance more than on hyperbole, and we expect institutions ostensibly concerned with truth rather than with power — journalism and academia in particular — to assist in achieving that transparency.

Alas, it rarely happens that way. It is fairly clear that the Academy, or at least the part of it from which the vast majority of our political and cultural leaders emerge, is populated largely by people, both professors and students, with an antagonism to conservatism even if they cannot articulate with any concision what conservatism is. And, although I do not care to wallow in the quagmire of debate over whether the media has a liberal or conservative bias, I can say, from my own observations, that the image of conservatism which emerges from long-term exposure to the media — and the one that emerges from long-term exposure to bits and pieces of the electorate informed by the media in places and settings as diverse as rural New Hampshire, Boston, coastal Florida, the San Francisco Bay area, on a college campus and in the community of a college town, within a military organization, at a Fortune 500 corporation, at an entrepreneurial startup, within various theatrical arts organizations, and among the congregation at a self-defined "open and affirming" church — is not one I recognize as either legitimate or helpful.

It is unfair and unfortunate, but true — and I credit my 17 year old son for pointing out to me what should have been obvious but was not — that, regardless of their core missions and stated goals, social and political movements are almost always branded by their most vocal and outrageous supporters. Thus, feminism is defined by its misandrist fringe; the civil rights movement was, for some time, tainted by the Black Panthers; Marxists who rally on behalf of social justice bind the ideal of social justice to socialism.

And, thus, in San Francisco 'conservative' means Jerry Falwell and Pat Robertson and John Hagee and the Mormon Church raging against homosexuality. In New York it is Newt Gingrich and Mitt Romney and Paul Ryan and a callous disregard for the poor. In Hollywood it is John Ashcroft and a new Puritanism. In academia it is Ronald Reagan and George W. Bush and an *aw-shucks* anti-intellectualism and incuriosity. In Europe it is Bush/Cheney/Rumsfeld and Imperial American hegemony. To the NAACP it is David Duke and the Klan and the silent racism of "red America." To the ACLU it is the NSA and Gitmo and the new American SS. To NARAL it is Ralph Reed and Rick Santorum and the Catholic Church and the campaign to outlaw both abortion and contraception. To the Sierra Club it is Exxon and BP, global warming, and the rape of the wilderness. To Gloria Steinem it is Todd Akin and the "war on women," chauvinism and the return of the 50's housewife. To Michael Moore it is conspiracy and power-lust and subjugation by the corporate aristocracy. To Al Franken it is Rush and his Dittoheads, a carnival of mindless conspiracy theories, anti-intellectual affirmations, boorish cynicism, and self-righteous puffery. To Ralph Nader and "the 99%" it is amoral greed, the rich against the rest of us. To my father-in-law, and to many honest and socially-conscious people like him, it is an underlying spirit of "meanness" that tarnishes any positives they might otherwise see.

And, of course, just as the American left includes a share of its own brand of radicals — its Marxists and eco-terrorists and anarchists and ethnic-separatists and misandrists and libertines and thought-police and public nannies and indiscriminate pacifists and naïve romantics and other nightmares of the right — so, too, all of those liberal nightmares, albeit exaggerated to the point of absurdity, *are* aspects of the broad face of an American 'conservatism.' That has been the nature of American politics over the last fifty years: both 'liberals' and 'conservatives' have created, and at some points regretted, awkward coalitions of convenience in their drives to wrest the agenda, and the control of the political process, from "them."

The question I want to ask is, "What lies behind that face?" Are these examples the core of American 'conservatism' or are they its fringe, its most extreme and antagonistic manifestations? Do they represent the intellectual heart of American 'conservatism' or its emotional and populist periphery? Do they represent the majority of American 'conservatives' or merely a collection of excessively vocal, and perhaps excessively powerful, minorities? And, if they are neither the core nor the heart nor the majority, what is the proper face of American 'conservatism' and how do we bring it into view?

For political reasons, the Democratic Party would like us to believe that's all there is and most 'liberal' stalwarts seem honestly to believe it. From the vehemence and extremity of 'liberal' opposition to the second Bush administration, even before it took office, it seems clear they always viewed the most recent 'conservative' President less as a human political opponent, representing a legitimate point of view, than as a ghoulish totem of every vile and frightening thing they have ever suspected about "the right."

I would argue the opposite is true. I would contend their view is of an ugly and exaggerated veneer on honest conservatism created by the dysfunction of the electoral process.

But that view (and the reciprocal view of Al Gore, John Kerry, Bill and Hillary Clinton, and Barack Obama on the part of 'conservatives') is reinforced by an arrogance in the self-proclaimed leaders both of 'conservatism' and of 'liberalism' — born of what Thomas Sowell called the "vision of the Anointed" — a conviction that their opponents do not merely differ in their judgment about what is practical, do not merely disagree in their perception of what is valuable, but are instead morally deficient and undeserving even of consideration. The distorting lens of that arrogance magnifies the fringes and diminishes the center.

But, if the perception of 'conservatism' by the 'liberal' stalwarts is distorted and exaggerated, what is the reality? If honest conservatives dispute the caricature of 'conservatism' that is portrayed, how would they portray it differently, not as a dry academic theme and not as a shallow campaign manifesto, but as a living political movement with philosophical consistency, enduring consequences, and immediate relevance to people's lives and electoral choices?

Conservatism in Theory

Conservatism and Liberalism

On its face conservatism is — conservative. That is, the term is deliberately descriptive, depicting an inclination to conserve what already exists and a reciprocal aversion to change. As such, the label "conservatism" is situational and describes policy rather than ideology: recall that in the waning days of the Cold War (and even now) the conservatives of the Soviet Union were the old guard of the communist party, a group that good American conservatives despised and vilified; and the original European conservatism was rooted in the defense of monarchy, class privilege, and religious authority, a thread of conservatism that died in America with the rebellion against English rule.

Conservatism is, by definition rather than merely by practice, in opposition to "liberalism" — the equally situational label for an antagonism toward stability, the propensity to throw over what exists in favor of something new. In that sense, conservatism is not only situational but "reactionary" in the most fundamental sense: conservatism is a reaction to liberalism and would not need to exist without it. With no particular impetus for change, there is no particular need to resist change.

Notwithstanding the pejoratives of modern political rhetoric, and one's personal biases about the suitability of "what exists" aside, that definition either of conservatism or of liberalism implies no moral or intellectual judgment. We may portray conservatism heroically as the defense of venerated and time-tested philosophy, culture, and tradition, an effort many American 'liberals' view as noble when practiced by ethnic minorities or recent immigrants within our society who resist assimilation. Or, we may portray conservatism critically as the defense of the status quo, which many American 'conservatives' view as noxious when practiced by those who resist any reform of longstanding welfare or affirmative action or environmental policies, or who view "stability" as the properly fundamental goal of foreign policy.

And, although the terms "liberal" and "progressive" are often treated as effectively synonymous in the western democracies, and particularly in America, that assertion of equivalence is mere presumption bordering on hubris. Even if "what exists" is disagreeable, a particular change may not lead, necessarily, to progress. It may merely make things equally disagreeable, or more so, in a different way. "Different" is not a synonym for "better," and "change" is not a synonym for "progress."

If we grant the progressives' conceit that their agenda represents "progress," then, to the extent that standing still precludes that progress, a progressive must be, to some degree, liberal. But not all change, and not all liberalism, is progressive. Standing still also prevents both regress and digress, along with an impetuous ramble entirely off the path into uncharted and perilous wilderness. And, even if you want to move rather than to stand, moving sedately and with caution allows you, at the very least, to examine the path for pitfalls instead of stepping blindly into them. Thus, conservatism can and should stand as a defense against regressive or misguided or reckless liberalism.

All of which provides some clarity but not much insight. It allows us to identify definitionally conservative or liberal policy positions on any particular issue, but it gives us no understanding of the philosophical differences between them and no basis, aside from personal desire, for choosing one over the other. Further, since most people who identify themselves as 'conservative' or as 'liberal' are motivated by some ideology beyond a simple opinion about change, per se, it is not, in practice, always even useful for distinguishing 'conservative' policies from 'liberal' ones. Both 'conservatives' and 'liberals' tend to be inconsistent about that: modern 'conservatives' are frequently not altogether conservative and modern 'liberals' are, all too often, remarkably illiberal.

We might take comfort in attributing such inconsistency to simple and correctible fuzzy thinking, and that certainly exists. Most people, 'conservative' or 'liberal' or otherwise, absorb political philosophies haphazardly from their environments and experiences more than they study them as intellectual systems. Dad grumbles about taxes. Mom volunteers at the food bank. Or, perhaps, it's the other way around. The mayor manages to keep potholes repaired, or he doesn't. The police catch the burglar that stole your stereo; or they hassle you and your friends while you hang out on the corner. Your social studies teacher tells you about social injustice. Your history teacher tells you about social disorder. You are poor, but you see other poor people work their way out of poverty. Or you don't. The cool people on TV support this candidate. The rich people in suits support that one. That candidate is young and handsome. This one is old and grumpy. Your peers make fun of you if you dislike what they like; or they make fun of you if you like something they think is odd or out of fashion. And all those things make you feel good or make you feel bad, make you feel helpless or make you feel inspired. Political preferences are as much the result of instinct or of feeling or of desire, or of indoctrination and habituation and peer pressure and tradition — with all the inconsistencies such unconscious conditioning entails — as of rational thought. Your gut does not urge you to be consistent. It urges you to be comfortable.

But even the truly thoughtful often seem inconsistent, so there must be something more to it than that.

In part, inconsistency arises from the fact that both 'conservatism' and 'liberalism' are, at times and as practiced, indistinguishable from self-interest. People who are doing well with things the way they are, or who are simply terrified of change, tend to want to keep them that way. People who are doing poorly with things the way they are, or who simply revel in innovation, tend to want to modify them or overthrow them.

Further, people are inclined to follow the most comfortable path in the face of ambiguity and much, in life and in society and in politics, is ambiguous. Even honest and rational appraisals of policy choices become entangled with biases when, as is generally the case, they depend on predictions and judgments rather than on observations and measurable facts. Prediction and judgment are necessarily subjective.

Both the ideological and the pragmatic fall prey to that subjectivity. In a perfect world morals and truth would trump desire, but the world is not perfect and neither are we. Did he vote against that regulation because he felt it would be counterproductive or because some company donated to his campaign? Did they donate to his campaign in order to bribe him or because they knew he already agreed with them and his opponent didn't? Does she really believe a budget increase will make the schools better or is she remembering the call bank the teacher's union staffed for her during the last election? And does the union really believe its own rhetoric when it proclaims it is advocating pay increases for teachers in order to improve things "for the children"? Would your position on school vouchers be different depending on whether your neighborhood schools were exceptional or appalling, or on whether you could or could not afford private schools for your own children? Does your view on what powers the government should wield vary depending on which party won the last election?

Whenever we assess motivation, there is room for suspicion that a particular choice fulfills desire rather than honor. When it fulfills both we can never know for sure — the one choosing may not even know for sure — which one was most important to the choice. And the fact that the contention between desire and honor is idiosyncratic, that it will play out differently for different people on different issues and at different times under different circumstances, only complicates things.

But, more fundamentally, inconsistency arises precisely because it is rare for any society to fully embody one complete and self-consistent ideological program or to be completely and consistently beneficial or detrimental to any person or group. To a 'pure' conservative or liberal, motivated strictly by a perception of the desirability of stability or change for its own sake, that would be irrelevant. To anyone else, motivated by some impenetrable muddle of principle and self-interest — that is, to most of us — "what is" will always be some jumble of good things and of bad things, of things we like and support and of other things we dislike and reject. Thus, most people will be, strictly speaking, neither liberal nor conservative but some amalgam of both. They will be issue-specific liberals or conservatives.

What, then, is a 'conservative'? And, in particular, what is an American 'conservative' (or, for that matter, an American 'liberal') a decade into the 21st century?

We must remember that almost all modern American political thought, both liberal and conservative, evolved from an original tradition that was, in its own context, liberal, a "classical liberalism" that represented a reaction to and a rejection of the old monarchical, aristocratic, and religious hierarchies of Europe. Our founding fathers were radicals, by contemporary European standards, and their radicalism became the foundational philosophy for our form of government and for our political culture.

Given their common genesis it should, perhaps, not be a complete surprise that American conservatism and American liberalism sometimes overlap or that American conservatives and American liberals sometimes contradict our ideological expectations. Historically, they are close cousins and share a common core of principles. Where, then, have they diverged?

Arguably, they diverged as American 'liberalism' imported evolving ideas and ideals about egalitarianism and "social conscience" and pluralism and communalism from various 19th and 20th century political philosophers and economists; while American 'conservatism' remained skeptical of such innovations in political and social thought, hewing more closely to the original liberal philosophy that emphasized individual autonomy while, simultaneously and perhaps inconsistently, calcifying around a variety of distinctly American cultural and religious norms.

As a practical matter, a 'conservative' might simply be someone who believes that, on the whole, "what is" is more positive than negative, that more of our culture and of our society and our government is worth preserving than is in need of improvement. That suggests a crude gradation in the measure of 'conservatism': the more one likes and defends, the more 'conservative' one may be; and a 'moderate conservative' (or a 'moderate liberal') finds both much that they wish to keep and much that they wish to change.

That depiction of 'conservatism' certainly fits with a general theme in recent political debate that conservatives are optimistic about America and its institutions while liberals are pessimistic. If you challenge more than you accept about America and its institutions — and *especially* if your primary method for expressing that challenge is outrage and accusation — then the charge that you "hate America" may be a wildly exaggerated form of an underlying truth. Certainly, a hallmark of modern American 'liberalism' has been its dissatisfaction with the way things are, its determination to change things for the better both politically and culturally. Certainly a hallmark of modern American 'conservatism' has been its presumption that America and its institutions are fundamentally sound: notwithstanding the very real and human sins of our history, or the very real and human flaws in our present that demand continued striving toward our ideals, or the very real threats to our future from a decidedly uncivilized and antagonistic world, the American experiment has been largely successful. It may yet be improved, through many small adjustments, and perhaps a very few large reforms, but it is at root worth protecting and nourishing.

Contrast that with the vocal and zealous "Left" (though not its modest and much more common cousins), the Ralph Naders and the Noam Chomskys and the Ward Churchills and the Louis Farrakhans and the Michael Moores and Oliver Stones and others who get a disproportionate amount of attention and to whom America and its institutions are corrupt at the core and unredeemable. To them, America and its institutions are built upon a foundation of, and designed to reinforce, racism and patriarchy and oligarchy and theocracy and greed and materialism and imperialism and militarism and puritanism and conformity. To them, the only justice would be in throwing out the whole mess and replacing it with something more enlightened and of their own design.

Again, such a characterization of 'conservatism' and 'liberalism' in strictly utilitarian terms may help us identify 'conservatives' and 'liberals' empirically from their policies and rhetoric but, in the end, it too is merely descriptive. And, while it perhaps suggests a general temperament or the muddled ideological cant of current politics, it is not a useful tool for detailed political or social analysis.

'Conservatism' and 'liberalism' represent *ideologies*, not mere *categories*. To understand either, we need to formulate a prescriptive statement of their principles rather than a descriptive statement of their effects. But what are 'conservative' principles in modern America? What convinces American 'conservatives' that "what is" is worth preserving? What are the ideological cores of American 'conservatism' and what philosophical and cultural assumptions inspire them?

Conservative Principles: A Summary

I am considered, especially when I lived in the San Francisco Bay area, politically 'conservative,' although "libertarian pragmatist" (with a small 'l' and a small 'p') might be a closer, but incomplete, approximation of my views. Despite relatively high early, but subsequently diminished, marks I gave him for his performance as Commander-In-Chief, I am no devotee of George W. Bush. I did not vote for him, either time, and I actually agree more with the standard 'liberal' line than with the last 'conservative' President on issues like abortion and school prayer and the death penalty and business subsidies. The converse is true on issues like school vouchers and social security and affirmative action. And on a great many issues I think both the Republicans and the Democrats are dangerous fools — all of which illustrates the pitfalls of using the terms 'conservative' and 'liberal' any more to communicate a consistent set of philosophical or policy choices, and especially to circumscribe the range of political options available to us.

If the notions of 'conservative' and 'liberal' have become ambiguous or inconsistent, how do we identify specifically 'conservative' principles?

Most attempts to understand political movements work forward from historical and philosophical underpinnings or focus on specific and narrow issues that mobilize political action. For American 'conservatism,' that includes the political and economic philosophies of John Locke, Adam Smith, Edmund Burke, the American founding fathers, Frederick Hayek, and Milton Friedman, as well as their predecessors and heirs and various theological sources; and it includes opposition to the New Deal, anti-communism, a backlash against the Great Society, the rise of the religious right with its social agenda, the rise of 'neo-conservatism' out of the depths of liberal disappointment, and now the rise of the "Tea Party" out of a concern over fiscal irresponsibility. That ground is well covered. Even casual research will turn up hundreds of such references to the ideological sources for variants of 'conservatism' and histories of various conservative movements. Any ideological defense of 'conservatism' will ultimately rest on those intellectual and historical cornerstones.

But 'conservatism,' as a modern phenomenon, is evolved from those pieces, not specified by them, and has, in many specifics, departed from them in the untidy ebb and flow of politics and of history. A review of those sources may explain and justify various threads of 'conservatism' but can neither explain why those threads are woven as they are, nor explain the seeming contradictions knotted into the cloth. To understand modern 'conservatism' requires an empirical and contemporary examination of the practice — including idiosyncratic reactions to the idiosyncratic forms of modern 'liberalism' — as much as an idealistic appreciation of the abstractions and the history.

If we set aside for the moment religious fundamentalists, who ally with a subset of 'conservative' attitudes in the same way Marxist fundamentalists ally with a subset of 'liberal' ones, and try to navigate through practical subtleties and inconsistencies to identify a working cross-section of modern American 'conservative' postulates and principles, we would include:

- The fundamental presumption that material truth exists, independent of any particular human belief or desire; that there is an objective reality antecedent to our experience of it.
- The fundamental presumption that human behavior tends toward certain norms which can be altered only with great difficulty and over long intervals — that human nature is both real and resistant to change — and that, in general, strategies for modifying common human behavior are more successful if they accommodate human nature than if they contradict it.
- The consequent recognition that human aspiration is unbounded, while both natural resources and human effort are finite; and that, therefore, the human condition is, and will continue to be, a struggle against scarcity.
- The acknowledgement that the characters of both man and nature, amplified by limits on human knowledge and understanding, guarantee chance and uncertainty will always be a fundamental feature of the natural environment and of human projects.
- The fundamental presumption that consciousness sets humanity apart from nature, endows it with both moral significance and moral responsibility.

- The fundamental presumption that moral truth and right exist independent of any particular human society; that moral principles are real and universal.

- The fundamental presumption that the individual, rather than society, is the prime moral agent, the basic unit of autonomy, the root measure of good, and the ultimate arbiter of value.

- The fundamental presumption that the individual is capable of making moral choices notwithstanding human nature, social and economic pressures, intellectual and emotional conditioning, habits, desires, or other vagaries of life. Human beings have the faculty of reason and the capacity for free will, and these empower us to overcome both natural and conditioned propensities and external compulsions, to decide to behave morally or not even in the face of proclivity or adversity and even enticed by reward or deterred by sacrifice.

- The consequent right of the individual to freedom of conscience and to the expression of that conscience, to make moral choices unfettered and to live with the consequences of those choices.

- The consequent right of the individual to freedom of property — the right to hold one's own body inviolate and, by extension, to hold and/or exploit the proceeds of one's bodily effort as one sees fit, rather than as the 'needs of society' or some other external moral claim dictate.

- The consequent responsibility to respect the rights of others to their freedoms of conscience and property.

- The consequent responsibility to be accountable for the external effects of our moral choices; and the responsibility to hold others to account for theirs.

- The consequent understanding that all other rights arise as consequences or logical extensions of the fundamental rights of conscience and property, the fundamental rights to liberty in mind and in body.

- The consequent understanding that rights may never be granted, they may only be taken away.

- The acknowledgement that individuals who disdain their responsibility to respect the rights of others can, thereby, forfeit their claims to respect for their own rights.

- The fundamental presumption that the primary concern of justice is the moral balance between action and consequence.

- The fundamental presumption that human individuals are morally equivalent and deserve equivalent respect and treatment under equivalent circumstances; that our treatment of others should be equitable.

- The recognition that human beings are, despite their moral autonomy, social in nature; that they will naturally, willingly, and necessarily form cooperative and collective communities for their mutual benefit — that they will naturally, willingly, and necessarily create, participate in, nurture, and be nurtured by society.
- The recognition that cultural and social norms — mores, traditions, customs, etiquettes, conventions, and so on — are both the social grease that allows civil society to function without excessive friction and the cultural glue which binds its participants together. As such they deserve a general respect and deference because of those roles even when some of their specific strictures seem arbitrary or personally disagreeable.
- The consequent recognition that the instinctive, thus primary and most generally beneficial, human social unit is the family.
- The fundamental presumption that it is possible for individuals, even embedded within a society, to act and achieve individually.
- The recognition that *human beings and human systems are fundamentally fallible and corruptible*, that perfection is not attainable and that, though we ought to strive for it, we should not depend on it from ourselves, from our leaders, or from our social institutions. As a result, it is unwise either to rely on social, political, or economic systems that are intolerant of error and malice or to allow a single individual or institution immutable authority over any important aspect of our lives.
- The recognition that human beings will act in what they perceive to be their economic, social, and moral self-interest; that while individually capable of great generosity and love they will, in aggregate, often behave with avarice and disregard for 'society' and with hostility toward 'the other'; and that, therefore, our institutions and social arrangements — including our economic, political, and legal ones — must be able to accommodate and survive such behavior.
- The consequent recognition that incentives matter; that, despite the restraint of ethical codes and the encouragement of good intentions, and regardless of any desires to the contrary, in the long run we will have more of what is rewarded and less of what is penalized.
- The consequent recognition that the dual human propensities to act in their own self-interest and yet to act in concert with others as social beings implies a fundamental human impulse toward

commerce; and that, when left alone to act on that impulse, the resulting "free market" of voluntary production, exchange, and consumption creates a robust, self-organizing, efficient, and adaptable economic system that effectively maximizes the productive potential of individuals and of society.

- The consequent recognition that any large-scale human social structure will inevitably suffer from irreconcilable disputes among its individual participants and between itself and other social structures; and that some form of constraining authority, with the power to enforce resolution of such disputes, is therefore necessary for the effective functioning of social institutions.
- The recognition that political authority — government — is fundamentally and necessarily coercive; and that it is the power of coercion which essentially differentiates it from other forms of social control — which defines it as political authority rather than as something else — and which allows it to be effective where other forms of social control may not be.
- The recognition that the power of coercion allows political authority to threaten individual liberty where other forms of social control do not.
- The recognition that human beings, left to their own devices and with no intervention from political authority, will tend to create, either deliberately or by fortuitous mutual reinforcement, voluntary cooperative endeavors — families, tribes, communities, churches, marriages, partnerships, guilds, businesses, clubs, traditions, mores — to satisfy their individual and communal needs; that there are alternatives to government for solving most everyday problems and that people will and do create them spontaneously when the need arises.
- The consequent understanding that the various voluntary institutions of a society, by exercising moral and practical restraint over the excesses of their participants, serve the same fundamental governing purposes as government itself and are at least as essential for the orderly and civilized functioning of society.
- The consequent understanding that the use of political authority, with its power of coercion, should be limited to purposes of such gravity that survival is in question, of such scope that unanimity is essential to success, or of such perverse incentive that voluntary cooperation is impossible. Because coercion is a threat to liberty, government should be the solution of last resort, applied only as a prerequisite to liberty or where liberty can be independently assured or in such extremes of threat that survival trumps liberty.

- The consequent understanding that the necessary and legitimate purposes of political authority — of government — with its power of coercion are: to protect the rights and enforce the responsibilities of individual citizens in their dealings with each other and with the state and to mediate disputes among them; to secure the citizenry and the state against aggression from foreign powers; and to administer what commons exist on behalf of the citizenry and for the general welfare of the society.

- The consequent understanding that citizens have a responsibility to support the political authority in its necessary and legitimate functions with both moral and material resources; but that the political authority, with its power of coercion, has an obligation to limit its moral and material demands to those purposes which are both necessary and legitimate.

- The recognition that efforts to guarantee a particular standard of "fairness" or "justice" in the distribution of material or political resources — efforts to enforce a state of equity rather than merely an equitable process — will be inevitably undermined by commerce and by natural disparities in talent, ability, knowledge, motivation, and desire as individuals pursue their own interests; and that, therefore, to be effective such efforts necessarily require both a high level of coercion and a pervasive and invasive scrutiny of individual behavior and of social transaction.

- The recognition that authority ultimately serves its own end and that power not only corrupts but attracts the most corruptible.

- The consequent recognition that concentrations of power lead inexorably to the corruption of power, and that the larger the concentration, the larger the corruption we should expect.

- The consequent recognition that compulsion inevitably will be resisted and subverted by those who are compelled; that any granting of authority toward the alleviation of 'unfairness' or 'injustice' for some necessarily involves a reduction in liberty for others; and that, therefore, efforts to achieve fairness or justice are more ethically undertaken by persuasion than by coercion, more effectively undertaken by incentive than by command, more reliably undertaken locally than globally, and more prudently undertaken in the private or civic spheres than in the political one.

- The consequent understanding that the rule of law — which implies not an abundance of laws but fair-warning, consistency, and equal treatment under law — provides the most effective and the least perilous procedural framework for achieving fairness and justice.

- The consequent understanding that the economic arrangement least destructive of individual liberty is one built around individual choice — a 'free market' constrained and regulated by the obligation to respect the rights of all participants, including the equitable and broadly beneficial use of the commons.
- The consequent understanding that the political arrangement least destructive of individual liberty is a constitutionally circumscribed democracy, whether direct or representative, with a strong separation of powers, with structural proscriptions against a "tyranny of the majority" over individual liberties, and with authority decentralized to the maximum practical extent.
- The consequent understanding that, while participation in international commerce and the general promotion of free markets and democracy beyond our borders is desirable and beneficial, we, as a society, have no moral standing to coerce others into adopting our favored social, economic, or political arrangements.
- The consequent understanding that, while collaboration in regional and global security, trade, and legal arrangements are desirable and beneficial, we, as a political institution, have no moral standing to subjugate our own sovereignty — and thereby the rights of our citizens — to any foreign or otherwise unaccountable authority.
- The acknowledgement that governments or societies which demonstrate both a willingness and a capacity to impose their own authority in place of our sovereignty, to coerce us into adopting their favored social, economic, or political arrangements, or to threaten the safety and liberty of our citizens and our nation have abrogated their responsibilities to respect our rights and have, thereby, jeopardized their claims to our own restraint.
- The recognition that, without a general societal commitment both to individual liberty and to civic responsibility, constitutional limitations on political authority cannot prevent the degeneration of democratic government into tyranny or anarchy; that the moral character of society and of individuals, their commitment both to respect for individual autonomy and to shared responsibility for the community, is what ensures ongoing respect for constitutional boundaries specifically and ongoing cohesion as a culture and as a nation generally.
- The recognition that human institutions that do not fulfill their functions well tend to dissipate over time, while ones that fulfill their functions well tend to remain vital; and that human institutions tend to evolve over time the better to match their processes to their function. Therefore, long-standing political, legal,

civic, social, and cultural institutions are precisely those which are likely to have evolved to fulfill their functions well and to have proven their worth through continued vitality. And, therefore, absent a fundamental change in the nature of man, society, or institutional purpose, it is more prudent to preserve those long-standing institutions than to replace them with something new and unproven.

- The recognition that human knowledge is imperfect, human behavior is erratic, and human institutions are organic; and that, therefore, the anticipated consequences of an institutional change are prone to differ from the expectation and the unanticipated consequences of an institutional change are as likely to make things worse as to make things better.

- The recognition that in human endeavors the predictability of individual and institutional responses to a given action are as important, both to success and to fairness, as the responses themselves.

- The recognition that human beings make decisions about proper individual and social actions based on their understanding of accepted rules for behavior and on their extrapolations from experience with prior actions; that, therefore, current processes and precedents will determine future actions; and that, therefore, the processes by which goals are achieved and the precedents they establish for future actions are at least as important as the goals themselves to a stable social community. Ends should not be invoked to justify means because means themselves have consequences beyond their current intent.

- The consequent understanding that, justice aside, the rule of law provides the substantial benefits of predictability, stability, and continuity, and is therefore superior to the 'rule of man.'

- The consequent understanding that long-standing political, legal, civic, social, and cultural institutions — including cultural traditions and social mores — are inherently valuable and, aside from their underlying purposes, provide the substantial benefits of predictability, stability and continuity; and that, therefore, they should not be torn down or emasculated merely to serve current intellectual fads, political whims, or ideological rigidity.

These last few principles, the belief in the importance of and the defense of established and stable institutions, are the ideological touchstone of 'classic' conservatism: the rejection of change for its own sake. But they are merely a subset of 'conservative' thought, and they are not the defining principles of the modern American 'conservative' movement.

In fact, many of the other principles were formulated during the Enlightenment as a reaction against the old social and political hierarchies of Europe and were, at the time, considered 'liberal' (or even 'radical') — "*classical* liberalism" (or "libertarianism") now that those social and political hierarchies are historical relics and the term 'liberal' has been appropriated for other purposes. They are conservative *only* in the sense that they happen to be the founding principles (and therefore the "what is") of the American state, which must be conserved in the face of the emergent *new* 'liberal' political philosophies of the 20th century.

I imagine many self-defined 'liberals,' if they've actually read this far, are scratching their heads, thinking of at least one specific item in that list, and musing either that the 'conservatives' they know of don't seem to agree with it or that they and their 'liberal' colleagues do. Or, perhaps, they are thinking both. I also imagine more than one self-defined 'conservative' thinking much the same thing in reverse.

And they are probably right. These principles are not all unique to 'conservatives,' nor are they consistently or persistently applied by those who call themselves "conservative." Moderate 'liberals' and moderate 'conservatives' likely share more of these principles in common than do the most moderate and most extreme of either 'conservatives' or 'liberals.'

But if you want to condemn present-day 'conservatism' as a broad movement, rather than condemning individual 'conservatives' or individual 'conservative' policy positions, this is the panoply of values and practicalities you must dispute.

The principles in this list, although they are general in their philosophy, primarily address in their particulars *political* conservatism — conservatism regarding the relationship between individuals and their government. *Cultural* conservatism — conservatism regarding the relationships among individuals and groups — is primarily an expression of 'classic' conservatism concerned with the preservation of cultural institutions or, more broadly, the preservation of prevalent cultural/social traditions and norms. As such, cultural and political conservatism are related but they are not identical.

Although cultural conservatism, for both philosophical and practical reasons, often presages political conservatism, the opposite is not necessarily true. It is common, and entirely consistent, that people have different philosophical and moral models for political relationships, based on power, and for personal relationships, based on interdependence. Many pragmatic and individualistic political 'conservatives' are, nonetheless, 'liberal' in their community, family, and personal conduct.

No doubt, a great deal of the modern conflict between 'conservatives' and 'liberals' in the political realm revolves around cultural issues. This is due in large part to the success of 'progressives' in the last century at politicizing cultural issues, at dragging government into the relationships among individuals and groups. Such confluence of politics and culture is unfortunate.

Traditionally, cultural conservatism and cultural liberalism, lacking the political power of coercion, coexisted, if not integrated and with mutual respect then at least in enclaves and with mutual forbearance. That tradition seems now often to have dissipated. We now often seem to be locked endlessly in a kind of cultural combat.

Nonetheless it is political principles which will determine whether and how cultural issues are to be resolved in the political arena, and so it is political principles that are of primary interest in a discussion of 'conservatism' as a political movement.

It is worth noting, however, that the distinction between the cultural realm and the political one is yet another source of inconsistency among both 'conservatives' and 'liberals': it is possible, and perhaps inevitable, that there will be those who embrace America's social institutions while rejecting her governmental ones, and vice-versa.

Categories of Conservatism

Although the list of conservative principles was presented as a thematically ordered and logical sequence of postulates and ensuing generalizations, the actual relationships between the various principles is much more complex than a simple linear progression might suggest. The drawing on the next page attempts (too well!) to illustrate some of that complexity.

You may, and probably should, throw up your hands in dismay or disgust at the apparent chaos. That would be a reasonable response were you to try to take in the drawing, all at once, as a blueprint for the system of conservative thought. But that is not the intent.

The drawing, other than merely making the point that this is all complicated, allows you to trace a single idea or policy through the tangle, to discover what its genesis is in principle and how it interacts with or reinforces — or contradicts — other ideas or policies. That is, it is useful for tracing the threads of conservative thought, rather than for comprehending the weave.

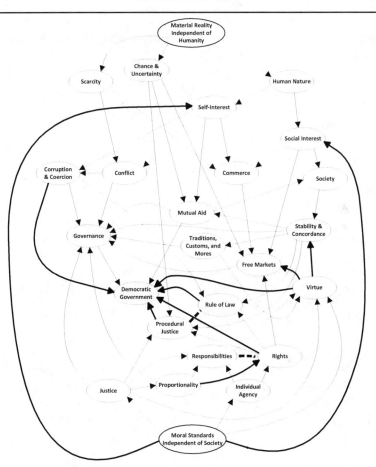

Relationships among conservative principles:

Ellipses represent principles; slender arrows represent implications and/or reinforcement between them; thick arrows represent constraints and/or directives imposed by them.

As an example, the desirability of free markets derives not from a single premise but from a combination of premises reinforcing each other: from the natural human affinity for commerce; from a commercial and social interest in maximizing the utility to be gleaned from available resources; from a recognition that natural chance and uncertainty undermine central planning; and from the natural human right to hold and exchange property. And the market, itself, is regulated (we hope) by the virtue of market participants and by social constraints that act to keep the market "free."

Combine the desirability of free markets with natural human tendencies toward corruption and conflict, with a moral desire for justice, and with a social requirement for stability, and we get a need for mechanisms of governance — which, in turn, and in conjunction with other non-economic considerations, implies the need for the specific institution of government. On the other hand, the presumption of fundamental and individual rights, the principles of the rule of law and of procedural justice, the human tendency to corruption, and the need for civic virtue constrain the forms that government should take (generally democratic ones) and the authority government should wield (generally as little as we can get away with).

In short, the postulates and conclusions in our list are linked in intricate and confusing ways that often obscure a visceral sense of pattern and consistency.

Anyone either defending or attacking 'conservatism' should acknowledge that the items in this list of principles are not intrinsically inseparable and may, at times, be in tension, or even in contradiction, *because they are not homogeneous*: they derive from several disparate intellectual, philosophical, spiritual, and cultural traditions. And that means different 'conservatives' applying those principles can come to drastically different conclusions on specific policy choices.

During the civil rights movement of the 1950s and 1960s, for instance, principles emphasizing individual liberty demanded radical change by overthrowing the existing unjust social and political structures, whereas principles emphasizing the conservation of stable institutions urged incremental change within the existing structures. And different aspects of the rule of law were argued on both sides: for "equal treatment under law" for individuals but also for respecting the a priori Constitutional limits on federal authority over the states.

That dichotomy was reflected in the way various 'conservatives' in Congress voted: people forget that the Republican party of that era voted 80% to 20% in *favor* of the Civil Rights Act of 1964; and that 'conservative' objections to it primarily concerned the ways in which it extended federal authority over the states in contravention of the enumerated powers of the Constitution, not a hostility to the underlying premise that civil rights should be enjoyed by all citizens.[1]

All this implies that a broad 'conservative' movement is bound to include people and groups who share only some of these principles in common or who prioritize them differently when conflicts arise. Even individual 'conservatives' will typically embrace overlapping but conflicting principles and will resolve contradictions in idiosyncratic ways that depend on their own internal hierarchy.

---

1 OK, I admit I resorted to *Wikipedia* for this: "Civil Rights Act of 1964," *www. Wikipedia.org*

In particular, we may group these 'conservative' principles into three broad categories with different philosophical roots and which receive different emphasis from different 'conservative' constituencies:

1.   *Classic Conservatism*: seeks to conserve established institutions because they form the basis of social stability and continuity, the necessary prerequisites for economic and cultural order, communal security, and civic harmony. This embraces both political and cultural aspects but is, in particular, the primary touchstone of traditional cultural conservatism, including a structural religious conservatism focused on religious tradition more than on religious doctrine. It is also the basis of one form of "Fiscal Conservatism" which is "conservative" in the strictest economic sense of conserving available resources and using them wisely and sustainably.

Classic Conservatism emphasizes the need to minimize disruption by favoring incremental changes over radical overhauls, and can, in some cases, embrace authoritarian political means toward that end when such overhauls are being propelled either by political power or by cultural activism.

Those who simply benefit from the status quo or who fear change for its own sake also gravitate toward this position.

2.   *Pragmatic Conservatism*: seeks to conserve established institutions because they function well, or at least better — or with less risk — than any proposed alternatives. It is particularly concerned with institutional evolution and with human nature — with the recognition of the shortcomings of human beings and human institutions in the exercise of power, and with the related understandings of what organizing principles and constraints must be built into a political or economic system to accommodate those shortcomings. It is also the genesis of certain forms of "Economic Conservatism" and "Fiscal Conservatism" which are concerned with the practical effects of fiscal and economic policies, concerned with wealth generation and productive efficiency.

Although there are definite philosophical aspects to their view of human nature and human systems, 'pragmatic conservatives' tend to think of themselves as empiricists more than as ideologues.

Given the practical focus on "what works well" — and given the inevitable disagreements over what we mean by "works well," and for whom — Pragmatic Conservatism can and does sometimes serve as an ideological basis for certain authoritarian political forms: despite its moral faults, authoritarianism can be particularly effective at achieving specific economic or cultural or social ends.

Pragmatic Conservatism can also be an intellectual cover for unmitigated self-interest.

3.   *Moral Conservatism*: seeks to conserve established institutions because they are "right," because they embody and adhere to desirable moral principles. In the American context that means, in particular but not exclusively, the principles of 'classical liberalism' — the principles asserted in the American Declaration of Independence concerning the place of the individual as the primary moral unit, the related understandings of rights and responsibilities, and a belief in the critical *and limited* role of government in securing those rights. "Free Market Conservatives," those to whom advocacy for the free market is a matter of economic liberty — a matter of moral right more than of practical effect — fall into this category. Some doctrinal forms of religious conservatism also fall into this category, particularly those driven primarily by concerns about the moral nature of society.

To the extent it is the principles of 'classical liberalism' that are under consideration, Moral Conservatives champion liberty over authority. However other moral platforms — and in particular moral platforms that emphasize some social (including theological) good over individual good — may lead to a morally-motivated embrace of more authoritarian political forms.

Viewed this way, it becomes clear that much of American 'conservatism' is conservative in only the narrowest sense, concerning itself with conserving *specific* existing institutions of particular perceived practical or moral value (and silent, or even liberal on others) rather than with conserving *all* institutions in principle. Further, even within a particular category, a divergent view of dominant concerns and interests — between the relative importance of political and social ethics, for example — can lead to dramatically different policy preferences.

Honest supporters and critics must also acknowledge that 'conservatism,' as much as any political movement and not necessarily more so, will attract support from opportunists who simply hope to benefit from certain 'conservative' policies.

Monolithic Conservatism?

We should not underestimate the subtleties (and ironies) of the coalitions possible among these 'conservative' constituencies. It is possible, for instance, to favor social utility over libertarian individualism as a moral ideal (or to have no moral goals at all beyond avarice) and, yet, argue in favor of the free market and preserving existing institutions from a strictly utilitarian standpoint — that a free market in a stable political and social environment will maximize the wealth of the nation. Similarly, it is possible to believe in the moral supremacy of the individual and, yet, embracing a rosy view of human nature, favor a more communal political and/or economic organization which depends heavily on the goodwill of each citizen.

It is also possible to care nothing for the preservation of institutions per-se, yet advocate the preservation of existing institutions because of some desirable moral principle embodied within them. Hence, someone might oppose eliminating the Electoral College from Presidential elections, not because they care either about tradition or about the integrity of the Constitution, but because it is one of the last remaining reminders that the Federal government was intended to be answerable to the states, as sovereign and independent political entities, as much as it was to the people as a whole.

And, in particular in this political environment, it is possible for religious-minded cultural conservatives to support politically 'conservative' policies and yet pay only lip-service to many of the traditional American conservative political principles like individual liberty and the rule of law. If they believe their long-standing, non-political institutions, their social mores and their cultural traditions, are under attack from 'progressive' political forces, then they benefit from a libertarian focus on limiting the governmental authority those forces can wield. If they want their religious principles to have more influence over public affairs, then decreasing the influence of government helps their cause. If they want their churches to thrive, a free market that allows them to accumulate wealth, and a small government that does not appropriate much of that wealth to serve its own purposes, leaves them more to tithe.

Ultimately, such diverse coalitions must fragment, but only when the broader movement has become successful enough to actually put its principles into practice — or unsuccessful enough to trigger finger-pointing and accusations over who is to blame for failure.

All of which is to point out that American 'conservatism' is no more monolithic than American 'liberalism.' It is merely, in the broad context of the 20th century political landscape, more defensive and less successful, so its fissures are less apparent from the outside. With recent 'conservative' electoral successes and catastrophes those fissures are likely to become increasingly apparent over the next few years, just as the fissures in 'liberalism' began to expand and fracture in the 1960s and 1970s.

In addition, those fissures will be accelerated by the fact that certain high-profile 'moral conservatives' and 'pragmatic conservatives' are, increasingly, not conservative in the traditional sense: in many ways they seek to reverse, or at least deflect, the 'progressive' changes of the 20th century. The farther those changes proceed, the more the attempts to reverse them begin to resemble counter-revolution than preservation of the status quo — the more liberal (in its regressive, reactionary form) those attempts appear.

This illustrates yet another source of inconsistency within the 'conservative' and 'liberal' movements: the descriptive terms "conservatism" and "liberalism" both designate outlooks relative to current conditions and naturally evolve with the political and cultural landscape; whereas the political labels 'conservative' and 'liberal,' like all political labels, tend to endure over generations even as the movements to which they are attached creep ever further from their origins.

Conservative Principles: A Discussion

At this point, no doubt, many of you are left scratching your heads or bristling over some of these declarations of principle. They are somewhat terse, necessarily so because they were provided as a summary and not as a discussion. They have been, therefore, both presented without context or nuance and proclaimed with bold confidence rather than offered with humility. They stand, unsupported either by explanation or by evidence, ready to be knocked down by any cogently-argued counter-principle or crushed by a righteous indignation at their effrontery.

It is only right, then, that I offer what explanation and evidence I may to buttress my boldness or, perhaps, to offer some humility. What follows is a restatement of the conservative principles as a narrative, rather than as list, and grouped within broad categories according to their general subjects to bring some sense of order to them, encompassing the general 'conservative' views of the nature of the world, the nature of people, the nature of morality, the nature and role of society, and the nature and role of government.

Material Truth and Reality

Material truth exists independent of any particular human belief or desire. More plainly, some things are objectively true and others are objectively false. Neither state is determined by how you or I perceive them and have even less to do with what we might wish them to be. They also do not depend on whether or not we can tell the difference with any certainty: enduring mysteries in both science and philosophy suggest that, in many instances, we may not be able to. But the fact that bounds on our own knowledge and intellect prevent us from seeing the truth doesn't make truth, itself, illusory.

The presumption that there is an objective truth is not undermined by sophistries about "my truth" and "your truth," or by any other arguments which rely on variance in human viewpoint or on the enigmas of human motivation. Human viewpoint reflects judgment about meaning, significance, consequence, desire, and value, convoluted assessments of internal mental and spiritual and moral landscapes intertwined with, and sometimes obscuring, straightforward assessments of external fact.

For that reason, the different "truths" that different people perceive, whatever personal significance they may conjure and however real they may seem in their effects, are more an indication of disparate personal values, interests and quirks — or of simple misinterpretation — than of any objective information about the nature of external reality. They signify more about the observer than about what is observed.

Similarly, demonstrations that truth is malleable and indeterminate based on semantic sleights-of-hand may amuse and score points at cocktail parties, but they don't convey any philosophical insight. A friend once sprung such a trap on me, describing a murder trial in which the coroner, the cop, and the killer, all charged with telling "the truth," were asked, "Why did this man die?" The coroner declared that he died because of a loss of blood through a hole in his heart; the cop declared that he died because someone shot him; the killer declared that he died because he was cheating on her. So which one of those was "the truth" about why he died? They propose three completely different explanations, yet aren't they all true? Doesn't that mean truth itself is not absolute but a product of viewpoint?

I would love to say that I brought my friend up short with an elegant rebuttal, but I don't think well on my feet, and the beers I had consumed and the comfortable chaise longue I was lying on left me stymied. It was only later that I could gather my thoughts into the proper response: those answers represent not three different "truths" about a single question, but truthful answers to three different questions.

The trap is in the ambiguity of the language used to ask those questions: although the *expression* of the question was the same for each witness, the *meaning* each took from that expression was conditioned by the context of their own knowledge and circumstance. The coroner understood he was being asked a question about biology; the cop understood he was being asked a question about circumstances and actions; the killer understood she was being asked a question about motivation. Had a priest been confronted with the same sequence of words — "Why did this man die?" — he may have offered yet another "truth" about sin and penance.

All those answers are, of course, interrelated by cause and effect. Each one represents the truth about some narrow detail, but only a portion of the entire truth about a broader question. There is only one "truth" about why this man died, but it is a narrative, not a fact, a narrative that includes all those elements in their proper relationships and sequence.

In other words, truth is objective but it may, nonetheless, be complex and messy and hard to pin down.

Human Nature

Human behavior tends toward certain norms. That is a statement about practical effect, not about moral value. You shouldn't take it as a justification for amoral conduct or as support for behavioral determinism. Rather, it is an acknowledgement of broad human tendencies rooted in ancient human biology and psychology.

Nor should you interpret it as a mandate for stasis. Human nature is rigid but not necessarily immutable. It can and does evolve. But evolution is necessarily protracted and unpredictable. We would be unrealistic and unreasonable if we presumed to steer it with any precision toward some desired end within one generation, or even within ten or one hundred.

As with any assertions about "tendencies" and "norms," assertions about human nature are more applicable to groups of people than to individuals. We cannot invoke human nature to make reliable predictions about what any particular person will do in any particular situation. But that is an observation about statistics, not about causality. It does not imply that human nature is a socially-created phenomenon, a matter of social conditioning. It merely means there is wide variation in the expression of that nature among individuals.

Certainly, societies also promote behavioral norms and resist change, but human nature is antecedent to social structure. Indeed, social norms may often be best understood as highly evolved strategies for controlling the more socially destructive tendencies of human nature.

That implies a certain synchrony between human nature and social norms, and it is easy to conflate the two when we are trying to explain human behavior. We should resist that tendency. Social norms are social constructs that we can alter by consensus when they become destructive or are no longer useful. To confuse them with human nature is to declare them beyond reach; and to confuse underlying human nature with social norms encourages futile and destructive attempts to reform humanity itself.

Material Needs and Resources

The human condition is, and will continue to be, a struggle against scarcity. Human desires will always outstrip our ability to fulfill them and, therefore, we cannot fulfill them all. We must make choices about what needs and desires are more and less important for our lives.

That doesn't mean material well-being has not been improving for centuries or will not continue to do so. Nor does it mean we must deplete any particular natural resource, imminently or even eventually. No doubt, as a society and as individuals we have become ever more adept over time both at utilizing the resources at hand more effectively and at identifying larger or alternative sources of those resources. No doubt, as a society and as individuals it is likely we will continue to do so. And, no doubt, as a society and as individuals we are materially better off by orders of magnitude than our ancestors ever were.

But dissatisfaction has less to do with what we have than with what we can imagine, and the human imagination is even better at creating new desires for the present and new aspirations for the future than it is at fulfilling old ones. Envision any possible level of resources available: there will eventually be disagreement over how to use them, and someone will be disappointed, and will resist, when someone else's preference is chosen over theirs.

Which implies yet another aspect of the human condition: conflict over the use of resources is the inevitable byproduct of the struggle against scarcity.

Chance and Uncertainty

Chance and uncertainty are fundamental features of the natural environment and of human projects. There are things about human behavior and natural phenomena we cannot predict. Therefore, even were we (improbably) to know with certainty how to manipulate that behavior and those phenomena to make them come out the way we want them to, they are beyond our ability to control.

A corollary to the presumption of uncertainty is that all human projects — even simply living your life — entail risk. We can reduce risk to some extent but we cannot eliminate it. Things break. Nature rages. People don't do what you expect. Circumstances arise that you never imagined or that you discounted as impossible. Institutions fail to fulfill their purposes.

The only certainty is that sometimes plans will go awry. It's best to be prepared for that, and it's best to build resiliency against that both into our own behavior and into our social and political institutions.

Moral Truth and Right

The Moral Nature of Man

Consciousness sets humanity apart from nature, endows it with both moral significance and moral responsibility. Beyond doubt, man and man's fate are entwined with the natural world. Biologically and materially we are animals like all others and we depend on the fruitful functioning of natural ecological processes.

But self-awareness, the knowledge of our own individuality and the self-focused aspiration — the spiritual purpose — it provokes makes us more than animals. It confers a moral status that transcends our ecological position. And other-awareness, the knowledge that, if we are distinct from others, then they, also, must be distinct from us, that they command their own spiritual purposes, places upon us a duty to acknowledge and respect their separateness and their own moral significance.

Moral Absolutes

Moral truth and right exist independent of any particular human society. More plainly, some things are morally right and some things are morally wrong. Which they are does not depend on what society you happen to live in. Slavery is wrong even in Medieval Europe and in the Ottoman Empire and in the American Confederacy and in the Aztec nation, all of which condoned it as an integral part of their cultures. Murder is wrong even if the victims are only Gypsies or only Tutsis or only Jews or only aborigines or only infidels, all considered less than human within the cultures that condemned them (or continue to condemn them). The subjugation of women is wrong even if the *Old Testament* or the *Koran* or some ancient tribal custom commands or blesses it. And neither those moral offenses nor any others can be transformed into virtues by consensus, or be legitimized by democracy, or be rationalized by invoking some social benefit or cultural paradigm.

The presumption of moral order does not depend on whether or not we think truth and right are God's commandment. It does not depend on whether we believe moral principles are Platonic ideals, independent of human nature, or practical imperatives derived from it. In fact, it does not depend on whether or not we can ultimately even perceive either truth or right with absolute certainty: the diversity of opinion on the details of moral values, not only between 'liberals' and 'conservatives' but even among 'liberals' or among 'conservatives' — and across societies — suggests it is likely we cannot.

But the lack of an objective and universal means for choosing among moral principles does not imply there is no valid choice. It is merely a reminder of the limits of human insight, a reminder that we should encourage moral debate, not stifle it by proclaiming it moot or irrelevant.

Put another way, we can acknowledge that our *understanding* of what is moral or immoral may be constrained by local and contemporary social accords — that *moral knowledge* will be relative to social and cultural knowledge and will, therefore, vary over time and between cultures — without presuming that moral principle itself must be similarly socially constructed rather than absolute. And that may lead us to moderate our judgments about the moral behavior of people from other cultures and other times because we recognize the limitations on moral knowledge that their societies impose upon them. Judged by modern standards, Thomas Jefferson was a hypocrite for having written with such eloquence about human liberty while at the same time owning slaves. But his moral obtuseness regarding slavery, a product of the contemporary cultural climate in which he and all his peers were immersed, does not mean he was wrong about human liberty. We may (or may not) forgive his sins because he acted out of an ignorance or pragmatism, rather than out of malice or disregard, without condoning those sins as, somehow, socially sanctified and virtuous.

In asserting that principles of truth and morality are universal, however, we must be clear and honest about the distinction between those principles and mere social mores. In many instances the contrary assertion — that "everything is relative" or that "morality is a social construct" — is actually a response to the failure to make that distinction. It is a reaction against attempts to elevate particular social convention, including and especially religious canon, to the status of universal truth.

If the idiosyncratic products of specific social history are asserted as moral principle then people cannot be faulted for recognizing the effects of social context on such "principle." And, perhaps, they cannot be faulted for concluding that all other moral principle (and truth itself) is similarly dependent on social context. The inference is exactly backward but it is not a wholly unreasonable response to such impudence.

Moral Agency

The Individual as Moral Agent

The individual, rather than society, is the prime moral agent. That does not mean society is inconsequential or that there are no higher moral purposes to which individuals ought to aspire or commit themselves. It merely presupposes that commitment to society, or to principle, is the choice and responsibility solely and entirely of the individual. It is not the choice or responsibility of some moral or intellectual elite; it is not the choice or responsibility of any biological or economic or social peer group; it is not the choice or responsibility of society at large; and it is not the choice or responsibility of some political institution, no matter how representative.

Aside from what some religious catechism may have to say on the subject, the presumption of individual agency is typically justified by philosophy: *humans have both individual moral value and individual moral authority; individual autonomy is, therefore, the morally proper arrangement of human affairs.* Many (including myself) accept and embrace that interpretation.

We must acknowledge, however, that if we cannot perceive truth or right with utter certainty then that assertion may be as objectively unsupportable as any other statement about moral absolutes. Although we may believe it as a postulate, we cannot prove it as a conclusive truth. Naturally, by the same reasoning, those who believe otherwise cannot disprove it, so debates about whether or not it is true rarely result in anyone changing his or her mind.

Nonetheless, even absent objective moral support, there are practical reasons to favor a presumption of individual autonomy.

The reality of sentience is foremost. Individuals have a sense of self. Individuals experience the consequences of actions both directly through their senses and indirectly through their higher mental faculties — through emotion and reason — and therefore have immediate and personal concern for those consequences. Society, as an agent, is not self-aware, can neither feel nor think, cannot experience, cannot reason, and is, therefore, indifferent to consequences except in the abstract, in the indeterminate and aggregated judgment of its individual members about how those consequences might affect its function or its evolution or the welfare of its citizens. Simple fairness would suggest that the agent most directly concerned with the outcome of an action ought to have primary authority over its course, and by that standard the individual ought to have precedence over society as the agent of moral choice.

Next is the question of "Who gets to decide?" If there is no objective and universal means for choosing among moral principles, then what person or group of people — what leader or prelacy or professoriate, or even what properly constituted democratic majority — is necessarily more likely to choose wisely than any other? Which one can claim a logical or moral privilege over others for their judgment? There is neither practical nor moral justification for subjugating the moral judgment of the individual to that of some authority.

Further, and as a consequence, honoring individual moral choice is, as a system, the most likely of the possible social arrangements to promote appropriate moral action. While some individual moral judgments may well be 'wrong' they will also vary from person to person and are unlikely all to be 'wrong' in the same way — nor is it likely that none among that variety will be 'right.' Moreover, in the case of error there is a natural mechanism for correction: although individual judgments are likely generally to conform to a moral consensus, those who disagree with that consensus are free to use their own autonomy and a level of effort determined by the value and confidence they place in their own beliefs to persuade others to their point of view.

If moral viewpoint were, instead, compelled to unanimity by some authority then a 'wrong' choice by the authority would be universally perpetuated and would be difficult or impossible to reverse.

More fundamentally, without moral autonomy there can be no moral accountability: you can't be held responsible for what you can't control. Humans, even engaged in communal activities or committed to higher moral purpose, think and act as individuals. They cannot do otherwise because they are each, ultimately, alone within themselves. Their every action represents an individual choice, even if that choice has been conditioned by society and circumstance or has been constrained by the coercion of despotism to be between moral integrity and physical annihilation. Ordered at the point of a gun to commit some moral offense, you must choose between sin and death. Agonizing as that is, it is still a choice.

If, then, we must act as individuals we must be individually responsible for our actions. And that requires that we acknowledge the individual authority to make moral choices.

Moral Choice and Moral Responsibility

The individual is capable of making moral choices. This does not contradict the presumption of a human nature or ignore the role of social conditioning, peer pressures, economic stresses, self-interest, self-preservation, and other "root causes" in explaining human behavior. Nor does it preclude forgiveness as a legitimate response to individual acts of moral abrogation.

But understanding and absolution should not be confused with approval and acceptance. The fact that we can predict some people will succumb to their baser impulses or explain their corrupt behavior as the ignoble convergence of innate nature and external influence does not make those impulses or behavior either worthy or tolerable. And forgiveness properly demands contrition and implies, at the least, an acknowledgement of offense. The inevitable need not be forgiven

Rights and Responsibilities

Freedom of Conscience

Individuals have a right to freedom of conscience. Although this implies great latitude in moral behavior it is not a moral free-pass. There is no guarantee that moral choices that rebuff societal norms will have pleasant or beneficial social consequences or that moral courage will be rewarded and moral cowardice punished. Both nature and society can be — and, alas, often are — unfair and even cruel. By claiming the right to freedom of conscience, we merely acknowledge the ideal of the individual moral right to make the choice and to bear the consequence.

Freedom of Property

Individuals have a right to freedom of property. Your body and your effort belong to you in the same way that, *and to no lesser degree than*, your mind and your conscience do. Therefore, so do the things you produce with them. The product of your labor is as much yours as the labor itself; just as no one has the right to force you to work on their behalf, so no one has the right to dictate what you do with what you produce by your work — you may keep it, or give it away, or sell it, or trade it for the product of someone else's effort — and no one has the right to take it from you. Further, that which you have taken in exchange for the fruits of your effort — what you've bought with the proceeds of your labor — is no less a product of that effort, and no less yours to control, than were the original fruits themselves.

Alas, property rights are frequently derided by placing them in an artificial opposition to "human rights" — by erroneously (or deceitfully) equating the human right of individuals to control property with some mythical right of property itself to special accommodation.

But property rights and human rights are not in opposition. They are two aspects of the same moral principle, for it is within this principle of the right to property, the principle of inviolability in one's own body and, by extension, of the effort one produces with that body, that the most fundamental human rights are rooted.

The right to your own life and the right to be free from enslavement are property rights to your own body and to your own labor. It is precisely because your body, the effort you exert through it, and the product your effort produces belong to you that no one else may appropriate them or destroy them without your consent.

Responsibilities

Individuals have a responsibility to respect the rights of others. Rights are not an open-ended claim to self-indulgence. They are a cushion of autonomy within which an individual may act, with flexible but definite borders where they come into contact — and especially into conflict — with the rights of other individuals. Thus, *rights and responsibilities are inseparable*, the complementary aspects of a single moral precept.

This is, at root, what we mean when we say that rights are "inalienable." Clearly, rights can be violated, abridged, usurped, or abrogated through coercion. They are inalienable not because they *cannot* be taken away by force but because they *ought* not be; because we all have, along with our own moral right to be free of coercion, a reciprocal and equal moral responsibility to refrain from imposing such coercion on others, whether acting as individuals or acting through the collective agencies of society or of government.

Moral Accountability and Moral Judgment

Individuals have the responsibility to be accountable for the external effects of their own moral choices and the responsibility to hold others to account for theirs. Individuals are individually responsible for their choices and their actions, and neither fortunate nor unfortunate circumstance, nor the anonymity of communal action, absolves them of that responsibility. Note that it is specifically external effects that require external accounting. Your internal moral welfare — the accounting of your conscience and of your soul — is your own affair.

The notion of a responsibility to hold yourself, and particularly to hold others, accountable for actions — a responsibility to accept judgment and to judge — can appear harsh to the modern Western sensibility. It is often characterized not as *exercising judgment* but as *being judgmental*, not as upholding a moral standard but as imposing a dogma.

But that characterization misses the point. Puritanism aside, a moral society cannot remain so if it refuses to recognize and acknowledge immorality when it occurs or to condemn its effects.

That is not just a practical matter of protecting us individually and collectively from moral harm. It is also an acknowledgement that social behavior replicates itself — that people, in spite of countervailing intellectual and moral principle, ultimately model their own social behavior on observation of what is sanctioned or condemned in the social behavior of others. *We will have whatever social behavior we will accept.*

Rights and Privileges

All other rights arise as consequences or logical extensions of the fundamental rights of conscience and property, the fundamental rights to liberty in mind and in body. Choose any right that Americans hold dear — the right to free speech, to be free from unreasonable searches and seizures, to peacefully assemble, to petition the government for redress, to bear arms, to due process, to privacy: they all, ultimately, amount to specific instances of the right to be spiritually, mentally, and physically autonomous and unbound.

Rights may never be granted, they may only be taken away. Rights are moral claims, non-negotiable and not contingent on circumstance. They are something you already have, yours through the simple virtue of being human, and you only lose them if someone takes them from you.

A grant, on the other hand, offers you something you do *not* already have, something neither available to you through the simple virtue of being human nor provided to you by nature nor produced by your own exertion. That is, a grant is something you must be given by someone else; and it, thereby, necessarily implies an effort on the part of someone else to provide it — effort on which no one has the right to make a moral claim. Thus, that which must be granted is a *privilege when offered*, a *boon when requested*, and a *plunder when demanded*.

You should not interpret that assertion without some sense of the abstract. For example, inasmuch as elections themselves are human social inventions, the right to vote is not "available to you through the simple virtue of being human" or "provided to you by nature" or "produced by your own exertion." It is part of a charter of government. But it is, nonetheless, properly construed as a "right" that is pre-existing, not granted by government. Through the simple virtue of being human, each of us is free to select which (if any) leaders we might follow, which (if any) authority to which we might accede, which (if any) cooperative to which we might delegate some part of our individual prerogative. Further, it is only coercion — of a bully or a tyrant or a mob or a government — that can keep us from exercising that choice. Hence, that choice can be taken away by coercion but, in the absence of coercion, it need not be granted. The right to vote is merely the way we honor and implement that choice within our particular political structure.

In contrast, the assertion of a "right to health care" or of a "right to food" or of a "right to shelter" or of a "right to a good job at good pay" — by which the claimants mean not the right to produce and hold those things for themselves but *the right to be provided with them* — is a claim on something that does not exist until someone else creates it. It is a claim that *cannot be fulfilled without someone else to provide the means*. To assert such things as "rights," then, is to assert a moral claim on someone else's effort. It is to enslave them to the fulfillment of your own needs or desires.

It may or may not be fair (and separately it may or may not be wise policy) for a wealthy society to grant such assistance to its less fortunate members (for the record: I believe it is both fair and wise). But we should never lose sight of the distinction: those grants are *privileges*, bestowed by a compassionate society and contingent upon the general availability of societal wealth. They are not *rights* with independent and inalienable moral substance.

Limitations on Rights

Individuals who disdain their responsibility to respect the rights of others can, thereby, forfeit their claims to respect for their own rights. This is a logical consequence of the duality of rights and responsibilities. Claiming rights without acknowledging responsibilities is both morally and practically unsupportable.

The principle is neither absolute nor irrevocable. Consequences ought justly to be proportional to action, and curtailment of liberty should be neither easy nor capricious. But some restriction on liberty is a reasonable and morally appropriate consequence for violations of liberty, and the more onerous the violation the more onerous may be the consequence.

This is not simply a matter of justice. It is, rather, an acknowledgement that we are both individually and collectively justified in acting to prevent others from abridging our rights; and that, for wholly practical reasons, acting to protect our rights is likely to require some form of coercive response to coercive provocation.

Justice and Equity

The Nature of Justice

The primary concern of justice is the moral balance between action and consequence. In the context of modern American 'conservatism' and its popular conflation with Christian fundamentalism, this typically brings to mind the *Old Testament* injunction of "an eye for an eye." For that reason, those who disagree frequently disdain it as a high-sounding pretense of civilization used to justify the ancient and uncivilized impulse for vengeance.

But in its original context, among the ancient tribal cultures of Palestine, the admonishment to take "an eye for an eye" was likely as much a constraint on vengeance as an inducement[1] — an eye for an eye *and no more* — and in its specific and complete text is explicit that administration of such justice is properly the province of society and not of the individual.[2]

In a modern context it is appropriately taken not literally but as a metaphor for the general moral principle of proportionality: that actions have moral as well as material consequences, that bad works should be punished and good works rewarded, and that both rewards and punishments should convey moral significance proportionate to the moral significance of the behavior that provoked them.

1   e.g. *The Meaning of the Bible: What the Jewish Scriptures and Christian Old Testament Can Teach Us*, by Douglas Knight and Amy-Jill Levine; HarperOne, 2011
2   e.g. Exodus 21 explains the punishment as part of a code of laws; Leviticus 24 prescribes the punishment should be meted out by "the congregation."

Despite the ancient Judeo-Christian roots of that particular phrasing, the notion of proportionality is not a strictly Western tradition nor is it the exclusive province of 'conservatives.' The Hindu and Buddhist concept of karma describes a sort of cumulative accounting of good and bad deeds that are settled in proportion, not as a measure of justice by any worldly authority but simply as the necessary and inevitable consequence of the natural cycle of life, defining your shifting moral position in the cosmos as you move through multiple mortal incarnations. In the West we express a similar, if more pragmatic, belief in the familiar aphorism, "What goes around comes around." And in a prescriptive form, rather than a reactive one, proportionality becomes the Golden Rule — "Do unto others as you would have others do unto you" — which has analogues in most cultures.

The ideal of proportionality is also intertwined with the moral duty to assume and apportion responsibility. We claim the right to liberty and the resultant right to any rewards that accrue from our actions, but that right attaches to an equivalent responsibility for the liberty of others and to a duty to accept the negative consequences our actions might bring. We hope (although, perhaps, do not expect) that both rewards and consequences bear some reasonable moral relation to what we did to earn them — that we will "be given our due" or "get what's coming to us."

Even those who view justice as something other than proportionality, who view the proper purpose of the political justice system as rehabilitation and redemption rather than as punishment, nonetheless often express satisfaction, and even glee, when some powerful anti-social villain — a corporate polluter or a market manipulator or a hypocritical televangelist or a corrupt public official — is brought down and "gets his just deserts." And their delight when some unsung hero is recognized and rewarded for his benevolence or courage is genuine and reflects more than mere empathy. The very notion of anyone "deserving" any particular fate, either prize or penalty, rests on an underlying presumption that there ought to be — that "justice" demands — some degree of moral balance in human affairs.

If you look up the word "justice" in a dictionary you will find, along with the concept of proportionality, mention of other moral concepts like impartiality and, in particular, equity or fairness. In my admittedly limited reading, often older editions placed more emphasis on proportionality while newer editions place more emphasis on equity and fairness, suggesting, perhaps, that the common understanding of "justice" has been in transition for some time. That may explain why the emphasis on proportionality in consequences might be considered a conservative interpretation.

The more modern emphasis on "equity" — which is often reduced in practice to the less nuanced demand for "equality," discounting any moral question of whether such equality is deserved — reflects political philosopher John Rawls' conception of justice as fundamentally equivalent to "fairness."[1] That is the intellectual root, if not the emotional and historical one, of the modern 'liberal' models for "social justice."

Rawls began his analysis from a notional "veil of ignorance" which isolates the individual from any knowledge of his own initial material circumstance, physical and intellectual abilities, emotional preferences, and moral character — factors Rawls presumed to be a priori conditions, beyond the individual's control and, therefore, beyond the individual's responsibility. That is, he started by assuming each person might be anything — sinner or saint, genius or dunce, prince or vagabond, producer or consumer, empath or psychopath — but that no one could know, nor could they control, which of those roles fate had assigned to them. He then imagined what people, reasoning from within such a state of utter ignorance and helplessness — in the dark about how fortune might favor or disfavor them, in the dark about their own individual material preferences or moral proclivities and powerless to change them — would agree was a "just" state of affairs.

To ensure their reasoning led to a coherent conclusion, Rawls presumed that people would be self-interested — that they would choose to arrange things in a way that would be to their benefit, regardless of who or what they might be. He presumed that everyone would prefer to avoid some really bad outcome, even if that reduced the likelihood of achieving a really good one. He presumed that, since no one could know whether they were good or bad, clever or foolish, talented or inept, they would be concerned more with what they might have in any moment than with how their fortunes might evolve over time. And he then used his guess as to what such people would choose for their social, economic, and political arrangements as his framework for a definition of "justice."

From all this, Rawls concluded that the primary concern of justice would be — and therefore ought to be — equality in the distribution of material, cultural, and political resources among individuals. Hence, he inferred individual actions and social arrangements may be judged to be "just" or "unjust" principally with respect to how they change that equality and not in any absolute sense. And, hence, he concluded the only morally mandated consequence for human action is that which is required to counter inequalities which might result. This is a modern echo of the exasperated

---

1 *Justice as Fairness*, by John Rawls; Harvard University Press, 2001. This is an update to the ideas first introduced in *A Theory of Justice* in 1971.

Alfred Doolittle, dustman and moralist of Bernard Shaw's *Pygmalion*, who lamented when challenged by his interrogators' notions of ethics:

> "What am I? I'm one of the undeserving poor: that's what I am. Think of what that means to a man.... I don't need less than a deserving man: I need more. I don't eat less hardy than him; and I drink a lot more.... What is middle class morality? Just an excuse for never giving me anything."

Despite what might seem an unbridgeable distance between these two versions of justice, they can coexist. If we think of "equity" and "fairness" in their traditional senses — which account for the moral component of merit along with the material component of equality — then the two differ only in their emphasis. But even if we think of "equity" and "fairness" in the newer and narrower sense, as mere synonyms for "equality," the difference need not preclude common ground. The fact that 'conservatives' conceive of justice in terms of moral consequence does not mean they place no value on equality. The fact that 'liberals' conceive of justice in terms of equality does not mean they place no value on moral consequence. But clearly the two groups value those ideals differently, and perhaps not consistently, and the fact that we attempt to describe both using a single word makes lucid and rational discussion of those differences more difficult than it might otherwise be.

We can think of Western moral values as having three facets: *Liberty*, *Accountability*, and *Equity*. As noted before, *Liberty* is the principle of human dignity, the idea that the individual has moral worth and an inalienable right to be left alone in certain fundamental pursuits, and has a concomitant responsibility to respect the human dignity of others. *Accountability* is the principle of moral responsibility, the proposition that we own the results of our actions and that moral choices ought to have consequences of proportionate moral import. *Equity* is the principle of human equivalence, that under similar circumstances we ought to treat people similarly, and which encompasses notions of fair dealing and impartiality and compassion.

We have traditionally subsumed accountability and equity (and occasionally liberty) together within the general rubric of "Justice," but that obscures the question of which takes precedence when the two are in conflict. If someone borrows more money to buy a house than he can reasonably pay back, he is likely to lose his house to foreclosure. *Accountability* might deem it appropriate that he make up for the demonstrable harm his irresponsibility causes the bank, its shareholders, and future borrowers who cover the loss in higher interest rates for their loans; certain notions of *equity* might deem it unjust that he must lose his home, or that the "rich" bankers are made whole while the "poor" homeowner ends up broke.

And all that ignores entirely the separate question of whether liberty or justice should predominate when the pursuit of one diminishes the other. If we decree, in the name of justice, that everyone must drive the same kind of car or buy the same kind of health insurance, then we will all, undoubtedly, be more equal. We will also, all, undoubtedly, be less free.

As an aside, even John Rawls' notion of "Justice as Fairness" — and even when reduced to the simplistic "Justice as Equality" — does not necessarily imply that justice requires utter equality in material status. "Justice" is a human principle that applies to human action, not to nature. To the extent that human activity increases inequality a follower of Rawls might invoke the cause of justice to demand regulation of that activity or to demand compensation for it. But justice — although not compassion — is silent on mere circumstance. Nature is not a moral entity. It can be unfair but it cannot be unjust.

The Nature of Equity

Human individuals are morally equivalent and deserve equivalent respect and treatment under equivalent circumstances. Or, as stated more succinctly (if less precisely) in the American Declaration of Independence, "...that all men are created equal." This augments the fundamental responsibility to respect others' rights with a more general charge to treat people impartially, fairly, and with compassion — to acknowledge and respect their basic human value along with their basic human dignity; to live by the Golden Rule.

That doesn't, however, mean we ought never to differentiate our behavior toward different people. Judgment about what differences in circumstance fall within the somewhat nebulous category of "equivalence" is a personal one. We generally favor those we love over those we merely like over those we don't know, and favor all of them over those we find insufferable. We voluntarily make promises to some, which we are then honor-bound to keep, but make no promises to others. We cooperate with those who reward us and shun those who offend us. We trust those who've dealt fairly with us before but are wary of those who have not.

We differentiate our treatment of others in these ways because we recognize that the circumstances of those various people are, in some ways, not equivalent. But we also recognize that equivalence is a continuum, not a boundary, and that, therefore, the differences in our treatment of others should follow a similar continuum. Equity also requires that *under roughly equivalent circumstances we owe others roughly equivalent respect and treatment.*

One aspect of this that deserves particular attention is its interaction with the concerns of justice. In judging moral equivalence, prior moral choices and the moral consequences they accrue are a legitimate consideration. *By their moral choices people differentiate themselves.* Equity, therefore, demands acknowledging such differences and respecting the accountability that justice requires. Thieves and murderers may have begun with a human claim to respect and treatment equivalent to that provided others but, by choosing to steal or to kill, they have debased their own circumstance and subordinated that claim to the demands of justice.

And, just as an obligation to be equitable does not negate the demands of justice so, also, it does not nullify the rights which define liberty. The demand for equity is not invertible: that you owe others a duty of respect and equal treatment does not imply a concomitant right on the part of others to extract respect and equal treatment from you. Those who shirk that duty are jerks; those who forcibly extract that duty from others are tyrants.

Individual and Society

Social Roles and Obligations

Human beings are, despite their moral autonomy, social in nature; they will naturally, willingly, and necessarily create, participate in, nurture, and be nurtured by "society." Although this implies that participation in society is inherent to human nature and is a fundamental, necessary, and productive component of human affairs, it also emphasizes that society is not, itself, a sentient entity with elemental moral status. Society is neither conscious nor purposeful. Rather, "society" is a label for the cooperative activity of socially oriented individuals, activity which attains moral status only through its participants, through its capacity for expanding the bounds and benefits of individual striving. Society is the product of human action but not its purpose.

This suggests that the "good of society" — reinforcement of its capacity to provide those benefits — is an important practical goal but, also, implies its importance should be measured in terms of individual, rather than communal, well-being. Society has no more and no less moral standing than its individual participants would as a mere collection of disengaged individuals. Aggregation of that standing does not transform its nature. Thus, it is neither the moral purpose of society to benefit its participants nor the moral purpose of its participants to benefit society.

Obviously, societies exist because participants expect to benefit from cooperation. If they consistently fail to do so, they will refuse to participate further and society will fragment or collapse, to re-form along more hospitable lines. To some extent, the mere existence of a society — the existence of a stable and accessible community to nourish innate human social yearning — is a benefit even if that society provides little specific material or spiritual reward. So the bar for what material benefits an individual expects to gain from participating in society may be fairly low. But he will expect some benefit.

We may fairly say, therefore, that the purpose of society *is* to benefit its participants. But that purpose is practical, not moral. And the opposite claim — that the purpose of the individual is to benefit society — is completely backward.

The question of how we should best account that practical benefit — of whether "the greatest good for the greatest number," or "how it treats those least among us," or "reward for the righteous," or "to each according to his contribution," or "to each according to his need," or "freedom of contract," or some other paradigm is the proper measure of a society's practical value — does reflect a moral rather than practical judgment and will, therefore, be a source of cultural variance and debate. But that moral judgment of value reflects on a society's practical effectiveness in fulfilling a particular set of moral goals, not on some underlying moral nature of society itself.

Certainly most people would consider a society effective at implementing an immoral conception of social benefit– say Nazi Germany — to be, itself, immoral. And certainly societies are not merely directed by such paradigms but reinforce them within the citizenry, so they not only serve immorality but perpetuate it. Yet, moral fault ultimately lies within those moral paradigms themselves, not within the working structures of the society. Even where those working structures incorporate morally objectionable methods and behavior, like the excesses of a police state, the society itself is not a moral agent but a neutral and peculiarly adapted tool for implementing the aggregated moral vision of its dominant participants.

To the extent that 'society,' in the abstract, is both inherent to human nature and generally beneficial to its members, there are compelling pragmatic reasons to favor and reward 'social' behavior over 'anti-social' behavior. And, therefore, there are also compelling pragmatic reasons to support and defend 'society' in its own right as a beneficial institution, distinct from the matter of individual rights and welfare. "Social responsibility" is a valid and worthwhile pragmatic goal even if it is not a moral obligation.

Moreover, to the extent that individuals are willing and able to profit from society, moral accounting and self-interest might also suggest a reciprocal obligation to invest in social beneficence, and might suggest that society may and should withhold its benefits from those who shirk that responsibility. But that defines the relationship between individual and society more as a covenant than as fealty. The concomitant moral duty accrues not to society per se, but to the moral principle of reciprocity, a variant of proportionality. That is, it is a matter of justice, of giving back in proportion to what you have received or may expect to receive.

Similarly, if individuals, in the name of equity or for some spiritual reason, assume a personal moral responsibility for the well-being of their fellow man, they may also derive a consequent personal moral responsibility for the well-being of society as a whole. But that reflects the moral self-perception of the individual with regard to other individuals, not the nature of society. And, as with other individual moral choices, that is an individual prerogative, not a collectively enforceable duty.

Although society has no particular moral standing beyond that of its members, and despite our earlier characterization of society as the "cooperative activity of individual moral agents," we must acknowledge that society is not merely the aggregation of its current and sovereign citizens, that society is more than the sum of its parts. Society, though not a conscious moral agent, *is* a self-organizing entity in its own right with its own forms, imperatives, and life-cycle.

It may not be properly asserted that society exists independently of its individual participants. The cultural and structural paradigms of a society exist in the minds and habits of its citizens as much as in any material or written or Platonic substance; and a society without citizens is a dead remnant of its original form.

But neither can it be asserted that society exists solely as a collection of contemporaneous individuals with no distinct and enduring character of its own. The forms, mores, traditions, and practices of society encode both structure and history, and replicate themselves through generations of citizens as a persistent and palpable gestalt. Society is a distributed embodiment of a culture, with history and with inertia, with a governing code of conduct, with an evolved practical wisdom, with mechanisms for reward and sanction, with a mimetic facility for regeneration and extension, and with power over the behavior and beliefs of its participants. In a very limited sense, those attributes, and particularly the mechanisms that allow for self-organization, self-perpetuation, and evolution, make society organic. But it is a rudimentary organism of instinct, not of intelligence, with no self-awareness and, therefore, no autonomous purpose or moral privilege.

Consequently, it may not fairly be said that individuals acting within a society are wholly autonomous. Society certainly imprints the individual as much as individuals construct society.

But that is a statement of practical effect, not of moral authority. It does not imply that individual moral autonomy is a fiction. The social imprint informs individual moral prerogative but does not usurp it.

Cultural and Social Norms

Cultural and social norms are both the social grease that allows civil society to function without excessive friction and the cultural glue which binds its participants together.

At the surface level, adhering to such norms of behavior is a matter of simple courtesy: they define a social and cultural "comfort zone" of roles, expectations, and obligations within which people generally can interact with confidence, without social risk or anxiety, and without reliance on moral courage or intellectual dexterity or emotional effort. A general respect for such norms allows people to go about their daily lives with a sense of security, without fear of distress or embarrassment, neither offering nor taking offense, neither implying a threat to others nor feeling themselves threatened. Violating such norms, whether for good reason or for bad, imposes an emotional and intellectual burden on others by forcing them out of that comfort zone and into an active negotiation over their own proper social and cultural conduct.

The strong-willed and the rebellious — and the merely arrogant — may scoff at the cost of such burdens but they are real and troubling to a great many people. There are certainly times and places where such an imposition is necessary or even desirable. But we must recognize that it *is* an imposition; and we must understand, therefore, that such breaches of social protocol, however pragmatically or morally justified, are also acts of aggressive self-indulgence.

But, at a more fundamental level, such norms are the very definition of "Society" and of "Culture," precisely what differentiates those integrative human forms from a mere collection of self-directed individuals. What is a culture if not a system of normative values and behaviors? What makes a group of people a society, rather than merely a crowd, if not a consensus about those normative values and behaviors? And what is it, if it is not accommodating those normative values and behaviors, which places the individual within a culture and a society rather than without it?

Behavioral norms are not the trappings and appendages of a culture. They are its essence. And, while certain social conventions may seem individually inconsequential or even insidious, as part of an integrated code of social behavior they embody the aggregated moral, material, and spiritual values of a society and of its underlying culture.

That does not imply that every individual more or tradition is a perfect embodiment of some cultural or moral ideal, nor that a system of mores and traditions is inevitably self-consistent, nor that cultural stasis is necessarily positive. It merely recognizes that the various mores and traditions evolved together as a cultural and moral system with a unique history of cause and incentive and compromise, and with idiosyncratic relationships between the individual elements. It, therefore, also implies that individual mores and traditions may not be as discrete as they appear, that they are knotted into the overall cultural web and may unravel it in unanticipated and harmful ways as they evolve — or as they are uprooted by social upheaval or by narrow efforts at cultural reform.

As with E.D. Hirsch's (oft misconstrued) assertion about cultural literacy and cultural canons,[1] the actual behaviors defined by cultural norms may be less important, in themselves, than the fact that they are *normative* — that they define a common and stable social behavioral framework that everyone within the culture and society understands, acknowledges, and shares. 'Liberals' have consistently disparaged and dismissed the "values" of the so-called "values voters" as mere religious dogma because they are so often defined, not in the abstract, but by reference to specific examples on which self-identified evangelical Christians happen also to assert strong opinions. But the theme that binds those examples together is not fundamentalist Christianity but a respect for normative behavioral codes.

As norms that define the limits of a cultural comfort zone, cultural mores must exist somewhere in the center between behavioral extremes and must be narrow enough to be non-confrontational — that is, to ensure behavior at the near margins is still, if not entirely conventional, at the least inoffensive for all but the most punctilious and the most subversive members of society. That is, norms must be *normal*, in the mathematical sense, not the psychological one — they must be well-matched to a cultural consensus; they must live near where the majority of people live. Hence, they must, by definition, appear constrictive to those inclined toward the avant-garde and decadent to those inclined toward the doctrinaire.

What frightens "values voters" about the 'liberal' world-view is not its assertions about what is "acceptable" but its assertions about what is "normal" — and, ultimately, its assertions about what we will hold up as our cultural ideal. "Family Values" is merely shorthand for the notion that public mores should be normative rather than inclusive; that not everything that is permitted is of equal moral or cultural or practical value and that passing

---

1 *Cultural Literacy: What Every American Needs To Know*, E.D. Hirsch, Vintage Books 1988

social judgment on extreme behavior is not only acceptable but desirable; that society should help the family unit socialize children to understand and respect the cultural norm rather than undermine it.

As long as cultural norms are well-centered between extremes of behavior, the boundaries of those norms need not, and generally will not, appear as bright lines dividing "good" from "bad" with precision. Rather they define the hazy periphery of a continuum that ranges outward from "conventional" to "acceptable" to "eccentric" to "impolite" to "distasteful" to "rude" to "offensive" to "vulgar" to "depraved" to "intolerable" to "evil." The precise location of those markers along the continuum is a matter of judgment and, in a highly heterogeneous society, the communal understanding of those locations will vary somewhat among its geographic and spiritual and intellectual and economic and cultural subsets — one man's eccentricity will be another man's convention. But, given the boundary between "good" and "bad" as a continuum, rather than as a sharp limit, those variations are tolerable. Behaviors along the continuum are encouraged or discouraged by a corresponding continuum of social rewards and social sanctions which may vary from community to community without causing excessive friction between them.

To the extent that such rewards and sanctions are socially imposed, rather than politically imposed, they will also generally be moderated by a cultural respect for privacy, a tacit conspiracy to ignore behavior that is neither overtly public (at least beyond the social enclave where it is accepted) nor calculated to draw attention to itself. It is precisely that kind of studied ignorance that has traditionally allowed subcultures from the eccentric to the depraved — red-light districts, the 'gay' community, artists' colonies, nudist retreats, communes, religious sects, individual eccentrics and malcontents, and so on — to exist as circumspect enclaves and with some modicum of freedom within a generally conservative culture. And it is precisely insolence toward that studied ignorance — either unwarranted scrutiny by those outside the subcultures of behaviors that are reasonably and deliberately circumspect, or the insistence by those subcultures on exhibition and flaunting of behaviors considered objectionable by the wider culture — that so often ignites otherwise quiescent social tension and intolerance.

Political reward and sanction are hardly ever quite so flexible. In the realm of power and law, the gray area between permitted and forbidden, between legal and illegal, is generally quite narrow. As a consequence, in a society governed by consensus rather than by edict — in a democratic society — that narrow line between legal and illegal is properly set on the continuum of behavior somewhere in the neighborhood between "depraved" and "intolerable" rather than closer to the norm, which leaves a broad range of unconventional (or merely anti-social) behavior subject only to persuasive social and cultural sanctions and not to coercive political and legal ones. Supreme Court Justice Potter Stewart famously declared that he knew pornography when he saw it[1] and refused to prohibit that which did not rise to a level of intolerability; but the fact that some things were legally tolerable did not, as least at the time, yet mean they were necessarily culturally acceptable in polite company or for unfiltered public display. "Tolerance" does not have to mean "approval."

As a normative force, culture is inherently and properly resistant to change. That is its material and ethical utility: to encode and preserve a "beneficial" behavioral standard so that it may persist across a society and over time. A culture represents the evolutionary wisdom of a society about the best paradigms and the best practices for living within the environment, including the feedback of its own historical moral frameworks, mores, and internal social structures, for which it evolved.

That does not mean that cultures are or should be static. As with any evolutionary system, the current cultural state is not necessarily the optimal one; it is merely the best, by its own quirky reckoning, that its unique history has encountered and incorporated. Further, to the extent that it *is* optimal, it is optimized for its peculiar historical environment and not necessarily for its contemporary one. Continuing cultural evolution is healthy; and the farther the environment — either external or internal — in which culture operates diverges from its historical basis the more important mechanisms for cultural evolution become.

But embracing the desirability of cultural evolution need not imply an animosity towards all cultural standards. And it certainly need not imply an animosity towards the very existence of cultural standards in principle. Evolution is a measured process of deliberative testing and replacement and, while over time it may result in dramatic change, such change accumulates from small increments rather than from radical transformation. Thus, cultural evolution is not inherently anti-conservative. It does not merely throw over obsolete behavioral norms but replaces them with culturally validated contemporary ones, keeping the cultural essence largely intact over the short term.

One of the great strengths of a generally democratic culture — separate from but augmented by democratic governance — is the opportunities and mechanisms it provides for cultural evolution. All cultures can evolve as technological and geo-political circumstances change around them.

---

1 *Jacobellis v. Ohio*, 1964

But extremely homogeneous cultures offer little internal social variance from which evolutionary change can emerge; and politically repressive governments that enforce cultural paradigms politically can halt overt changes at least for a time. In both cases the failure to evolve quickly enough to adapt to the external environment will eventually result in social collapse or revolution.

But cultural evolution need not comprise merely an acquiescence to external pressures. It can, instead, result from an internal enlightenment, the recognition that certain changes, either imported from other cultures or adopted internally from the cultural perimeter, are culturally or socially or materially or morally beneficial. Such enlightenment may result simply from innovation, from a willing embrace of a newly discovered way of thinking or behaving that offers unambiguous advantage — from an evolution in our conception of what is possible. Technologically driven change often follows that pattern.

Such enlightenment may also, however, cascade from prior intellectual, emotional, spiritual, or moral enlightenments, from an evolution in our conceptions of what is wise, or good, or sacred, or right. Both the American Revolution and the American civil rights movement of the mid-twentieth century were such cases: decades of moral and intellectual evolution resulted in a new enlightenment about human dignity and equality; and that moral and intellectual enlightenment drove cultural and political structures to evolve as well. The cultural enclaves and individual eccentrics that are tolerated at the periphery of democratic societies provide precisely the cultural dissonance that catalyzes such change; and the significant distance between the cultural norm and political constraints on behavior leaves room for that avant-garde to develop and to make itself heard throughout the culture.

The first two sources of cultural evolution — adaptation and innovation — are largely pragmatic and, although such changes always engender conservative resistance, it is often modest. Since any advantage offered by such change may be measured against traditional standards of "good," and often against strictly material ones, both the opportunity for disagreement and its scope are somewhat limited.

The intellectual/emotional/spiritual/moral cascade, however, often induces extreme resistance as it seeks to transform not merely behavioral norms but the very standard of "good" itself. It is one thing to say that certain forms of self-expression are not as harmful to social concordance as we once thought and ought to be upgraded from offensive to merely eccentric; it is something else entirely to declare, if the cultural understanding has always been the opposite, that the right to self-expression has a higher moral value than social concordance. In appearance, such a cascade is more a "cultural reform" than a "cultural evolution"; and, as a process typically driven by moral rather than practical concerns, such "cultural reform" will often attempt to force our conception of normative behavior in one large step far out to some cultural extreme.

One unfortunate consequence of "cultural reforms" which push cultural and social norms away from the consensus behavioral comfort zone and toward the extreme is that they narrow the range of the behavioral continuum between "acceptable" and "intolerable." That similarly compresses the range of corresponding social sanctions, and exaggerates the variations between cultural subsets. When the behavioral continuum becomes squeezed so narrowly that those two cultural markers nearly overlap — when, for instance, admonitions to 'tolerance' and 'freedom' (and against 'prudery') allow public sexual mores to be set by the sensibilities of the most licentious rather than by the sensibilities of the broad center; when "acceptable" public sexuality becomes almost indistinguishable from "pornography" — then the continuum degenerates into a de facto bright-line limit. In such circumstances, even minor variations between cultural groups over placement of the boundary become major sources of social friction because the boundary defines not the gentle slope between civilization and anarchy but the edge of the abyss, a precipice dividing unassailable approbation from utter condemnation. And, when that precipice moves so far that some begin to demand approbation for what others still consider depraved and intolerable, friction will devolve into bitter conflict.

To some small extent that situation can arise naturally from normal cultural evolution: if different groups within society view the continuum of behavior through different moral lenses then different groups will likely evolve at different rates, and some will race ahead and others be left behind as the center of consensus shifts.

But social friction is exacerbated when such shifts are not the result of an evolving social consensus at the center but are, rather, propelled from the cultural fringe through a self-proclaimed assertion of intellectual or moral superiority. When, for instance, an avant-garde cultural clique dominates the flow of information — dominates academia, media, and entertainment — then their cultural preferences tend to be asserted as the normative baseline for public discussion, notwithstanding the cultural distance between those preferences and the broader cultural norm. The way people behave on TV and in movies and in music videos and in modern novels strays far from the way people behave generally across broad swaths of America; but if you got your sense of American culture from magazines and popular web-sites and cultural commentary in newspapers and on television, you might come away thinking Beyoncé, not Morgan Freeman, is closer to the cultural center.

If some form of cultural excess becomes the normative reference against which alternatives are measured, then the adherents to the cultural norm begin to appear as advocates rather than as defenders, as reactionary rather than as honorably conservative. As a result, the cultural norms exhibited and promoted and reinforced in the public square tend to be dragged outward from the center toward the uncomfortable edge almost by default, and without a corresponding evolution in the underlying cultural consensus.

And when those cultural shifts are reinforced or resisted with political power, either by establishing actual bright-line legal limits where none previously existed, or by moving existing bright-line legal limits away from their natural place on the behavioral continuum, or by eliminating bright line limits entirely, then the inherent malleability and adaptability of localized and non-binding social sanction is completely lost. Every disagreement over placement of the legal limit is elevated to the status of a life-or-death struggle for some cultural ideal — to the status of a "culture war."

Family

The instinctive, thus primary and most generally beneficial, human social unit is the family. That recognition represents a practical judgment, not a moral one. Although there may be separate moral or theological or traditional arguments either for or against a family-focused social order, the practical primacy of family as a social unit is a product of human psychology, not of any moral ideal.

The fundamental advantage of family as a social unit is its intimacy. The idealized Norman Rockwell family is both loving and supportive, intimate in an emotional sense. Families which approximate that vision of the ideal to some greater or lesser extent are still more the norm than our cynical popular culture –in its fascination with the extreme and the insolent and in its disdain for the ordinary and the civil — would lead us to believe. Forging emotional bonds and commitments is both innate and necessary for personal psychological well-being. We will naturally favor those with whom we have such bonds and privilege such commitments over others with a less emotional basis. And such emotional intimacy certainly reinforces the benefits and the mechanisms of family as a social unit by intertwining personal with communal welfare and by inspiring sacrifice for the common good.

But even families short on such emotional connections can function as quasi-effective social units. The most socially useful intimacy of family is demographic, not emotional: it is the bonds of similarity and familiarity, operating on a modest and, therefore, personal scale, which naturally forge a collection of individuals into an integrated social organism. This reflects two practical propositions:

- All other things being equal, your own well-being is more likely to be aligned with the well-being of those with whom you know you share common traits and circumstances than it is with the well-being of strangers.
- Long-term observation of others, and experience with their skills and quirks, makes you far more likely to evaluate — and to exploit or to accommodate — those alignments constructively.

In other words, if the family does well you will probably do well, too, and you know the family intimately enough to have a pretty good idea of how you can both contribute to the family's success and benefit from it. If that stranger does well, then...who knows?

It is precisely such common characteristics that draw and hold a family together, so such connections may be assumed of family members whereas they must be laboriously and haphazardly discovered among outsiders. The bonds of family are given to you as a child and passed on by you as an adult to your own children, without need either for effort or for risk. You know uncle Zeke and he knows you, if not directly then at least from the stories you've both heard since you were a kid. He has a pretty good idea he can trust you to work diligently, not only because he's heard about all your school triumphs over the years but also because, if you don't, he can ask your dad to tell you to shape up. And you can trust him not to short your pay for the same reasons.

Naturally, in any heterogeneous and socially mobile culture we are likely, eventually, to accumulate experiences outside the family and to discover others with whom we share common interests and characteristics. And, having discovered common connections with others beyond the family, it is natural to begin to consider some of them, as well, to fall within the "family" umbrella. Hence, the "extended family," the best friend who is "like a brother" or the mentor who is "like a father"; and, hence, the joining of families by marriage.

But those friends are likely to share more in common with you than they do with the rest of your kin. You have bonded with them because of time spent together, because of shared interests, because of particular synergies in your personalities. But your family has not spent that time with them. Those shared interests may be precisely the ones your siblings neither understand nor appreciate. Those personality traits you find endearing may grate on your parents. And your friends have ties to their own families that may draw them away from yours. For those reasons, such person-to-person familial extensions tend to be less stable as collective social institutions than the familial core.

In the extreme, of course, some individuals may find so much more common ground with their friends than with their relations that they minimize, or even sever, the traditional family ties in favor of their new peer group. To the extent such voluntary groupings function as self-reinforcing and mutually-beneficial social units they, too, may be considered, at least for practical purposes, "family." However, such groupings, based as they tend to be on idiosyncratic and contemporary personal preferences rather than on broad and inheritable characteristics, tend not to persist over generations in the way traditional biological family units do.

It is, naturally, possible to forge other kinds of social units by conscious acts of will, either by imposing legal obligations or by convincing participants to embrace some extra-personal and common purpose. People join clubs and participate in local government and "rally 'round the flag." Extension of the family to higher-level structures — to the tribe or to the village or to the nation — or more abstractly to a perhaps vaguely-defined "community" — is also a natural human process that increases the potential of the social benefit.

But we must recognize that such extension also entails a cost to the individual. The more diffuse the similarities and the less tangible the familiarities among participants in the social structure — the less intimate it is — the less that structure can or will accommodate and support individual needs or preferences. Your family may or may not understand you and adjust itself to your needs; the Congress most definitely will not.

The source of that cost is more fundamental than a mere failure to live up to the ideal of loving your fellow man. Regardless of moral obligation or emotional commitment, the less you know about an individual and his circumstances the harder it is to accommodate them; and the more diverse the individual needs and desires that a community must accommodate, the less flexibility it has to accommodate them all. At some point, when the needs and desires of individuals within a community diverge so much that they pull the community in opposite directions simultaneously and it has to choose one over the other, the advantages which accrue to the individual and to society from similarities and familiarity among citizens disappears.

We should note here that the notion of a family unavoidably implies a social hierarchy, a social structure of levels defined by degree of social proximity or distance. If you afford some small group of individuals — the family (or the tribe or the village or the nation) — a greater consideration in social affairs then you must, conversely, afford others a lesser. The family, therefore, is the highest level of a social hierarchy that descends through decreasing degrees of intimacy, through clubs and associations and neighborhoods and communities and towns and other ever more distant, and sometimes overlapping, economic and social and political units, down to the level of the state and the nation and beyond. And, although all those social levels provide some degree of social benefit, as the highest and most intimate level of the social hierarchy the family will generally provide its social benefits to the individual the most flexibly and with the greatest immediacy.

But, if the fundamental function of family is as the most intimate and most privileged level in a hierarchy of social relationships, then a familial social organization is, at root, at odds with communal social structures which depend on a generalized embrace of egalitarianism or of a superseding duty to the whole of society. Such social structures, with their global notions of social obligation, are antithetical to hierarchies. If we are all brothers equally, then none ought claim from the few or offer to the few a privilege on loyalty and commitment; and if our principal duty is to the whole of society, then offering special and higher status to an intimate group of kindred must be a violation of that duty. It was not an accident that both Lenin and Hitler created youth organizations oriented toward devotion to the state and with the purpose and effect of alienating children from parents and of emasculating family ties.

If the family is the natural and most generally beneficial social unit, then there is great reason for government to avoid undermining its ability to function. That doesn't necessarily mean, in the common parlance, that government should "support families," but neither should it be hostile to them or allow its policies unintentionally to disrupt their beneficial function. Government may not be "family friendly," but it ought, at least, to be family neutral.

Despite the tenor of current political debate, neither the recognition of the primacy of family as a social unit nor the specific advantages that lead to such primacy imply anything about how a family is or ought to be constituted. Family, as a functional unit, is defined by its capacity for binding its participants together through empathy and by its ability to adapt its own structures to the needs of its members. Natural biological imperatives make, and will continue to make, families built around genetic linkage — and particularly around parents and children and siblings — the cultural norm because those linkages provide an ingrained and particularly compelling basis for commonality and empathy. And, to the extent that we find value in cultural norms, per se, *because* they are normative, we should respect and, perhaps, favor "traditional" family structure as a cultural institution.

But genetics is not the only source of familial virtues, and the assertion that a family is defined by some traditional biological form, rather than by its function, reflects a concern with cultural stability — or with a particular and narrow view of some "natural order" — more than with practical social utility.

Individual Autonomy and Achievement

It is possible for individuals, even embedded within a society, to act and achieve individually. This does not deny that human beings are social creatures or minimize the benefit they derive from interactions with other individuals and from general social structures. Nor does it deny the inequities among individual circumstances.

But, declaring that humans operate within and benefit from a context, whether a social matrix or a primordial jungle, is neither insightful nor noteworthy. The social context in which individuals operate is but part of a broader environmental, material, cultural, intellectual, historical, and moral background against which individual efforts play out — a background inherited by the individual and largely beyond his control, a background shared broadly by other individuals and neither designed to support any particular individual's efforts nor particularly concerned with their results.

Thus, to assert, as some do, that individual achievement is a myth because individuals work in a social context or begin with disparate advantages and handicaps is to confuse *achievement* — advancement resulting from a fusion of intent, imagination, skill, effort, and persistence within a pre-existing context — with *accomplishment*, the measure merely of the end-state of their efforts. And to assert on that basis that "society" has a claim on the fruits of an individual's achievement or, for that matter, on his accomplishment because it would have been impossible without "societal support" is like asserting that the air has a claim on an individual's life because he could not live without breathing.

Where there *are* specific social, cultural, or material conditions designed and provided to enhance or retard specific individual efforts, the distinction between individual achievement and communal achievement can and does blur. That is, for example, the basis of a particular 'conservative' critique of affirmative action (that it undermines an individual's claim to respect for his/her personal achievements) and forms a rational basis for some useful public programs, from support for scientific research (in which results derived from public funding are to be public resources) to ROTC or AmeriCorps scholarships (in which private tuition support is to be paid back in public service). And where benefits and handicaps are both intentional and unjust — the result, for example, of long-standing and institutionalized racial prejudice — the resulting taint on individual effort can be severe.

But, even in such contexts, individual achievement, however tainted, does not completely evaporate into a communal mist. And such contexts are not as common as they are often asserted to be. They are not extinct. But they are also neither pervasive nor nearly as seminal as they once were. In most cases the benefits and handicaps an individual faces are incidental rather than intentional, widely distributed among the population rather than narrowly focused on the individual, and properly viewed as the neutral launch point and raw material from which achievement may be wrested.

It is undeniable — and undisputed — that those who begin, for whatever reason, from a more fortunate circumstance are likely to end similarly. It is undeniable and undisputed that focusing attention only on outcomes — on test scores or on grades or on performance or on wealth — may undervalue the achievement and the potential of those who lack such advantage. And it is also a reasonable moral proposition that those thus favored ought at least to acknowledge their advantage and, perhaps, to "give back" by assisting those at a relative disadvantage.

But fulfilling moral obligations is an individual prerogative; and to acknowledge advantage is merely to argue for finding better ways to evaluate individual potential and achievement when potential and achievement are at issue. Neither the existence of advantage nor some social duty to pass it on bolsters an argument for denying that individual achievement exists, nor does it bolster an argument for devaluing accomplishment itself in circumstances where accomplishment — the skill of the surgeon or the reflexes of the pilot or the knowledge of the scholar or the acumen of the leader or the effectiveness of the teacher — ought to be of primary concern.

Human Frailty

Human beings and human systems are fundamentally fallible and corruptible. As a result, it is unwise either to rely on social, political, or economic systems that are intolerant of error and malice or to allow a single individual or institution immutable authority over any important aspect of our lives. A practical corollary of this is that coercive authority which seems benign, or even benevolent, under today's just and visionary leaders may seem perilous and malevolent under tomorrow's benighted and ignorant ones. 'Liberals' who espouse the expansion of government programs and power seem to forget that two of the last eight Presidents were 'conservatives' they considered misguided, and another three of the eight, spanning 20 of the last 40 years, were 'conservatives' they considered either stupid, or cunningly evil, or both. The FBI authority to investigate domestic "subversive" activities abused by Richard Nixon was established two decades earlier by Harry Truman; had Jimmy Carter managed to create a nationally mandated and coercive energy conservation strategy it would have been implemented by Ronald Reagan; if Bill Clinton had succeeded in socializing health care under a government umbrella George W. Bush would have become our Doctor-In-Chief. I suspect none of those are what the supporters of such policies had in mind.

Nor, I suspect, are those 'conservatives' who trusted in John Ashcroft's discretion in applying the terms of the Patriot Act to "terrorists" (or in President Bush's equivalent discretion on NSA wiretaps) as sanguine about the discretion of Barack Obama's appointee, Eric Holder, nor would they have been as sanguine about any successors appointed by John Kerry or by Hillary Clinton.

Human Motivation

Self-Interest

Human beings will act in what they perceive to be their economic, social, and moral self-interest. This does not presume that trust, generosity, and even altruism don't exist. On the contrary, in a wide range of circumstances many people, or even most people, will prove gracious. Hurricanes and earthquakes strike and Americans open their wallets. However, we must acknowledge that many people will behave otherwise under the best of circumstances, and under bad circumstances even the most gracious tend to narrow the scope of their generosity to their own immediate community or family. In the most extreme circumstance, under threat or deprivation, tribalism and self-defense is still the natural and widespread human response. And in any circumstance there are human predators who will abuse our trust, generosity, and altruism to their own benefit and against ours.

It is important to emphasize here — because this is so often either misconstrued or willfully misrepresented — that the proposition that people are self-interested is not a mere assertion of greed. Certainly the classical market theories of economics are based on the presumption that people will make economic decisions based on economic self-interest, but self-interest cannot and should not be understood only in terms of material wealth because that is not how people behave. Honest and intelligent economists understand that. People have a great many interests — in self-preservation, in the safety and security of their loved ones, in comfort, in their sense of self-worth, in self-image, in public image, in legacy, in ideology, in justice, in moral accounting, in piety, in spirituality, in adventure, in beauty, in truth, in joy — and they may sacrifice material gains, or even personal safety, to pursue those interests they value more.

We should also acknowledge, notwithstanding the derisive nature of arguments to the contrary, that although these other interests are not material they can often be valued in material terms. We, in fact, assign such value all the time.

For example, what is the material value of helping the less fortunate? Those of us who give to charities for that purpose estimate such a material value, conditioned by our own economic circumstance, whenever we write the check: most of us would like to give more, but given other interests in things like supporting ourselves and our families, providing a nurturing home, and even in securing some creature comforts, we do not. Why? Because, in some intuited sense, we judge the marginal cost to those other interests to be higher than the marginal benefit of more charitable giving.

That does not mean that either charity or those other interests are, in any real sense, more material than they are moral or spiritual or emotional or intellectual. It simply reflects the fact that, when we make tradeoffs among our interests, we must somehow evaluate them on the same scale. When the tradeoff involves material interest, either as a consequence or as a medium of exchange, then economic value is a natural language for evaluating cost and benefit.

That also suggests a source of contention that is fundamental to any policy decisions in the political realm: there is, literally, no one "right" answer to the question of how much of our resources should be dedicated to any particular non-economic policy.

Any policy, even if it is intended to do good, will create costs as well as benefits. If both the costs and the benefits are purely material (and if they are accounted clearly and honestly), the optimal tradeoff between cost and benefit is clear. But if either the benefits of the policy or its costs are moral, or spiritual, or intellectual, or cultural or somatic, then assessing them in material terms will be necessarily subjective and idiosyncratic. When, as is almost always the case, the distribution of costs and benefits among citizens is uneven, that subjectivity will inevitably lead to disputes over those assessments. And those assessments are further complicated when, as is almost always the case, the resources available for implementing the policy are limited and/or also needed to support other policy goals.

Incentives

Incentives matter; we will have more of what is rewarded and less of what is penalized. If we reward indolence and penalize productivity, some number of people will choose indolence over productivity and a larger number will shift their efforts incrementally away from useful activity and toward idleness. As we mitigate the costs of irresponsibility by extracting succor for the irresponsible from those who behave responsibly, we devalue responsibility and make irresponsibility more attractive.

That incentives matter is true in absolute terms, as we all identify patterns of what behaviors bring us the most and least happiness. But the effect of incentives is also amplified by a perception of contrast — by an observation that others are receiving more or less than we are for the same degree of physical or emotional or moral effort — because such contrasts evoke our sense of justice and injustice along with our assessment of self-interest.

That incentives matter is a pragmatic statement, not a moral one, an acknowledgement of the way people behave not a prescription for how they ought to behave. Over short periods and in exigent circumstances it is possible to override this natural inclination, to convince the bulk of people to ignore perverse incentives and to sacrifice for some notion of the greater good. But for most people that kind of concentrated moral fervor is not sustainable in routine circumstance and over the long haul.

That this is a pragmatic, rather than moral, axiom does not imply it is wholly insulated from any moral consideration. People respond to incentives pertaining to moral as well as material behavior, and sometimes the two overlap. If you consider sloth or waywardness to be not merely unproductive but morally objectionable, then a concern with incentives that encourage sloth or waywardness takes on a moral dimension. That is inevitable, but unfortunate inasmuch as it tends to transform tightly-focused discussions about incentives into open-ended, contentious, and emotional debates over appropriate and inappropriate moral aspirations.

Commerce

The dual human propensities to act in one's own self-interest and yet to act in concert with others implies a fundamental human impulse toward commerce. This is a pragmatic acknowledgement that a "free market" is a direct product of human nature and is, for that reason, the most effective practical system ever envisioned for improving the overall human material condition through the conversion of natural resources and human effort into individual and societal wealth.

The evolution of commerce at the individual level into a society-wide economic system depends critically on the acknowledgement and enforcement of the individual right to property — the right of each individual to consume or to accumulate or to exchange or to aggregate with others that which they themselves produce. Without that key acknowledgement, both the incentive for individual participation in commerce and the self-organizing mechanisms for wringing the maximum benefits from such commerce are undermined and the productive potential of the system is diminished. This practical defense of property rights is separate from — but complementary to — the philosophical defense of property rights as a manifestation of individual moral autonomy.

The evolution of commerce at the individual level into a society-wide economic system also depends on some social mechanism for enforcing commercial agreements and for discouraging fraud and coercion — for holding participants accountable for their promises and constraining their excesses and predations. At the individual level, those who fail to fulfill their agreements or try to gain advantage by using force will lose the trust of potential trading partners and their opportunities for future commerce will wane; the system will self-regulate. At the level of a large and complex society, however, much of commerce becomes practically anonymous. As a result, those self-regulating mechanisms become much less effective and some external mechanism for regulation and enforcement of contracts — typically but not necessarily a mechanism of government — becomes necessary. Again, this specific practical requirement on behalf of large-scale commerce is separate from but complementary to a general moral responsibility to respect others' rights and to hold ourselves and others morally accountable for actions.

Governance and Government

The Need for Governance

Any large-scale human social structure will inevitably suffer from irreconcilable disputes; some form of constraining authority is, therefore, necessary for the effective functioning of social institutions. Where there is society there must be governance because human interaction will always lead to conflict as well as to cooperation — and conflict without governance devolves into anarchy and violence.

In purely voluntary associations — the bulk of human social behavior — governance is most often achieved cooperatively through consensus and social pressure: those who fail to fulfill their responsibilities to other individuals or to the group may be refused cooperation or ostracized or ejected; and one who disagrees with a ruling of the group or its leaders either accepts it as a condition of continuing membership in the group or leaves to find another group more attuned to his or her needs.

However, when association with a 'society' is not purely voluntary — when, for instance, a pervasive community and culture is so widespread and so dominant as to constitute a "nation," as to allow no practical means of independence from it — those sanctions may be both impractical and draconian. In such cases the forms of governance must be more formal and the governors must have the authority to enforce their edicts on those who would not willingly comply.

The Dangers of Governance

Political authority — government — is fundamentally and necessarily coercive. This is, in one sense, a tautology. If the power of coercion is what differentiates political authority from any other form, then any form of control that is coercive must be, by definition, political even if it appears otherwise. But that implies either that any relationship imposing limits on our behavior — every relationship — is political or that "coercion" cannot be understood as a mere diminishment of options but, more specifically, as a consciously-imposed constraint which precludes the free exercise of the rights to conscience and property — typically through the mechanism of violence (actual or threatened) or of deception. In other words, coercion is an *action* not a *circumstance*; it is *determinant* rather than merely *persuasive*; and it constrains your *rights*, not merely your *choices*. Coercion is not a synonym for persuasion. Coercion is defined in the difference between being convinced grudgingly to do something because the consequences are less objectionable than the consequences of any alternatives, and being tricked into doing something without realizing it, or being forced to do something under threat of bodily harm or imprisonment.

The power of coercion allows political authority to threaten individual liberty where other forms of social control do not. We must note and acknowledge that social pressures and economic circumstances can and do have an intense constraining effect on individuals; and we must note and acknowledge that some individuals haven't the physical, mental, emotional, spiritual, or material resources to surmount those constraints. For those individuals, the conceptual distinction between political and non-political controls may be irrelevant in practice.

Nonetheless, the distinction is real. External circumstance can be changed to a greater or lesser extent through individual talent, ingenuity, and effort; and the weak may at least enlist the support of the strong and the like-minded to help them circumvent economic or social constraints — or retire from the field to avoid them. But political control always implies the threat or application of force to ensure compliance, leaving even the talented and the wise and the ambitious, the strongest and the strongest-willed — and those among the weak they have chosen to assist — at its mercy.

Social Institutions

Human beings, left to their own devices, will tend to create voluntary cooperative endeavors to satisfy their individual and communal needs; there are alternatives to government for solving most everyday problems. Although there are exceptions, these endeavors tend to grow or shrink to match the scope of the problem they are intended to solve and tend, therefore, to be particularly responsive to the needs of their participants. They also naturally develop their own internal structures for governance, so they are not entirely devoid of political aspects. But the particular governance mechanisms they employ are varied, consensual, and adapted to their specific tasks. Thus their voluntary nature, their limited scope, and the variety of consensual governance mechanisms they employ distinguish them from the overarching — and coercive — political structure associated with government.

The various voluntary institutions of a society serve the same fundamental governing purposes as government itself and are at least as essential for the orderly and civilized functioning of society. As a result those who favor weaker government tend to favor stronger voluntary social institutions, customs, and mores — and the traditions which sustain them — and those who, for either legitimate or self-serving reasons, wish to emasculate traditional voluntary social institutions, customs, and mores often favor stronger government.

The Purpose of Government

The use of political authority should be limited to purposes of such gravity that survival is in question, of such scope that unanimity is essential to success, or of such perverse incentive that voluntary cooperation is impossible. That is, we should avoid the use of coercion — we should avoid the application of government and of law — unless we really have no choice because voluntary cooperation is either impossible or insufficient to protect us from grievous harm.

The necessary and legitimate purposes of government are: to protect the rights and enforce the responsibilities of individual citizens; to secure the citizenry and the state against aggression from foreign powers; and to administer what commons exist on behalf of the citizenry. All these are manifestations of a basic proposition: enjoyment of liberty ought to be a matter of right, not of individual power, and the moral basis for political authority is the deployment of collective power on behalf of individual liberty.

Different people will prioritize these purposes differently, and judgment of their relative importance changes with circumstance — whether or not, for instance, threat from a foreign power is perceived to be imminent. But most 'conservatives,' though acknowledging certain commons (the global atmosphere, for example, or the structures of society, or the machinery of government itself) may be inevitable, would place administration of the commons at the bottom of the list, would oppose attempts to expand the scope of the commons at the expense of individuals, and would support attempts to reduce the scope of the commons by judicious identification and designation of property rights wherever practical means of doing so were available.

Of particular note in the current environment is the friction between protecting liberties and protecting security. On the one hand, a state which tramples individual liberty in the name of security loses its moral claim to sovereignty. On the other hand, a state which has lost its sovereignty to internal or external aggression — to crime or invasion — cannot fulfill its necessary function, cannot prevent the aggressors trampling individual liberty. The optimum boundary between liberty and security will tend to drift with the level of perceived threat and will always be contentious and elusive.

This illustrates a fundamental contradiction regarding government: the protection of liberty *generally* always requires some reduction in liberty *specifically*; and the ideal compromise between the two is indeterminate, a matter of judgment rather than of fact. In a perfect world, liberty would persist effortlessly as individuals and societies acknowledged their responsibilities for the liberty of others. In a perfect world, liberty would require no protection. But the world is far from perfect, and those who would circumscribe liberty succeed narrowly, even when they fail broadly, by forcing us into such compromises.

The Political Responsibilities of Citizens

Citizens have a responsibility to support the political authority in its necessary and legitimate functions; but the political authority has an obligation to limit its demands to purposes which are both necessary and legitimate. The citizens' responsibility to the political authority is another consequence of the duality of rights and responsibilities. If government is necessary to secure the rights of citizens within a social context then citizens have a responsibility to support that endeavor.

But the inverse is also true: a government which exceeds that mandate to the point where it, itself, threatens the citizens' rights not only forfeits its claim on the citizens' fealty but earns their active enmity.

The Limits of Distributive Justice

Efforts to guarantee a particular standard of "fairness" or "justice" will be inevitably undermined by commerce and by natural human disparities; therefore, to be effective such efforts necessarily require a high level of coercion and an invasive scrutiny of individual and social behavior. Any program to ensure some level of distributive justice over an extended period of time requires either a priori restrictions on the right to produce, hold, and trade resources or post-priori confiscation and redistribution of resources after the exercise of such rights has, as it must, perturbed the favored distribution.

Suppose each of 100 of us starts with $10, a perfectly equal and "fair" distribution. You have a particularly lovely singing voice, so each of the rest of us agrees to pay you $1 to perform a concert. Or, perhaps, you are particularly adept at growing tomatoes and you sell each of us a tomato for $1, which we then eat. You end up with $109, while each of the rest of us ends up with $9 and a pleasant memory or a full stomach. All well and good, but tomorrow we all wake up with that memory fading quickly, hungry, and with only $1/12$ of your wealth. By next week, the memory and the full stomach will be gone but the wealth disparity will persist.

Will we still consider that fair? Maybe not. Should we then demand your wealth be "redistributed" to make us all even again? Or should you never have been permitted to collect for the effort you put into singing or growing tomatoes in the first place? If so, what coercive agents of the state will be required, and what authority must they be granted, in order to enforce that policy?

In either case, had you known what the outcome was to be, had you known that what you collected for your effort today would be taken away from you tomorrow in the name of fairness, would you have bothered to put in that effort in the first place? And, if you had not bothered, would we all be better or worse off for never having been inspired by your music or sustained by your food?

The Nature of Power

Power Corrupts the Powerful...

Authority ultimately serves its own end; and power not only corrupts but attracts the most corruptible. Lord Acton famously observed that power corrupts.[1] We commonly presume that such corruption must spring from some submerged (or purposely concealed) avarice which surfaces when access to power creates an opportunity for profit. That is, we presume power seduces through latent greed with the lure of material or psychological or spiritual reward. We presume that an underlying ethical weakness causes people to give in to temptation. And we presume, therefore, that we can inoculate ourselves against that seduction by demanding the greatest

[1] Letter to Bishop Mandell Creighton, 5 April 1887; from *Historical Essays and Studies*, ed. J.N. Figgis and R.V. Laurence, Macmillan 1907

integrity of those entrusted with power and by specifically circumscribing the potential for personal gain.

Alas, as often as not our attempts to inoculate ourselves against moral fault in our leaders fall short of expectation. People are remarkably adept at hiding their own moral failings, even from themselves, and at bending or circumventing rules intended to prevent them from getting what they desire. And, as with any human enterprise, such attempts to control behavior are at the mercy of the law of unintended consequences, sometimes increasing rather than decreasing our vulnerability. Campaign finance laws intended to insulate politicians from special interests created the infamous 527s and PACs which have so roiled recent election campaigns. Rules which protect us from unscrupulous building contractors increase the arbitrary authority, and the opportunities for corruption, in municipal zoning and building departments. No one has yet devised a way to erect perfect institutional barriers between avarice and power, and we should not expect that to change.

But, even if it did change, power would still corrupt. Avarice is not the only, or even the primary, source of power's corrosiveness. Whether power is sought for selfish ends or for magnanimous ones, those who wield power ultimately realize two things: that to continue to do so they must defend their hold on power against the strivings of others who would supplant them; and that, however much authority is theirs already, acquiring more would enable them to achieve their ends faster and more effectively. That is, they realize that to continue to *use* power they must continue to *have* power, and the more power the better.

The temptation, then, to turn some part of the power they wield toward sustaining and expanding itself is relentless and overwhelming. Few can resist such temptation for long, if for no other reason than that it can be so easily rationalized as serving a noble end: "*I must continue to hold power in order that I may continue to wield it on behalf of my righteous purpose. It is not for me. It is for my cause!*"

But once authority is turned toward perpetuating itself — once the exercise of power becomes focused on internal goals rather than external ones, directed away from the ends that may be achieved and toward the means, and in particular toward the agent, that would achieve them — the line between the magnanimous and the selfish begins to blur. That is the nature of power: the righteous man may seek power in the name of some higher good, but the act of achieving and exercising power inevitably elevates his own status; and the more he protects and expands that power in the name of others the more benefit he accrues to himself. Moreover, the more he identifies his own continued hold on power with the good he desires — the more he convinces himself that he is necessary and not merely sufficient to the achievement of that good — the more effort he exerts on his own behalf and the less effort remains to be exerted on behalf of his original goals.

The effect is amplified by the fact that those most likely to oppose his authority — and those, therefore, most actively seeking to usurp it — are precisely those benefitting the least from it. Those who benefit from others' exercise of power have no pressing need to wield it themselves.

Hence, the self-justifying reasoning that convinces those in power of their own indispensability is often accurate and, therefore, self-reinforcing: those trying the hardest to replace the powerful would *not*, in fact, use that power to pursue the ends that the current office-holder desires. Those holding the reins of power often *are* indispensable to their cause, not because no one who agrees with them could exercise that power as well, but because those who agree with them are not the ones striving to wrest power from them.

Whether it seduces through avarice or arrogance, the corrupting effects of power are exacerbated by self-selection among those who seek out power in the first place. Who tends to seek power? Those most adamant about the goals they wish power to achieve; those most convinced of their superior ability to wield power wisely and effectively; those with the greatest personal ambition, who desire not only that their noble ends be achieved but that they be the one to achieve them; those whose ends are less noble than covetous. Power is a magnet for the most zealous and the most self-aggrandizing among us — precisely those most likely to fall victim to the self-justifying redirection of power toward sustaining and extending itself.

...and Power Corrupts the Powerless

Concentrations of power lead, inexorably, to the corruption of power; the larger the concentration, the larger the corruption. Naturally, if power seduces those who wield it then more power concentrated in their hands can only increase its seductive potential. That is the second half of Lord Acton's axiom: that absolute power corrupts absolutely. But a concentration of power has an effect on the broader society in which it operates quite beyond its effect on those who wield it.

We must recognize, foremost, that there is no such thing as a neutral exercise of power. If the exercise of power does not induce changes in behavior then it was either superfluous or ineffectual — no exercise of power at all. By definition, an exercise of power is coercive. It disadvantages someone or some group by causing them to change behavior, by making them do what the powerful want them to do rather than what they want to do themselves.

The disadvantaged will, naturally and legitimately, resist. The more inequitable, or excessive, or capricious, or imprudent, or costly the commands of the powerful seem the more determined that resistance will be. People don't like being told what to do and they will rebel against being forced to do things which cause them harm.

Conversely, for those whose interests align with the interests of the powerful, the exercise of power will provide an advantage by changing the behavior of others. Those fortunate enough to reap such windfalls will encourage them as earnestly as those who must pay for them will resist.

Hence, aside from its effect on those wielding power, any exercise of power will generate and assign costs and benefits within the broader society, costs and benefits that result from a human act of will rather than from a neutral interplay of circumstance and ability. Both the existence of winners and losers in that transaction and, more importantly, the fact that the allocation of such roles is the result of a conscious choice, rather than of fickle fate — the fact that someone powerful got to *choose* who would win and who would lose — create a broad incentive throughout society to influence that choice, to pursue and attain influence over those whose will determine such outcomes. That is, they create a broad incentive to pursue and attain influence over those who wield power. If the whims of the powerful can determine whether you will prosper or wither, then you would be smart to try to get them on your side and you would, arguably, be foolish not to.

Thus, power not only seduces those who wield it but entices attempts at seduction by those under its sway. This is not some unfortunate and minor side-effect of exercising power. It is an inevitable and indivisible aspect of the dynamic by which power is used: *power corrupts not only those who wield it but those upon whom it is wielded and, in fact, corrupts the very environment in which it exists and any institutions or systems in which it is exercised.*

When power is concentrated into some central authority, rather than dispersed, that tendency to corruption is exacerbated by several factors. First and foremost is the scope of activities over which concentrated authority can be brought to bear. Power is never dormant. It tends to be applied whenever and wherever it can be, which implies that the more power that can be wielded the farther it will reach into the affairs of those under its purview. The result of this ever larger scope of activity is ever more opportunity, and ever more incentive, for corruption. Further, when the power being applied is centralized rather than dispersed, the opportunity to reap a large benefit from a single act of corruption is amplified to the extent that a corrupted official exercises wider, rather than narrower, jurisdiction.

In addition, concentrated authority implies not only a wider scope for its actions but a deeper one. That is, not only does a concentrated authority induce more changes in behavior but each individual change can have a larger and more deleterious effect. Hence, the incentive for corruption — the incentive to mitigate or to reinforce that effect by purchasing influence — grows along with the opportunity for it.

In particular, it should not be a surprise that, as government becomes more powerful and more intrusive, as it takes upon itself authority to allocate ever more of society's resources to its own ends and to redistribute those resources among its citizens according to some politically-determined scheme, those citizens, as individuals and in aggregate as corporations, will try ever more strenuously to influence governmental choices in their favor. It would be truly remarkable if that were *not* the case.

This leads to a practical corollary to our general rule: *a larger and more active government will be a more corrupt government.* To constrain corruption in government you must constrain the scope of government. There is no other way.

Finally, centralized power is more prone to corruption because it eliminates alternatives. Dispersed power creates its own opposition: it creates the possibility of a clash of interests, the powerful acting against the powerful and the possibility of those unhappy with the exercise of power switching allegiances and jurisdictions to avoid the worst of its predations. But centralized power is monopolistic power, with no rival and with effectively unlimited scope. It is inescapable. And, because it is inescapable, it almost *demands* attempts at corruption as the first and only line of defense against its arbitrary edicts.

At the level of practice, rather than structure, concentrations of power result in increased corruption for a much more mundane reason: a broader scope for the exercise of power requires a larger organization to support it; and a larger organization requires more people for its operation and can, therefore, exercise concomitantly less scrutiny over the abilities and ethics of each individual that it hires. That is, the potential for corruption increases with the size of the organization because it becomes more likely that some of those hired to exercise power will be particularly prone to corruption. Three stories in the *New York Times* from a single day, the 21st of March 2008, illustrate the point: a New York City crane inspector was indicted for fraudulently reporting an inspection on a crane that was never inspected and that later toppled; an INS agent was arrested for having demanded sex of an immigrant in return for issuance of a Green Card; and State Department employees were fired for having illegally accessed candidate Barack Obama's passport records. All of these abuses of power were the result of corruption at the lowest possible level in a gargantuan power structure; and yet all of these abuses of power had, or could have had, far-reaching, and potentially disastrous, consequences both for the individuals over which power was exercised and for society generally.

Although 'conservatives' tend to focus on government when talking about the dangers of concentrated power we must, in fairness, acknowledge that the dangers of concentrated power extend to private organizations as well. Corporations, universities, churches, newspapers, and other organizations which exercise economic or cultural or moral power are not exempted from the ill effects of power by the fact that they are private rather than public agents, even if they are nominally "non-profit" agents of the "public good" rather than operating purely in pursuit of self-interest. Unless such organizations are reinforced by government with some delegated political authority, their power cannot be literally coercive — that is, they cannot actually force anyone to do what they want by threatening them with physical harm. But concentrated economic or cultural or moral power, even if not technically coercive, can be nonetheless determinative for a great many people. The fact that people are free to choose among bad alternatives does not negate the observation that better alternatives might be available but for the power such organizations can apply.

Nonetheless, by its nature such power is distributed rather than centralized, and to a greater or lesser degree people submit to the authority of private organizations voluntarily and can escape that authority if it becomes too oppressive. If Exxon is despotic you can switch to Shell or, in the extreme, ride a bike instead of driving.

The same cannot be said of the federal government; and the greatest danger of privately held power lies in its ability and propensity to coopt governmental power on its own behalf.

Political and Economic Arrangements

Scope and Mechanisms of Governance

Compulsion inevitably will be resisted and subverted by those who are compelled; any granting of authority toward the alleviation of 'unfairness' or 'injustice' for some necessarily involves a reduction in liberty for others; and, therefore, efforts to achieve fairness or justice are more ethically undertaken by persuasion than by coercion, more effectively undertaken by incentive than by command, more reliably undertaken locally than globally, and more prudently undertaken in the private or civic spheres than in the political one. Cooperation, rather than regulation; motivation, rather than authority; limited, rather than expansive scope; standards, rather than laws: that is the ideal. Coercion should be reserved for circumstances when those have already and demonstrably failed.

The Rule of Law

The rule of law provides the most effective and the least perilous procedural framework for achieving fairness and justice. This requires that law be discernible a priori to those subject to it, that enforcement of law adhere to the a priori understanding of its terms, and that within the same context the law be applied in the same manner to all people and at all times. It is incompatible with ad hoc decisions by regulators or courts attempting to achieve some desired end, be it self-serving profit or selfless justice; it is incompatible with after-the-fact clarifications or changes-of-heart by legislators, regulators or courts that apply some new standard of behavior to actions already taken; and it is incompatible with differential treatment by legislators, regulators or courts based solely on the presumption that some are more or less 'deserving' than others.

The Free Market

The economic arrangement least destructive of individual liberty is one built around individual choice — a 'free market' constrained and regulated by the obligation to respect the rights of all participants. This is both a pragmatic proposition and a moral one: the fact that the free market is, by its synchrony with underlying human nature, the best known producer of general economic well-being is, itself, fortuitous and momentous but not its primary benefit.

Constitutional Democracy

The political arrangement least destructive of individual liberty is a constitutionally circumscribed democracy, whether direct or representative, with a strong separation of powers, with structural proscriptions against a "tyranny of the majority" over individual liberties, and with authority decentralized to the maximum practical extent. This, too, is a moral proposition. It is, in fact, frequently neither as pragmatic nor as immediately effective as some other arrangement might be: consider Congressional gridlock — and that it was said in defense of Mussolini's Fascism that he made the trains run on time.

A corollary to the desirability of democracy is the general proposition that, in order to keep that democracy accountable to its citizens, any authority citizens delegate to government should be retained at the lowest level that allows it to be effective — that is, if the local government can do something effectively, then the authority to do it should be held locally and not delegated to the state government; and, if the state government can do something effectively, then the authority to do it should be held by the state and not delegated to the federal government.

We often forget — notwithstanding President Lincoln's soaring rhetoric in his *Gettysburg Address*[1] — that, in the original design of our Federalist system, the individual state governments were the acknowledged "governments of the people" while the federal government was a government of the States. In our modern context, we might more wisely push even that down a level and say that our local governments should really be recognized as the "governments of the people," given that the government of even the largest state at the time of America's founding[2] oversaw a population that would today represent a modestly-sized city; and the federal government in 1789 asserted authority over a population that would nowadays be equivalent to the population of a mid-sized state.[3]

Interactions with Other Societies

International Politics and Commerce

While participation in international commerce and the general promotion of free markets and democracy beyond our borders is desirable and beneficial, we have no moral standing to coerce others into adopting our favored social, economic, or political arrangements. That doesn't mean attempts to convince others to be more like us constitute "cultural imperialism." Persuasion is not coercion, and we have some good reasons to suppose that many of our cultural, economic, philosophical, and political preferences are, in fact, objectively better than what may be found elsewhere. But it does mean respecting others' right to reject our overtures.

Although this is stated in terms of international policy, *it is equally applicable among the states of the United States and among the towns within individual states.* Just as America has no moral standing to coerce people in Botswana to behave more like Americans, so New York has no moral standing to coerce the people of Texas to behave more like New Yorkers

---

1 Which proclaimed, in reference to the sovereignty of the federal government which had been successfully defended at battle of Gettysburg, that "...government of the people, by the people, for the people, shall not perish from the earth."
2 Virginia, at -550,000 people; from *Century of Population Growth: from the first census of the United States to the twelfth, 1790-1900*, U.S. Census Bureau, 1909
3 -4 million people; from *Historical Statistics of the United States, 1789-1945*, U.S. Census Bureau, 1949

and Washington, D.C. has no moral standing to coerce the people of the 50 different states all to behave more like each other.

Collective Security

While collaboration in regional and global security, trade, and legal arrangements are desirable and beneficial, we have no moral standing to subjugate our own sovereignty — and thereby the rights of our citizens — to any foreign or otherwise unaccountable authority. This applies rather obviously to international organizations, like the United Nations and, in particular, the International Criminal Court, which would claim legal sovereignty over actions of American citizens not only abroad but, in cases and on some subjects deemed the province of "international law," even within the bounds of the United States.

But it is also the basis for the original Federalist design of the American polity, itself, which divides sovereignty between the federal and state governments and limits the authority of the federal government to specific enumerated powers that have a clear national scope; and it reflects the analogous division of sovereignty and responsibilities, within the states themselves, between the various governments at the state, county, and municipal levels.

At root, this reflects the general principle stated earlier: delegated political authority over individual behavior should be retained at the lowest possible level that allows it to function effectively, because the farther that delegation gets from the affected individuals the less accountable it can be to them. There is no good reason for a state-level law when a local law will serve the purpose; there is no justification for imposing a uniform Federal standard for something when variance from one state to another causes no unmanageable harm; and there is never a credible argument for delegating our own national sovereignty to international organizations whose actions and governance are so far removed from any semblance of oversight by the American citizenry that assertions they operate by the "consent of the governed" cannot be anything more than wishful thinking.

Sovereignty and War

Governments or societies which demonstrate both a willingness and a capacity to impose their own authority in place of our sovereignty have abrogated their responsibilities to respect our rights and have, thereby, jeopardized their claims to our own forbearance. Or, in simplistic terms: as long as you keep your political and societal pathologies within your own borders we have no right to interfere; if you export them to us we claim the right to repel them and to ensure you cannot export them again.

As with violations of individual rights, violations of national sovereignty should be neither capricious nor disproportionate — nor are they always wise even given sufficient justification. But, there are instances in which they are both justified and the least damaging among bad options. War is always a horrible policy; but it is often not the worst possible policy and it is, alas, on occasion the best policy we can muster.

It is worth noting that the determination of what constitutes a threat to our liberty, safety, and sovereignty can be the subject of great contention, even among 'conservatives' or among 'liberals.' At the least, however, it is fair to say that in the modern era of global economic interconnection, increasing dependence on fragile technological infrastructure, instant communications and real-time transportation, and increasingly powerful weapons, threats that might once have seemed remote now seem suddenly imminent — or seem likely to become imminent with alarming rapidity and scant warning — and the traditional 'conservative' urge to security through political isolation is receding.

It is also worth noting that notions of how to respond to external aggression — or to the potential for aggression — are in flux. In particular, there is a recent recognition, now almost a maxim, that more-or-less democratic governments, so far without exception, resolve disputes with each other relatively peacefully; whereas non-democratic governments often do not. Although the libertarian right asserts we have no moral standing to coerce others into adopting our favored political arrangements, and although the relativist left asserts doing so amounts to cultural imperialism, it has become a default policy goal among both mainstream 'liberals' and mainstream 'conservatives' that the best way to ensure long-term security, and, ultimately, to avoid war is to convince our enemies and potential enemies to embrace democracy. The major contention between 'liberals' and 'conservatives' on that point is how best to go about that enterprise and whether, and when, some particular level of peril and urgency makes it appropriate and necessary to do so at the point of a gun.

Moral Discipline

Without a general societal commitment both to individual liberty and to civic responsibility, constitutional limitations on political authority cannot prevent the degeneration of democratic government into tyranny or anarchy. A society of purely self-interested individuals or tribes will function as a society of warring factions striving for advantage, not as a nation. And, in the absence of internalized moral constraints or a sense of social obligation, individuals or tribes who gain control of political power will use it to undermine both liberty and the rule of law for others.

To function as a nation — politically or socially — requires the personal and collective discipline to subjugate immediate self-interest or narrow tribal-interest to a higher goal of collective national good. In a constitutionally circumscribed democracy, having prudently denied the state authority to impose such goals and such discipline, these virtues must arise voluntarily from the citizens and must be fostered by the civic and cultural institutions of society.

It may seem a contradiction that the individual has a right to autonomy but that the individual must subjugate that autonomy to some notion of the "common good" in the name of preserving political order and social cohesion. But the contradiction is not as vast as it might appear.

In the first place, in a social setting the individual right to autonomy is constrained by the individual responsibility to respect the rights of others — the minimum standard of the "common good." If you choose to live alone on a deserted island your autonomy is effectively boundless; when you choose to interact with others you choose to constrain your own autonomy to accommodate theirs.

Further, we have already acknowledged that the practical need for governance to secure liberty against anarchy implies its own additional set of moral responsibilities, and that accepting and enjoying the benefits of society entails honoring additional and reciprocal practical social obligations. Taking a broader view, one might also consider that common interest and personal interest converge in the long term, that living in a politically and socially stable democracy is in one's long-term interest (either directly or through one's descendants) even if the short-term actions required to maintain stability and democracy are counter to one's immediate interest.

More importantly, however, recognition of the importance of a generally moral society is a statement of how we ought to behave *socially*, not a prescription for enforcing that behavior *politically*. The political protection of the freedom to do *as you will* is not a social exemption from the duty to do *as you should!*

There is no contradiction in advocating both liberty and the moral use of that liberty. Quite to the contrary, the existence of political liberty makes social and cultural institutions that reinforce the moral bases for the exercise of liberty all the more vital: if people are to be free to act, then it is imperative both that *they know how to act morally* and that *they aspire to do so*.

Traditionally it was presumed, even by those like Thomas Jefferson[1] who was otherwise famously at odds with religious authority, that only religion, or at least a religious outlook, could provide the moral framework and discipline necessary for such a civic-minded society. Why would that be so? Because it, alone, provides the four necessary ingredients for maintaining a civic-minded moral consensus *en masse*: 1) a self-consistent moral framework derived from an objective and unambiguous moral authority — God — emphasizing the moral value of both individual and community; 2) a nominal *non-political* governing structure — the clergy — acknowledged as the social custodians of moral authority and responsible for moral education and for resolving moral disputes; 3) a morally homogeneous and collegial social community — the congregation — to reinforce moral behavior through peer pressure and through social rewards and penalties; and 4) an omniscient observer and judge — again, God — to reinforce moral strictures out of public view, to encourage moral consistency and habits of moral rectitude.

As such, it is not the specifically theological aspects of religion that are important to democracy but the *social* ones shared by most of the world's major religions: the recognition of individual moral value even within a social environment; the emphasis on duty to a community and to a higher moral purpose; and the social reinforcements, both supportive and punitive, that promote individual moral behavior despite temptation to act immorally. For that reason it is religion as a general social institution, not any particular religion or any particular religious doctrine, that is valuable.

Further, it is not necessary or, perhaps, even desirable for everyone to adhere to the same religious tenets, nor even for everyone to be religiously observant. It is sufficient that generally religious moral teachings are widely enough followed and respected that they can exert their beneficial social effects across all faiths and even on the non-observant.

We may argue the question of whether religion truly is necessary to a moral society. As a godless heathen who, nonetheless, embraces a well-considered moral code, I would like to believe that such moral discipline may be founded on philosophy, or on some form of secular civic creed, rather than on religion per se: a study of political philosophies could provide the necessary moral frameworks under the guidance and governance of academic philosophers; a civil society which allowed itself to be concerned with such things, and to be critical enough to enforce them, could provide the social reinforcement; our own well-conditioned consciences could provide

1 "And can the liberties of a nation be thought secure when we have removed their only firm basis, a conviction in the minds of the people that these liberties are the gift of God? That they are not to be violated but with his wrath?" — Thomas Jefferson, *Notes on the State of Virginia*, 1781

the omniscient observer and judge. Certainly for some individuals that is sufficient.

Observing the state of our increasingly secular culture, however, I admit to a disappointed and discomfiting skepticism in that regard. Academic methods and the environment of the academy reward novelty over consistency, and encourage — perhaps demand — debate and divergence, rather than consensus and convergence, in the understanding and acceptance of moral frameworks. And the ideal (though perhaps not the practice) of reason over passion in such secular and academic debate seems unlikely to engage, on any large scale, the emotional commitment required to ensure general compliance with moral stricture. In the absence of the unambiguous moral authority provided by a God, the canon and institutional and educational supports provided by a clergy, the social reinforcement of a collegial congregation, and the external omniscient observer judging private behavior, it may well be impossible to instill in people generally the kind of moral commitment, consistency, and, most importantly, concordance required for such social discipline.

If such an authoritarian backdrop is necessary for moral discipline, what but a church (broadly conceived) can provide it?

The obvious alternative authority available for moral direction and education — the one seemingly advocated ever more often and ever more strenuously by the secular forces within our society — is the state itself. In one sense this is not radical. American governments, through the mechanism of public schools, have traditionally augmented the moral framework taught in homes and churches with practical civic guidance on the responsibilities of citizenship and patriotism, and calls for a broader role in moral education merely extend that role.

But even limited education on the mechanisms of civics has at times been controversial. Is voting a right or a duty? Is it more patriotic to support the government or to question it? The prospect of the state indoctrinating our children on their duties to the state presents a conflict of interest at odds with the notion of "government by the people" — and such limited efforts are a far different endeavor than fundamental moral education.

Setting aside the contentious question of whose moral vision should become official and monopolistic state policy under such an arrangement, conferring upon a single institution both primary moral authority and political power inevitably undermines liberty. It is one thing to enforce moral authority by imposing social sanctions or threats of spiritual sacrifice on transgressors; it is quite another to enforce moral authority with the power of arrest and imprisonment, to enforce moral authority at the point of a gun. In the middle ages the Catholic Church exercised both moral and political authority in Europe and the combination led to the Inquisition and other human catastrophes. More recently, socialism, in its various guises, prescribed the converse arrangement, the state acting as moral authority, moral educator and adjudicator, and omniscient observer. In practice where it has been tried around the world — and predictably so — the universal result has been political tyranny, moral decay, and the utter loss of both liberty and civic values.

These disastrous examples should not be surprising. Enforcement of moral discipline is an authoritarian process in the most rigorous sense: at its very foundation is an unassailable assertion of moral authority. It is logically impossible for a government "by the people" — a government accountable to and controlled by its citizens, which presumes as its moral basis the consent of the governed — simultaneously to be the source of moral authority and control for its citizens. Either government is morally accountable to its citizens or citizens are morally accountable to their government. It cannot work both ways.

But, although government should not, itself, wield moral authority, neither should it unduly obstruct or undermine the exercise of moral authority by the non-political institutions of civil society, that do wield it. If the purpose of government is to defend liberty against anarchy, and if moral virtue is necessary to that enterprise, then government should do what it can within its constitutional constraints to provide a political environment in which social and cultural institutions facilitating moral virtue can thrive. What it should not do, lacking its own independent moral authority, is to favor one such institution or moral framework over another — except in the singular case of resisting institutions and frameworks which advocate the overthrow of those democratic constitutional principles upon which the government is founded.

Institutional Stability

The Value of Institutions

The recognition that human institutions that do not fulfill their functions well tend to dissipate over time, while ones that fulfill their functions well tend to remain vital; and that human institutions tend to evolve over time the better to match their processes to their function. Therefore, long-standing political, legal, civic, social, and cultural institutions are precisely those which are likely to have evolved to fulfill their functions well and to have proven their worth through continued vitality. And, therefore, absent a fundamental change in the nature of man, society, or institutional purpose, it is more prudent to preserve those long-standing institutions than to replace them with something new and unproven. Although this sounds like a doctrinaire assertion of the status quo, it is actually more akin to the "precautionary principle" that 'liberal'-leaning environmentalists use to argue against things like genetically-modified crops: we know that what we have now generally works and we don't know for sure what dangers lurk in the changes you are proposing. So why not just play it safe?

Unanticipated Consequences

Human knowledge is imperfect, human behavior is erratic, and human institutions are organic; therefore, the anticipated consequences of an institutional change are prone to differ from the expectation, and the unanticipated consequences of an institutional change are as likely to make things worse as to make things better. This comes directly from the assumptions that chance and uncertainty rule the natural and human worlds, and that human beings are inherently fallible. What we don't know can hurt us.

Predictability

In human endeavors, the predictability of individual and institutional responses to a given action is as important to both success and fairness as the responses themselves. If we want to be able to accomplish anything over a time-frame longer than the next few minutes or the next few days, we need to be able to plan. We need to be able to guess with reasonable confidence what is likely to happen if we make an investment of resources or of time or of passion into some project. And we can't do that in an environment of continuous social or economic or political — or legal or regulatory — turmoil.

Precedent

Human beings make decisions about proper individual and social actions based on their understanding of accepted rules for behavior and on their extrapolations from experience with prior actions; therefore, current processes and precedents will determine future actions; and, therefore, the processes by which goals are achieved and the precedents they establish for future actions are at least as important as the goals themselves to a stable social community. The ends don't justify the means because the means, themselves, create consequences and determine future ends.

The Rule of Law

The rule of law provides the substantial benefits of predictability, stability, and continuity, and is therefore superior to the 'rule of man.' Aside from any moral considerations, the rule of law mandates both fair notice when rules are to change and consistency in their application, which makes it relatively predictable and stable. Hence, it facilitates planning for the long-term and promotes a durable social contract.

Stability

Long-standing political, legal, civic, social, and cultural institutions are inherently valuable and provide the substantial benefits of predictability, stability and continuity. Therefore, they should not be torn down or emasculated merely to serve current intellectual fads, political whims, or ideological rigidity. Uncertainty, volatility, and disruption are not benign, so they should not be ignored or dismissed as irrelevant. Anxiety over uncertainty, volatility, and disruption should not be disparaged as an infantile artefact of timidity and fear. And the prospect of creating uncertainty, volatility, and disruption should be reason enough to pause for reflection, and perhaps to relent, when you are feeling a rebellious urge to change things, even if that change might be for the better.

Conservatism in Perception

I began this book with the complaint that 'conservatism' is misunderstood and misrepresented in modern America, and then assigned myself the task of correcting those misunderstandings and misrepresentations by exploring what 'conservatism' actually is and does. Thus far, that exploration has focused on the theoretical underpinnings of 'conservatism': on the philosophical and moral bases for 'conservative' beliefs and on the assumptions, about the natural world and about human nature, which undergird those moral philosophies. I have enumerated principles and presumptions that 'conservatives' value. I have categorized those principles and presumptions according to their philosophical roots. I have provided arguments to support those principles and presumptions and have explored some of the subtleties and nuances of what they imply. And, to make those discussions clearer, I have attempted to organize those principles and presumptions into broad subject areas based on which aspects of human experience they address.

But political philosophies operate in the real world of people and events, not in some Platonic world of abstract essence. In the transition from theory to practice, the meaning of a political philosophy is filtered through human perception and conditioned by human concerns, by the practical subjects to which it must be applied and the social and cultural environment within which it must operate.

Any attempt, then, to understand American 'conservatism' must contemplate not only what principles are in play but how those principles are perceived and mapped onto everyday politics and policy.

In the process of examining 'conservative' principles I have used a few concrete applications of those principles as examples. But that is all they were — examples, intended as illustrations of the theory, not topics in and of themselves.

It is now time to expand on those, to discuss some of the observable and common ways in which 'conservative' principles are applied (or mis-applied) in practice, and how that practice is perceived both by self-described conservatives and by their critics.

This discussion of how 'conservatism' is perceived and practiced is organized into three sections:

- A discussion of specific accusations that are commonly leveled against 'conservatives,' of stereotypes commonly applied to 'conservative' policies, and of specific groups of 'conservatives' who commonly draw particular ire from their political and cultural opponents.
- Discussions of Capitalism and of Social Responsibility, two topics which loom large in the imaginations of those who vilify 'conservatism' and 'conservatives.'
- A discussion of personal traits and tendencies often associated with individuals who describe themselves as conservative and which may help explain their attraction to a 'conservative' political philosophy.

The Critics' View

Against the Stereotypes

Since opponents of modern 'conservatism' routinely classify it by reference to its most extreme elements and stereotype it by identification with its most obnoxious supporters, it is worth a bit of effort to note some commonly discussed items that, while identified with certain 'conservatives' in the modern American context, are not in the general list of core 'conservative' principles. This brings me back, alas, to my original complaint — the persistent need to explain 'conservatism' by what it is not. Nonetheless, if the goal is to broaden the general understanding of 'conservatism,' the exercise is both necessary and worthwhile.

To that end, here are a few of the notable absences from our statements of principle:

There is nothing there about the Bible. It is undeniable that religion is an enormous factor in American 'conservatism' at present, and a broad 'conservative' belief in the importance of moral virtue to civil society — not to mention a conservative deference to tradition — implies sympathy for religion generally if not for any specific religion. In addition, specifically religious 'conservatives' tend to be vocal and passionate, and they therefore form a strong base of support for 'conservative' candidates in elections.

But the same was true with respect to 'liberalism' of the religious 'liberals' at the core of the movements for civil rights, "economic justice," and "peace" which were synonymous with 'liberalism' in the sixties and seventies and beyond. The Reverend Martin Luther King, Jr. (father of the American Civil Rights movement); Father Robert Drinan (not merely a peace activist, but a Democratic Congressman); the Reverend William Sloane Coffin (disillusioned anti-communist and CIA officer turned civil rights activist, designer of the Peace Corps training program, and vocal critic of the Vietnam war); the Reverend Jessie Jackson (both an agitator for various racial justice causes and a Presidential candidate for the Democratic Party); Father Gustavo Gutiérrez Merino (coiner of the term, "liberation theology"); Pope Francis (whose pronouncements on a variety of contemporary political controversies have delighted American 'liberals'): no one on the left objected that these clerics were irrigating their political gardens with ideas from the tainted well of religious faith. American 'liberals' embraced these religious leaders without hesitation, as often as not *because* of their religious credentials rather than in spite of them.

As with those religious 'liberals,' the faith of religious 'conservatives' has led them to cultural and political positions which are not themselves bound to religion; and, as with 'liberals,' many 'conservatives' arrived at those positions for reasons having nothing to do with religious belief. Conservative religion certainly overlaps political 'conservatism' but it does not define it.

In addition, much of the current religious 'conservatism' is more cultural than theological and its intersection with politics is not only at odds with many aspects of political 'conservatism' but is largely driven by a perception of political persecution — a perception that cultural 'liberals' have been using political mechanisms to attack fundamentally social and religious institutions which must now be defended politically.

There is nothing there about sexuality or family arrangements, except in the general (and sometimes contradictory) principles of maximum liberty for the individual to decide on such matters and the fundamental importance of stable and well-defined social arrangements to cultural cohesion. It is undeniable that there are identifiably 'conservative' cultural and religious values and taboos governing those issues, values and taboos which undergirded long-standing non-political social regulation and which have now been undermined by the sexual revolution and by evolving social conventions about marriage and family. People who value and want to preserve those cultural and religious traditions, or cultural and religious traditions generally, are conservative by definition, at least in the cultural realm.

But, such doctrinal cultural conservatism aside, there is also a legitimate and largely pragmatic conservative concern about the increasingly deleterious effects of having, over the last forty years, politicized what are fundamentally matters of culture. And those who find the politicization of culture, and the assertions of governmental authority that make it possible, to be a danger to both individual liberty and social concordance, regardless of its particular cultural targets, may resist that trend without any specific concern for cultural traditions in and of themselves.

In the context of American 'conservatism,' saying that cultural traditionalists are 'conservative' does not imply that all, or even most 'conservatives' are cultural traditionalists. And, as with explicitly religious 'conservatism,' the modern trend toward political activism on these issues is in large part a reaction to a perceived use of political power by "progressives" to weaken or tear down many of the non-political social institutions that formerly moderated sexual and family behavior.

There is nothing there about racism or misogyny — excepting, again, the general principles of liberty for the individual and the rule of law, which would tolerate neither as politically-enforced policy — nor, indeed, is there any mention at all either of race or of gender. There are no statements in those principles about the superiority or inferiority of any individual or group based on anything other than behavior.

Yes, 'conservatives' undeniably assert that some types of behavior are superior to others. Yes, 'conservatives' undeniably assert that inferior behaviors should be sanctioned, for the most part socially rather than politically. But they make no assumptions about who can or cannot, will or will not, behave in superior or inferior fashions. And they do not prescribe behavior that is, somehow, incompatible with or unavailable to members of any particular group. 'Conservatives' do not ask women or ethnic minorities to "behave like white men." They ask everyone, white men included, to behave like free, autonomous, responsible human beings.

Elimination of official racism and misogyny imposed by political means, and the censure of unofficial racism and misogyny throughout society, are two of the great 'progressive' successes of the twentieth century. The many who objected at the time were, on those narrow issues, at one time and by definition conservative — meaning, simply, that they resisted the cultural change.

But that was a long time ago: it has been 50 years — many social generations — since the cultural explosion of the civil rights movement and the passage of the original Civil Rights Act. Our current president (and the last two 'conservative' secretaries of state) is African American, as is one of our nine Supreme Court justices. Our popular culture is arguably dominated by a hip-hop ethos which emerged from the African American community. Our most recent Secretary of State (and current front-runner for the next Democratic presidential nomination) is a woman, as was the last 'conservative' Secretary of State, several Supreme Court justices, the entire Senate delegation from California, and the nearly all the Senate and Congressional delegations and the Governor of libertarian-leaning New Hampshire.

No doubt, prejudice and inequality remain. Humans are tribal, and we have not yet fully tamed that lamentable part of our natures. But, at this point, the agenda of those unreformed supporters of Jim Crow and a "woman's place" is much better described as revolutionary than as conservative. No one should doubt that those few are at odds with many of the principles of 'conservatism' and with the vast majority of modern 'conservatives.'

'Conservatism' can be criticized on this topic for its principled, and sometimes infuriatingly inflexible, insistence that political power should not be used to enforce cultural change or to regulate interpersonal affairs. To many modern 'liberals,' precisely because they have spent decades trying to use the blunt instrument of law to eradicate social "intolerance" from our culture, that sounds like an infuriatingly inflexible insistence on maintaining the status quo. But it is not.

It is, rather, born of the understanding that government authority, once granted, is exceedingly hard to revoke. It is born of the understanding that the authority to regulate inter-personal behavior, to enforce cultural enlightenment on the philistines, can easily be turned to more disturbing subjects of regulation. It is born of the understanding that, at some point and on some topic, we will find we are all philistines.

Unfortunately, what passes for 'racism' and 'sexism' in the modern 'liberal' lexicon is often merely hysterical mischaracterization of policy differences concerning tradeoffs between freedom and fairness, of philosophical differences over the proper measure of justice, of differences in perception of the relative costs and benefits of particular cultural and political choices — or, worse, is simply a rhetorical tactic for shutting down debate on those subjects through an assertion of moral condescension. If you define *any* critique of affirmative action, or of immigration policy, or of welfare, or of any other policy — or of a President who happens to be African American or of a candidate who happens to be a woman — as ipso facto evidence of "racism" or of "sexism," then you need not defend the policy against that critique. You can, instead, simply declare the critique morally reprehensible on its face and, therefore, unworthy of attention. To do so is dishonest and anti-democratic. But it is, alas, effective.

There is nothing there about patriotism or nationalism, though for obvious reasons patriots and nationalists tend to appear conservative in the classic sense. Certainly, given the long-time dominance of America and American interests in the world, a devotion to country or nation might lead one to conserve the institutions that led to that dominance on the presumption that a dominant nation is more secure than a dominated one. And patriotism, in particular, is primarily recognized in its defensive guise — as the *defense* of country rather than more generally as the *love* of country — which is descriptively conservative even if not ideologically so.

But, from the very beginning, American patriotism has been broader than the specific assertion of national interest. The original American "Patriots" were both revolutionary and decidedly unpatriotic, at least in the view of the government and culture — the British Empire — which had heretofore claimed sovereignty over their territories and their loyalties. That there were clearly strains of geographic and economic nationalism mixed in with the political liberalism that fueled the revolution does not diminish the fundamental distinction of the American nation: that it was born as much a philosophical entity as a sociological or cultural or geographical one (and much more so than as an ethnic or religious one) and that American patriotism has always been driven as much by fealty to a political ideal — the ideal of power in service to the individual rather than the other way around — as by a fealty to country or to nation or to government. It is telling that the oaths sworn by American government officers, both military and civilian, is "...to support and defend the Constitution of the United States..." — to support and defend not the executive or the legislature, not the government per se, not the physical integrity of the homeland, not the social or cultural integrity of the nation, but the embodied political ideals on which the country was founded.

In that sense, American patriotism is not so much 'conservative' as 'conservatism' — in particular the form of moral 'conservatism' which concerns itself with those founding ideals, with individual liberty and democracy and the rule of law — is patriotic. And, in that sense, certain forms of 'liberalism' (and, alas, of 'conservatism') which would place the individual in service to power in the name of some superseding social good — may be fairly and accurately described in the American context as *un*patriotic.

Unfortunately, politicians seeking electoral advantage, particularly self-identified 'conservative' ones, have used the idea of patriotism, though not its substance, as a club with which to pommel those who simply disagree with their policy prescriptions. That is both divisive and dishonest, and the dishonesty and divisiveness are exacerbated by the fact that there is a particular brand of myopic nationalism — the flag-waving, America *über alles* variety, which is presumed by 'liberals' to define the political "far right" — that masquerades as patriotism.

But the "far right" is the product more of grievance and anxiety and pathology than of any 'conservative' ideology. 'Conservatives' who parade such faux patriotism as an electoral strategy diminish both the understanding of and respect for the real thing.

Equally unfortunately, however, the "far left" often seems incapable of distinguishing between that bastardization of patriotism and the genuine article, which renders their criticisms and denunciations of patriotism itself, and their claims to be the "true" patriots, an absurdist caricature. Both in the denunciation of any patriotic fervor as mere jingoism and in the equation of "true patriotism" strictly with some 'progressive' egalitarian ideology that they deem to be good for us, they prove their ignorance of American patriotic traditions.

In a time of emergency, and particularly in a time of war (broadly defined), patriotism may very well require an unquestioning answer to "the call," the momentary suspension of individual judgment in deference to the best judgment of our leaders in the face of crisis. That is the patriotism both of 'conservative' demagogues and of 'liberal' bombasts — to one an ideal, to the other an abomination — used to panic their opponents with moral sanctimony. It is also a legitimate and necessary — *but temporary* — response to calamity: the patriotism of exigency.

It is not the patriotism of governance, which demands skeptical examination, individual judgment, and a willingness to accept personal responsibility both for the national interest and for our ideals of individual liberty — and to which neither 'liberals' nor 'conservatives' can claim exclusive title.

That said, however, acting to influence the course of national policy and acting to undermine its legitimate implementation are fundamentally different things. There is a difference between constructive criticism aimed at altering disputed policy and mordant criticism that seeks primarily to direct blame for unpopular results or to craft electoral advantage by undermining the current political authority. There is a difference between decorous critique that endeavors, amidst its censure, to uphold national dignity and national interest abroad, and supercilious denunciation that recklessly undermines national moral authority and subverts established policy goals. There is a difference between unselfish acts of protest designed to illuminate and highlight policy distinctions, and sanctimonious acts of sabotage designed to impede or counteract the legitimate efforts of national agents. And there is a difference between pointing out flaws and inconsistencies within a fundamentally decent society in an effort to correct them, and using those flaws and inconsistencies as a rationale to condemn that society wholesale as corrupt and barbaric and beyond salvage. The former represent patriotism at its best. The latter approach perfidy.

To the extent that either 'liberals' or 'conservatives' fail to distinguish between the two they leave themselves open to a legitimate charge of being "unpatriotic." With the most recent extremes of political polarization — with 'conservatives' or 'liberals' setting policy unilaterally and 'liberals' or 'conservatives' criticizing it with particular bitterness — and with an occasional excursion into the realm of subversion, of self-righteous "public servants" actively undermining policy in the practice — the charge has been flung about almost thoughtlessly and with abandon.

There is nothing there about compassion (or a lack of compassion) because 'conservatives' tend to view compassion as a personal virtue, not a political one, and question the ethics and wisdom of consigning it either to orthodoxy or to compulsion by politicizing it.

That statement does not imply, as popularly characterized, that 'conservatives' are callous and mean. Some probably are but most are not, and those concerned with moral and civic virtue take their responsibility for the general welfare of society and of their fellow man quite as seriously as the most kind-hearted 'liberal.'

That statement merely corresponds to four general propositions:

- that compassion encompasses a moral judgment not only about need but about merit;
- That compassion is squandered on those who will accept no responsibility for improving their own circumstance.
- that moral judgment is the right and responsibility of the individual and, so, concrete decisions about 'compassion' — who to help, to what extent, and what resources to remove from other uses to do so — are, as both practical and moral choices, an individual prerogative;
- that the authority to requisition resources in the name of compassion is, in practice, indistinguishable from the authority to requisition resources for less admirable causes, or from the authority for limitless other types of coercion, and is, therefore, a threat to liberty generally.

It is true that a 'conservative' political philosophy *permits*, as a natural variant of human behavior that must be reluctantly accommodated in our political arrangements, 'callousness' and 'meanness.' But it does not mandate them or even condone them.

'Conservatives' are not, in principle or in practice, opposed to a compassionate society. They merely presume that a compassionate society is one in which most individuals wield personal resources, both time and money, in support of personal compassion, rather than one in which resources are forcibly extracted from individuals to support public compassion.

There is nothing there about greed except to acknowledge that people will generally act in what they perceive to be their own interests, however they may define them, and the presumption that they ought to be free to do so bounded by their responsibility to respect the rights of others. Although individual 'conservatives' (and 'liberals') may have varied opinions on greed's moral nature — and there seems to be a great deal of debate even over precisely what 'greed' is — there is no moral judgment per se attached to that acknowledgement. It is merely an empirical observation of human nature, one which must be accommodated in choosing forms and practices for our communal institutions.

As with choices about 'compassion,' the choices of what interests — economic, political, spiritual, emotional, familial, tribal, social, cultural, aesthetic, ethical — should take precedence in determining self-interest in any given interaction are moral decisions to be left to the individual. And, as with 'compassion,' we can acknowledge that a 'conservative' political philosophy *permits* greed without presuming that it necessarily mandates or condones it.

'Liberals' often equate 'conservative' support for free markets with a slavish devotion to the "God of the profits" — with an ethic of no ethics beyond the bottom line. That attitude certainly exists, and people who have it often identify themselves as 'conservative' — although that may be simply a matter of contrast rather than of doctrine. But that attitude is not by any measure universal, and there is no particular support for it in 'conservative' philosophy. The pursuit of wealth is not a 'conservative' principle; it is merely human nature. And the pursuit of wealth above all else reflects not a 'conservative' moral value but, rather, a paucity of moral values that many 'conservatives' find abhorrent.

The moral justification for the free market is liberty, not profit. The practical justification for the free market is productivity, not avarice. Within the narrow bounds of the market, profit is both the incentive to participate and the measure of success and, in economic terms, represents the excess productive capacity that improves our standard of living and allows us to invest in the future. But profit is the *byproduct* of economic liberty, not its *purpose*.

There is nothing there which mandates, or even suggests, that business should receive any more (or any less) consideration from government than individuals. Business is the natural expression of the human desire for more than an individual can produce alone, and one of the fundamental forms of apolitical cooperation. It has no independent basis as a moral entity but represents, within the limited scope of its activities, the collective moral will of its individual participants.

As do individuals, businesses must live within the moral constraints of fundamental rights and responsibilities and within the legal constraints of our political system. Since a corporation is a legal fiction not a moral one — created by government to simplify the task of negotiating our complex legal system in the conduct of a large-scale enterprise — it has a formal existence and "rights" under law but in the end it, also, is no more than the collective expression of its shareholders and employees and has precisely the moral standing that they would as a group of individuals without the corporate penumbra.

Since business is both a voluntary, cooperative action of individuals and our primary mechanism for expressing our productivity and creating wealth — meaning the goods we all consume, not individual fortunes — it is a reasonable presumption that needless interference with its activities would be unwise as well as a restriction of liberty for its participants. Conversely, it is also a reasonable presumption that creating a general environment conducive to the conduct of business and to the creation of wealth would be wise. However, that is not a wholesale prescription for eliminating all regulation or for subsidizing either specific businesses or business in general. It is merely a broad and pragmatic lens through which political actions affecting the conduct of business should be evaluated.

To be fair we ought to note that, although business is the natural expression of human cooperation to increase productivity and wealth, it is not the only possible one. People who say dogmatically that "government doesn't produce anything" are not only wrong but must be blind as well, since evidence of specific items like roads, buildings, police and court and national defense services, the postal service, and various forms of social insurance that the government has produced are all around them. Those things exist; they (for the most part) have value; and they were, indeed, produced by government.

But the fact they were produced by government doesn't, necessarily, mean that was the only way they *could* have been produced. Some things — particularly police and court and defense services that depend for their operation on the sanctioned use of force — are pretty clearly the proper and unique province of government. But private enterprise builds roads.

Private enterprise builds buildings. Private enterprise ships packages. Private enterprise provides various kinds of insurance. Those things would exist even if the government had never touched them. The mere fact that government *does* produce something doesn't mean that it *must*, or even that it *should*.

More fundamentally, government has no mystical power to create bounty from the void. Government production, like private production, consumes resources and entails costs in order to produce its benefits. Government is not free, and it draws the money it spends to produce its benefits from the same pool that individuals and corporations do.

Moreover, decisions about costs and benefits within government reflect concerns of power as much as of productivity and are enforced by collective coercion rather than evolved from individual preference. Thus, there are reasonable economic grounds for criticizing the relative efficiency with which government can produce wealth, and reasonable moral grounds for lamenting the amount both of personal liberty and of private economic productivity that must be sacrificed, not only through direct regulation but indirectly through incremental taxation, for it to do so. Although there is no specific 'conservative' principle requiring government benevolence toward business, there are both economic and moral grounds for favoring, whenever practical, business-based activities to government-based ones.

There is nothing in there that requires, or even recommends, the application of 'conservative' political principles to interpersonal or community relationships. Political principles regulate the acquisition and application of power, and it would indeed be a narrow and cynical vision of human nature to assume that all our communal endeavors — family, friendship, community, religion, business, art, academe — were primarily relationships of power rather than of nurture. There is a thread of 'conservative' thought, led by advocates of Objectivism, that favors applying political principles to personal relationships, but even among 'conservatives' that is considered a part of the fringe.

But if we postulate that it is inappropriate to apply political principles to relationships that are based on nurture, we might also propose the converse: that it would be unwise to presume principles of nurture are necessarily applicable to political relationships. That is, perhaps, the primary dividing line between 'liberals' and 'conservatives.' Most 'conservatives,' like most 'liberals,' believe in values like "giving back to the community" or noblesse oblige or "lifting up the downtrodden." They just don't believe those values form secure and reliable principles for governance.

The Religious Right

Beginning early in the last century, and building slowly to a frenzy in the nineteen sixties and seventies, the 'liberal' part of the American intellectual and political classes — although not necessarily the generally more moderate 'liberal' politicians and electorate — were suffused with, and arguably bedazzled by, the rhetoric and ideals of Marxism, the remnants of which can still be heard among the most vocal advocates of "the left." Poverty, once viewed as the unfortunate result of a dysfunctional economy or of indifferent misfortune or of injudicious personal behavior, was re-envisioned purely as the result of oppression by capitalist robber-barons; war, once thought to result from a complex interplay of national prestige, social hegemony, tribal division, moral fervor, political power and economic advantage, was now recognized to revolve primarily around corporate profit. Traditional notions of social mores and civil order were revealed to be not practical rules for minimizing interpersonal conflict and social upheaval but merely hidden mechanisms for herding the masses into their bourgeois fantasies. Western society, both American and European, was finally understood not to have evolved fitfully to match changing circumstance but to have been conceived consciously and purposefully by and for the wealthy and the powerful, solely for their own enrichment — and the time was nigh for the poor and the downtrodden to re-conceive it in their own image.

It was, in some ways, a natural alliance: the superficial end-goals of Marxist socialism — an egalitarian distribution of economic resources and political power — coincided both with the modern 'liberal' (and ancient Christian) ideals of distributive justice and with a growing unease (voiced by, among others, the 'conservative' president Eisenhower[1]) over the ascendance of concentrated private economic power in public affairs.

There was, of course, as much or more divergence between Marxists and mainstream 'liberals' as there was convergence, but the convergence encompassed ample common goals and common language to obscure the differences for a time. If the moral rigidity of socialist rhetoric seemed incongruous in a pluralistic democracy, it also seemed comfortably remote; if the mechanisms of socialism — concentration of political power and coerced subjugation of individual desire to the social good — seemed dangerous to some civil libertarians, many concerned with social justice seemed both confident in the ability of democratic institutions to temper those dangers and apprehensive about their ability to temper the dangers of the presumed alternative, the law of the jungle in the guise of a free market;

---

1 "In the councils of government, we must guard against the acquisition of unwarranted influence, whether sought or unsought, by the military-industrial complex," from his televised farewell address, 17 January 1961.

and if 'conservatives' objected to the consequent need to enforce a moral transformation of individuals and society toward a collective embrace of distributive justice itself — well, that could be dismissed as a demonstration not of their respect for individual moral autonomy but, rather, of the moral impoverishment of their ethos of greed.

Over the course of a century, aided by spectacular failings both in regulated (and politicized) "Capitalism" and in European nation-state politics, and both propelled by and propelling related cultural and economic upheavals, this alliance of convenience between mainstream liberalism and the Marxist fringe succeeded in transforming the landscape of American political thought and of American government: witness the New Deal, Social Security, the Great Society, Medicaid, AFDC, and all the other policies and agencies of the welfare state, along with the expanded tax system which supports them; and the labor movement, the civil rights movement, the feminist movement, the consumer rights movement, the sexual revolution, the gay rights movement, and other modern ancillary movements, social revolutions, and cultural upheavals they aroused. All these were rooted in a legitimate (and, in many cases, long overdue) desire for justice but they were also catalysts for the ascendance of "group rights," identity politics, and a diminution of standards for personal responsibility; for the ascent of the regulatory agency as a principle instrument of governance, with its assertion of rules without legislative debate, its presumption of guilt, and its draconian powers of "civil enforcement"; and for the transformation of the courts from arbiters of fact and law into agents of social justice, with the consequent expansion of federal authority over the states, erosion of the constraints of the Constitutionally enumerated powers, decreasing coherence between the text and the application of both Constitution and statute, and explosion of litigation as an instrument for the mitigation of simple inequity.

But the success of their program also exposed the fissures between mere 'liberalism' and the more radical socialist agenda. For where 'liberals' paused occasionally to ask "How far have we come?" and "How much is enough?" socialists merely rushed ever onward demanding "farther" and "more."

'Conservatives' took full advantage of the dichotomy between the wild rhetoric of the left and the more cautious electorate, and it may be that the refusal of the 'liberal' establishment to unequivocally disassociate itself from its most extremely socialist spokesmen was the genesis of the modern 'conservative' resurgence. To many, the socialist formulation of social good over individual needs or desires sounds more reasonable as a template for personal ethics than as a template for political authority, and more onerous in the practice than in the theory.

For the most ardent socialist declarations resemble nothing more than fundamentalism: they espouse a structured and idealized view of the moral world, enforced adherence to a dogma of revealed truth, unquestioned allegiance to a centralized moral authority, a zealous and comprehensive evangelism on behalf of their egalitarian gospel, and an intractable and virulent intolerance of and opposition to anyone who believes or behaves otherwise.

Unfortunately, just as Marxist fundamentalists had a natural affinity for modern 'liberal' ideals that allowed them to attempt a hijack of 'liberalism' in the sixties, so religious fundamentalists recognized in the eighties a natural affinity for certain 'conservative' ideals and formed an equally strong alliance with a conservative movement on the rebound. And, as it was with fundamentalist economic socialism, fundamentalist theocratic socialism is on the verge of hijacking — and destroying — an honorable and valuable political tradition.

For the agenda of the religious right, for all its self-identification with 'conservative' principle, is socialistic at the core. Their conception of the social good is theological rather than economic (as in Marxism) or nationalistic (as in Fascism), but they are characterized by the classic socialist values: the moral primacy of [God's] society over the individual; an unassailable [Biblical] moral structure which identifies not only how individuals should behave but what is good for society and who may be accounted the enemy of moral order; the mandate to reform and re-form society and individuals to conform to that moral structure; the willingness to subjugate any individual desire or liberty — theirs and yours — to the greater social-moral vision; and a promise of a future paradise — in this case an actual Heaven, rather than merely the heaven-on-earth of Communism or The Fatherland — once the enemies of moral order have been re-educated or eliminated.

Just as most 'liberals,' yearning for an ideal world of social justice, are not truly Marxist socialists, so most religious conservatives are not true theocratic socialists. But, for the moment, the language of theocratic socialism seems able both to speak to concerns about cultural stability and about the moral nature of society that had been ignored or ridiculed by the preceding generations of 'liberal' thinkers, and to galvanize political action on their behalf.

And just as the more moderate 'liberal' electorate felt confident that American democratic systems could rein in the excesses of their Marxist compatriots, so now — though perhaps decreasingly so — moderate 'conservatives' seem confident that those systems can rein in the excesses of their theocratic ones. Given where we are and how far we've come in the last 100 years, is it unreasonable to feel that the path from here to theocratic socialism is longer, less certain, and more obstructed than the remaining path from here to Marxist socialism? Is it unreasonable to feel that it is, therefore, less likely to be followed to the end and less dangerous? Even one who abhors the destination may, perhaps, pardon many non-theocratic 'conservatives' for concluding it is not.

Nonetheless, the fact that we seem unlikely to follow the path to its end does not nullify the hazards of the journey. 'Conservative' socialism is ultimately no more palatable than 'liberal' socialism and should be resisted as fiercely.

The problem, for non-religious 'conservatives,' in disassociating themselves from the religious right is threefold. The first and most obvious problem is purely pragmatic: the religious right votes in large numbers and votes primarily for 'conservatives'; but their support is predicated on their perception that 'conservative' candidates share their concerns. Hence, as a purely political calculation, and in the same way that moderate 'liberal' candidates pledge allegiance to organized labor, even non-religious 'conservative' candidates try at the least to avoid antagonizing the religious right — which reinforces the association between the religious right and the public image of 'conservatism.'

But the other problems are ideological. The first is that the 'conservative' concern for the moral nature of society — the recognition that social and political cohesion in a free society depends on a prevalent moral virtue — makes 'conservatives' generally sympathetic to institutions, including religion, which provide moral authority and guidance, even if they are uncomfortable with theology per se. To the extent that modern secular hostility to religion — and, in fact, to any institution which asserts and exercises moral authority — seems to undermine those sources of moral authority specifically and shared cultural values generally, it not only subverts religion itself but threatens those democratic political structures which depend on a prevalent moral virtue among citizens. Even non-religious 'conservatives' feel the urge to rise to the defense of institutions which provide moral guidance.

More broadly, non-theocratic religious conservatives — the rank and file of the religious right rather than its zealots — are not merely poseurs. They are genuine conservatives in the classic mold, defending cherished social institutions that they perceive to be under threat from a political liberalism run amok. It is one of those compelling ironies of modern life that the religious right, perhaps as a social movement and certainly as a political one, is largely the product of 'liberal' excess. One need not have religious motivations to find those excesses disturbing — one can be a social conservative without being a religious one — but for better or worse the religious right has been the primary catalyst over the last three decades for bringing critique of those excesses into the public debate.

On the whole, social conservatives, religious or otherwise, are responding to widespread 'progressive' success in using the political process to tear down traditional social structures and social controls, which has done much to undermine traditional value systems. Some of the results have been worthy and long-overdue: only the most ardent patriarchs really want to force women back into the kitchen and the nursery; only the most ignorant bigots really want to push African Americans back into the segregation of Jim Crow; only the most zealous theocrats really want to imprison homosexuals back in the closet. But the particular 'progressive' process that wrought those liberties also wrought a social cost: a general debasing of intellectual, artistic, and cultural standards; the fragmentation and factionalization of society and politics; a degradation in civility; a coarsening of language; a devaluing of personal propriety and dignity; a loss of cultural sanction for degenerate behavior and a consequent protrusion of the private sphere, including both overt and eccentric sexuality, into the public sphere; a subjugation of personal liberty to an idealized egalitarian vision of distributive justice; an emasculation of the sense of personal responsibility, with a resulting diminution of civic participation and a decline in family commitment and the work ethic.

Even if 'liberalism' is not the proximate cause for all this — and certainly there have been many other demographic, economic, historical, and cultural forces at work — 'liberalism' and the 'progressive' agenda were a driving force moving it forward, often without regard for, or even with open admiration for, the collateral damage to social cohesion and cultural paradigms. Worse, the 'progressive' project has been so successful in changing the intellectual and cultural tableau that even to mention those costs, to suggest that perhaps we've gone too far in breaking down social mores and cultural taboos, now evokes derision and hostility from large segments of the academic, political, and cultural elite.

All this would be troubling enough to social conservatives if it was merely a cultural quarrel, a matter of free choice in the "marketplace of ideas," but it is not. Increasingly, as traditional social and cultural controls have been eviscerated new political controls have supplanted them — controls which have then been used to reinforce the cultural changes that spawned them. Non-judgmental divorce laws truly freed many from the pointless despair of permanently failed marriages but they also undermine the social significance of a personal vow and reinforce loosening sexual mores and the decay of the family unit; various welfare programs, a lifeline for the struggling poor, do the same when, in the name of "fairness" and "dignity" and tolerance for "non-traditional lifestyle choices," rules reward single parenthood with increased subsidies and penalize marriage with the opposite. High marginal tax rates fund some worthwhile government programs, but they infringe on economic liberty and they promote the decay of the work ethic by reducing the recompense for work, as do welfare rules that reward indigence and punish enterprise. Social services and economic assistance funded by taxes provide a stable and secure safety net for those in poverty but they also undermine the sense of shared civic purpose and moral responsibility by disconnecting benefactor from benevolence, by replacing altruism with compulsion and philanthropy with expropriation. Changes in tort laws that allow more access to the courtroom for the victims of corporate negligence also undermine the notion of personal responsibility by fostering the rise of a litigation culture; the same is true of criminal justice and social service systems which hold society to blame for acts of crime and self-indulgence, and of affirmative action policies that muddle the distinction between individual and collective grievance. Child-care subsidies and family leave policies reduce barriers to mothers who choose to work outside the home, but socialization of the direct costs must be borne in part by those who choose not to; and tax increases to pay for those and other government lifestyle supports force a few who would otherwise choose full-time motherhood into the work force to pay for them. Taxpayer funded public schools are the great leveler that provides academic and cultural education and opportunity to everyone equally, but that ubiquitous cultural (and increasingly moral) education includes promotion of morality-free sex, social justice at the expense of liberty, moral relativism, cultural relativism, the moral and practical equivalence of traditional and eccentric "lifestyle choices," environmental spiritualism — and such inclusion seems to be at the expense of traditional academic achievement. Taxpayer funded public universities provide a route to intellectual growth and upward mobility for the children of the poor and middle-class, but their humanities and social-science departments (and those of their private counterparts) seem to be devolving into re-education camps to reinforce "progressive" dogma. Arts subsidies that make traditional culture broadly available to the public and catalyze inventive new artistic endeavors also support, legitimize, and promote art which dignifies incivility and undermines tradition and authority; regulators' healthy respect for free speech and artistic license blinds them to many forms of indecency on the public airwaves. Courts, understandably frustrated with the slow and messy path to social justice provided by legislative and electoral processes, use judicial fiat to re-define marriage as gender-neutral and surgical procedures as fundamental human rights, and thereby undermine the rule of law.

Many of these are unintended consequences of otherwise well-intentioned and just policies, and even social conservatives — or at least those driven primarily by cultural rather than religious concerns — would eschew a new Puritanism, notwithstanding their portrayal in the national media. But, on these and many other issues, social conservatives have increasingly found the avenue of debate and compromise closed to them: with cultural transformations and costs they contest locked into place by acts of political power rather than by social consensus, and with their concerns dismissed as beneath contempt by the political and cultural elite who dominate the public discussion, their only remaining prospect for influence is through the acquisition and exercise of countervailing political power.

If *social* conservatives generally concern themselves with broad and discomforting social changes, specifically *religious* conservatives have an additional and narrow focus: perception of an increasing political hostility to religion, and in particular to conservative Christianity. This is not only about prayer in public schools or the Ten Commandments in the courthouse. It is about a broader modern understanding of the "wall of separation between church and state" that has systematically excluded all theological discussion and even personal expressions of faith from the public square.

The evidence to support such a perception is thin: by most accounts religion, especially conservative religion, is flourishing in America. Religious spokesmen are quoted routinely in the media on a range of subjects — if generally as representatives of the "right wing" — and appear to be influential in policy discussions within the Republican Party. In fact, aside from a general disdain for conservative religious beliefs among the intellectual and cultural elites, the perception of hostility comes primarily from one source: the education of children. And education is the focal-point for religious concern because, in the last 40 years, the government has more and more taken on responsibility for moral, not just academic and civic, instruction.

Some of this is seemingly innocuous or undertaken with sincere high purpose: needle exchanges and public service advertisements advising condom use to reduce the spread of AIDS; public service advertisements to convince people not to smoke; 'Earth Day' to celebrate saving the environment, and 'Black History Month' to foster role models and a sense of place and culture for African Americans, and 'Take Your Daughter to Work Day' to foster a sense of career possibility in young girls. Some of these are inoffensive even to religious conservatives, and a few are supported by them. But along with their practical messages all contain moral lessons — smoking is decadent, women should aspire to career over motherhood, "safe sex" is an acceptable alternative to sexual abstinence, clean needles are an acceptable alternative to chemical abstinence, saving the environment is a spiritual calling — that are stamped with the imprimatur of (and supported with tax dollars by) the government. They set the tone and the message: government is the teacher and arbiter of moral values. With government pervasive and growing, if you disagree with those moral lessons you cannot easily opt out or shield your children from them, especially when they are reinforced in the public schools.

And if these indirect governmental moral lessons are sometimes bothersome, the public schools themselves are ground zero in the war over moral education. There the children of religious conservatives learn by example that prayer — even personal and private prayer — is disruptive to civic order and that the Bible is a banned book; in science classes they learn that the biblical stories of creation and the flood are not merely unscientific but intellectually ridiculous and worthy mainly of outright contempt; in English and arts classes they learn that crude language, defacement of cultural icons, and anti-social behavior are to be valued for their "authenticity," that contrarian viewpoint, not beauty or truth, makes art valuable, that plebeian, not transcendent, vision makes art relevant; in social studies classes they learn that patriarchy is evil while "non-traditional" family structures must be treated not merely as tolerable but as normative, that modern Americans must atone for the ancient sins of colonialism and chattel slavery and for the hypocrisy of the founding fathers, and that non-Christian religions — as representations of cultural diversity — must be treated with a deference and respect never accorded their own; in health and sex education classes they learn that homosexuality is "normal," that masturbation is healthy, that promiscuity and hedonism are OK as long as you practice "safe sex," and that abortion is a solution to the problem of unintended pregnancy — and they are offered free condoms if they choose to act on what they've learned. If parents of those children object to what the public school teaches and choose to try to change it, they are accused of corrupting the purity of the curriculum, of substituting faith for fact, of imposing their narrow agenda on society. If they choose to abandon the public schools for a more tolerable option they are offered no support in that choice — they must bear the cost of both the public schools and the alternative — and are, in fact, often treated as if they are committing cultural child abuse: remember that it was the public education establishment, at the genesis of the home-schooling movement, that tried to prosecute parents for leaving the public school system; and, in the argument over school vouchers, schools with curricula circumscribed by religious values are routinely described as balkanizing, promoters of ignorance, and detrimental to a shared civic culture.

It is hard for those of us who are not religious, or for people to whom religion is an activity for Sunday morning and an occasional wedding or funeral, to understand the depth of passion all this induces or to take the alarmist rhetoric seriously. If you generally agree with what the schools are teaching, or if you see religious and moral instruction as a discrete activity that you take on when the need arises to counteract a particular school lesson, then it must seem paranoid and overwrought. But if you experience religion — or for that matter any moral philosophy — as a constant force in your life, inseparable from your daily routine and at play in every decision and action, these kinds of indignities are not trivial, they are fundamental.

More generally, the "wall of separation" between church and state has seemingly come to mean that religious beliefs — and *only* religious beliefs — are to be excluded from the discussion both within government and in any setting touched by government — which is, increasingly, every setting not actually inside a church. "Neutrality," in this case, is not neutral. That is not a problem if the discussion is about tax rates or trash pick-up but when the government takes upon itself the prerogative for moral action, moral regulation, or moral instruction, excluding one particular moral viewpoint from the discussion specifically because of its genesis disenfranchises those to whom that moral viewpoint is dear and impoverishes the moral dialog.

The contention that government cannot — as is, for instance, the argument from the opponents of school vouchers — act in any way that even indirectly benefits religion, regardless of the original purpose of the action, is in practice hostile to religion. When mention of God is prohibited in valedictory speeches or other student-controlled content; when students are prohibited from uttering a prayer aloud, of their own volition, in the lunchroom or before a class or a test; when classrooms or other public spaces may be used after-hours for almost any kind of interest-group or event meeting except a religious one; when religious texts, even when freely chosen by the student, are ruled unacceptable for reading exercises or reading tests solely because they are religious; when previously awarded publicly-funded scholarships are revoked on the grounds that the recipient chooses to study theology rather than biology or sociology or African-American Studies or mathematics or women's studies or English or history or philosophy; when public benefits like vouchers for education or social services are available to any otherwise qualified group except those with religious affiliations, or abandoned entirely when it seems religion might benefit; when otherwise context-appropriate quotations about nature or spirituality or duty or law are removed from public spaces merely because they have religious origins;

when non-Judeo-Christian texts and icons are found acceptable as cultural relics but Judeo-Christian texts and icons are unacceptable as religious ones; when it is affirmed as appropriate for the professorate to instruct us on suitable policy preferences based on secular moral judgments but condemned as inappropriate for the clergy to instruct us on suitable policy preferences based on religious moral judgments; when politicians are either praised or vilified in the media for upholding moral principle based solely on whether the principle derives from secular or religious tenets; when any indication that a personal political choice was motivated by religious conviction rather than by secular principle becomes a reason to ridicule and denigrate the choice as an act of "theocracy"; when acts like these banish religion as an acceptable subject for consideration in public, then not just religious conviction but religious viewpoint is silenced in public life.

The issue is not political advocacy or persecution of religion itself; the issue is political restraint on the public expression of personal and political preferences solely because they are based on religious belief rather than on some secular moral paradigm. Even when these and other policies are eventually reconsidered or overturned, as they most often are, they signal to the devout that their views are unwelcome, that, even as freedom of expression and freedom of action for the formerly marginalized are expanding at an unprecedented rate, the expression of religious values ever more often requires prodigious effort and determination to break through the "wall of separation."

Luckily, as is often the case, the scope of these depredations has been exaggerated by the sensitivity of those most affected, and those most affected overcompensate. We are not yet close to the French ideal of a total abolition of religious expression from public life. Our political candidates, even the 'liberal' ones, still feel the need for public demonstrations of their religious commitment, at least when the cameras are rolling. Religious viewpoints are widely available and widely heeded in policy debates. Religious leaders, even 'conservative' ones, are routinely sought out by the press and by politicians for comment on issues with moral dimensions. Church attendance, at least in the growing charismatic churches, is robust. There is no sign that religion is vanishing from the public square.

Which is why even religious 'conservatives' don't need theocratic socialism: its benefits are illusory. In fact the threat it represents will soon, if it has not already, become more destructive than constructive in advancing not only 'conservatism' generally but specifically religious interest as well.

In the late 1970s, when the religious right arose as a political force, 'conservatism' was reeling from the social and cultural chaos induced by the previous two decades and from the corruption of its purported champions. Its alliance with the religious right was an act of desperation and revitalization. That alliance is no longer necessary or wise. Social conservatism can stand on its own as a brake on the worst excesses of the "progressive" social experiment, and would be more persuasive to other 'conservatives' — and to moderate 'liberals' — without the specter of theocracy as a shadow lurking behind it.

Neo-Conservatism

Neo-conservatism has taken on an almost mythic role in current political discussion, primarily because of its purported role in driving the war in Iraq specifically and American foreign policy (and domestic security policy) generally in the post 9/11 world. It is now evoked by 'liberals' as the moniker for a shadowy conspiracy of statists, a "neo-conservative cabal" at the heart of the government which has seized power in some kind of silent coup. Such imagery may be useful politically, but it both overstates the facts and misses the point.

A neo-conservative has been famously characterized by the so-called "Godfather of Neo-Conservatism," Irving Kristol, as "A liberal who was mugged by reality." Michael Scully, editor of *The Public Interest*, described a neo-liberal, in contrast, as "A liberal who was mugged by reality, *but who has declined to press charges*,"[1] indicating an attitudinal distinction between neo-conservatives and neo-liberals that masks their common genesis.

Neo-conservatism seems not so much a separate philosophical entity from other types of 'conservatism' as it is a separate path to many of the same general conclusions. Neo-conservatism is not a new intellectual formulation from political principle; rather, it began — as did neo-liberalism — as a pragmatic reaction by disillusioned 'liberals' to the failures of 'liberalism' and of 'liberal' government, beginning in particular with the American Left's flirtation with Soviet socialism and hardened by the failure of the "Great Society" to deliver on its most idealistic promises and by the seeming determination of a generation of 'liberal' American leaders to lose the Cold War.

The primary neo-conservative (and neo-liberal) argument against 'liberalism' is practical: it doesn't work; that is, the benefits it creates consistently fall short of its goals and the costs it imposes are consistently

---

1 Reported by William Kristol in "Where Do We Go from Here?" in *The American Spectator*, December 1981; has been attributed elsewhere to MIT economist Lester Thurow and to Irving Kristol himself. Richard Starr, Deputy Editor of *The Weekly Standard*, has my eternal gratitude for graciously tracking down the citation after I, a complete stranger, sent him an unsolicited e-mail asking for his help in resolving the ambiguity.

out of proportion to those benefits. But where neo-liberals are chiefly concerned with the financial ramifications of 'liberalism' and often align with free-market conservatives in an effort to achieve 'liberal' goals for social and economic justice through market mechanisms, neo-conservative concerns extend also and much more to cultural, political, philosophical, and moral costs, so their alignment with 'conservative' policy is much more complete. To neo-conservatives, the sin of 'liberalism' is not its activism but its utter failure to appreciate, or even to acknowledge, the importance of things like social and cultural stability, economic liberty, and the immorality and injustice of totalitarianism.

Having concluded on practical grounds that 'liberalism' is a failure, neo-conservatives find intellectual support for that conclusion in the same philosophical and economic frameworks that motivate other pragmatic and cultural 'conservatives.' Much of the language of neo-conservatism is indistinguishable from other forms — thus raising doubts about whether neo-conservatism really exists as a distinct political movement or is merely a subtle variant or a self-serving myth (Irving Kristol himself described it as a "persuasion," and it is often used as a universal pejorative by 'liberals' in an attempt to discredit specific objectionable policies).

However, neo-conservatives, unlike their more traditional counterparts, believe as 'liberals' do in the potential for instigating and guiding human progress — in our duty and ability to make things better. They are merely skeptical of 'liberal' government as a competent means to that end. In particular, the primary and most consequential neo-conservative criticisms of the experiments in 'liberal' government of the 1960s and 1970s were not of the underlying intent but of the extent to which 'liberals' ignored the detrimental financial, social, and political consequences of their policies — the extent to which their cost-insensitive and morally-neutral social and foreign policies undermined the nation in the name of humanizing it.

That has practical consequences. If neo-conservative opposition to 'liberalism' is a matter of pragmatism, rather than ethics, then neo-conservatives can be convinced to 'liberal' action by a sufficiently persuasive practical argument. They are not uncomfortable with state power and state action per-se but merely with state power and state action that returns too little benefit for the very real cost; and in particular their views on individual liberty and society more resemble those of the activist left, which emphasizes responsibility for "the good of society" (in whichever idiosyncratic form) over individual autonomy, than they do those of the libertarian right. The combination of such 'liberal' impulses with traditional 'conservative' concerns for social and moral issues can be alarming both to traditional 'liberals' and to traditional 'conservatives': it brings with it a willingness to assert state power both in defense of traditional moral and social structures under 'liberal' assault (remember the "Defense of Marriage Act"?) and in support of American interests and moral values abroad. It is also ironic, for in the current political climate these 'liberal'-minded neo-conservatives are considered by proper 'liberals' to be 'ultra-conservative' — the far fringe of the "right" — precisely because of their liberalism, because of their willingness to break with the 'conservative' policy conventions of the past and to use the political power of the state to push forward their agenda.

The comfort with liberal action can be seen in their activism on behalf of cultural tradition and social stability, but it is most evident in neo-conservatives' dealings with national security. While they agree with traditional 'conservatives' that national security is a primary and legitimate function of government, they also tend to view national security as an arena in which the government can be particularly effective and should, therefore, be particularly active. However, they believe as other conservatives do that to be effective it must take a sufficiently pragmatic view of its goals, of its opponents, and of the limits of the "global community" as a coherent partner for collective security.

In particular, neo-conservatives embrace the view that extending state authority beyond the natural scope of a single 'nation' both dramatically increases the risk of tyranny and dramatically decreases the sense of shared interest and moral consensus that could make it effective — hence their aversion to international pseudo-governmental agencies like the UN and the International Criminal Court. This, combined with a pragmatic and expansive view of 'national interest' — a 'liberal'-like conviction that the spread of democratic institutions around the world is both an inherent moral good and practically necessary for long-term peace and prosperity — makes neo-conservatives break with more traditional 'conservatives' (and with modern pacifist and multiculturalist 'liberals') in advocating an activist, autonomous, and ideologically expansionist foreign policy. Again, there is considerable irony in the fact that, in the current foreign policy environment, it is 'conservatives' who are most eager to disrupt the status quo, to reinvent the world order along more agreeable lines, and 'liberals' who have reacted to that eagerness by rediscovering the benefits of stability and the balance of power.

But to identify neo-conservatives with that agenda is not to assert they are necessarily the root of it, especially in the current political environment. We should not underestimate the degree to which the attacks on New York and Washington in September of 2001 radicalized the political center, both 'liberal'- and 'conservative'-leaning. Notwithstanding the view from the 'left' that terrorists and terrorism should be prosecuted rather than assaulted, nor its protests about American complicity in "creating terrorism" and the need for "multi-lateral" and "holistic" responses, most people viewed those attacks as acts of war and were conceptually comfortable with responding as such — and were correspondingly frustrated at the lack of a traditional enemy "state" on which to focus that response. In that regard neo-conservatives offered an intellectual vision for such a response that others could not, a philosophical rationale for assertive unilateral action and a strategic (and, ironically, "holistic") goal — the conversion of our enemies, broadly envisioned, to democratic values — that arguably undermines the philosophy and culture underlying and unifying global terrorism rather than merely assaulting or prosecuting its individual agents.

Notwithstanding the sideshow of debate over whether or not Iraq's acquisition of WMDs was either imminent or inevitable — and the latter claim by the Bush administration was often misinterpreted by its opponents as equivalent to the former and derided on that basis — that democratic transformation of the Islamic world was the real goal and motivation for invading Iraq. And, notwithstanding the claims to the contrary after subsequent elections, the frustration with the invasion on the part of the broad American public had less to do with doubt about the wisdom or desirability of that goal and more to do with our failure to deliver on it.

Libertarianism

"Libertarianism" is the modern word for what was, at the time of the American Revolution, considered 'liberalism' and is now sometimes called "classical liberalism" — the doctrines of individual liberty and limited government scope embodied in the American *Declaration of Independence.* The fundamental tenets of libertarianism are the moral primacy of the individual, the consequent individual rights to conscience and property, and the consequent individual responsibility to respect the rights of others to conscience and property.

As such, libertarianism is primarily a political philosophy: it prescribes how people, individually or as a "society," may — and, more importantly, may not — exercise coercive power over each other while remaining true to the goal of maximum individual autonomy. That has economic and social implications, from advocacy for free markets to defense of free expression and free association to a generally non-interventionist foreign policy but, in terms of personal morality, libertarian philosophy imposes only a minimum — and political — ethical standard: respect the rights of others; do not coerce them into behaving against their own desires. It neither prescribes *nor proscribes* any higher moral goals — no duties to the greater society or to the downtrodden — nor does it prescribe greed and egocentrism. It is, in fact, largely silent on personal moral values and compatible with a wide range of moral and religious beliefs.

On the surface it might seem that the prescription for the exercise of coercive power must be to forbid it entirely, and that is certainly the ideal. However, in addition to its moral foundation, libertarianism acknowledges many of the pragmatic lessons about human nature and human behavior that appear in our list of 'conservative' principles. Thus, it acknowledges that some people and some societies will not respect the rights of the individual to autonomy; it acknowledges, therefore, that anarchy is as hostile to liberty as is tyranny and that, for people *en masse*, a civil society is a practical prerequisite to liberty; it acknowledges the need for governance — albeit limited in scope — to protect individual rights from those who would usurp them and to enforce individual responsibilities on those who would shirk them; and it acknowledges the individual responsibility to support government in that necessary (but limited) endeavor.

But, in acknowledging the necessity of government, it also recognizes the danger inherent in government: that, to perform its legitimate functions, government must have coercive authority, authority which reduces individual autonomy even when properly exercised and which imperils it when not. The measure of the moral authority of government, then, is the balance it strikes between diminishing liberty through its coercive authority and enhancing it through its protection of rights and enforcement of responsibilities.

The fundamental purpose of government is the preservation of liberty, and a balance detrimental to liberty overall nullifies its moral authority. In general, libertarians consider that the statement of principles in the American *Declaration of Independence* and the balancing of federal against state sovereignty, the division between legislative and executive and judicial authority, and the constraints of enumerated powers in the original American Constitution — *excepting* the egregious and (in the context of its time) politically expedient tolerance for slavery — are, with all their shortcomings, about the best prescription ever conceived for a practical government that strikes the proper balance.

Libertarians are fond of proclaiming they are neither 'liberal' nor 'conservative' but something else entirely — a "third way" of thinking about political philosophy. In some senses that is a valid description given the proclivity of both the modern political left and the modern political right to think of government as a tool for re-forming or ossifying society in fashions that suit their ideological and policy preferences. To libertarians, government is a tool only for protecting individual liberty, and a crude and dangerous tool at that.

Certainly in their philosophical consistency and rigor, libertarians are at odds with 'conservatives' almost as often as with 'liberals.' And there are libertarian factions on both sides of the 'liberal'/'conservative' divide. Aside from their attitude toward the libertine excesses liberty makes possible — as cause more for relish or for regret — the difference between them tends to be their judgment on which is the greater threat to liberty: the accretion of old power within expanding and "unaccountable" institutions — for instance the transformation of corporate economic power into political power — or the appropriation of new power in the name of the social good — the extension of regulatory and legal coercion ever deeper into our economic, intellectual, social, cultural, interpersonal, private, and even moral lives.

Nonetheless, most people seem to think of libertarianism as some extreme form of 'conservatism' and that view also has merit.

Libertarianism is the prototype for our definition of 'moral conservatism': conservative in practice but not in principle, unconcerned with institutional stability per se but striving to defend the specific ideals and institutions on which the country was founded against modern conceptions of activist government. It treats economic liberty as a human fundamental, equal and complementary to intellectual and political liberty rather than as an inferior cousin to be sacrificed on the altar of economic or social equity. And its ideological opposition to the use of government as an instrument either of social change or of social inertia places it at the opposite pole from the more socialist aspects of modern 'liberalism' (and of theocratic 'conservatism'). In both its adherence to America's founding principles and its opposition to an activist 'liberal' agenda, libertarianism fits comfortably within the descriptive definition of conservatism and within the broad 'conservative' ideological framework, even if it shares that position uncomfortably with other 'conservative' constituencies which place far less emphasis on individual liberty. What makes libertarianism seem extreme is not so much its *philosophy* as its *adherents*.

In part, libertarianism seems extreme because the Libertarian party, with its message of minimalist government, tends to attract anarchists, people happy to make claims on liberties but reluctant to acknowledge either corresponding responsibilities for the liberty of others or the importance of a civil society to that cause. These are narcissists, libertines more than libertarians. Their dismissive attitude toward responsibilities indicates a fundamental gap in their understanding of the libertarian moral framework, but their policy preferences overlap the libertarian prescription of reduced government authority and so they muddle understanding by inaccurately identifying themselves as libertarian.

In part, moreover, libertarianism seems extreme because a vocal subset of political libertarians are also social libertarians, Objectivist admirers of Ayn Rand who carry the ideal of individualism, liberty, and self-reliance from politics and economics into the domain of social and personal interaction. In their view, the political proposition that others must respect your rights to conscience and property, that they can have no moral claim on you, implies a reciprocal personal moral proposition: that, beyond the admonition to respect their rights, you can have no moral duty to others or to society. Where the narrower political libertarian ethic is silent on individual moral duty and can encompass many views on the subject, Objectivism asserts a specific personal moral code: self-reliance is a moral virtue, compassion breeds dependency, nurture is a matter of contract, and social conscience, far from being a moral obligation or even a moral positive, is actually a moral vice.

All this has no direct impact on Objectivists' political policy prescriptions. Limited government is limited government regardless of your personal moral view. Nonetheless, even one who agrees with Objectivists' social philosophy might acknowledge that it makes them — and by extension all libertarians (and all 'conservatives') — appear callous and contemptuous of lesser mortals, traits socially disagreeable on their face and widely despised in modern 'liberal' culture.

But much of the perception of libertarians as extreme arises because so many libertarians seem to be idealists in the same way that communists are idealists. They begin by imagining a system in which government is largely unnecessary because individuals can behave with moral perfection; they then convince themselves it is only the corrupting effect of the existing power structures — of Capitalism for communists, of Socialism for libertarians — that is inhibiting such universal moral behavior. Their resulting policy prescription is to eliminate the existing power structures — to eliminate socialist government — as quickly and as thoroughly as possible that the ideal libertarian world may emerge naturally from the void left behind. It is the political equivalent of "If you build it, he will come."[1]

But of course many people — and many societies beyond our borders — will not behave as moral libertarians even if most do. And among those who try to behave morally there will be disputes over how moral principles apply to a given circumstance, particularly as growth in population and technology have pushed ever more of our interactions beyond immediate social groups and into the anonymity of mass markets, mass culture, and mass politics. Government must exist for precisely those reasons. And in the political and social climate today, after almost a century of increasing

---

1 From the movie, *Field of Dreams*, 1989

dependence on government, increasing government power, and, most importantly, increasing insinuation of modern 'liberal' ideals of social justice and communalism and political control into the philosophical and intellectual fabric of society, many people would not know how to behave as libertarians even if they wanted to. As a culture we've lost the habit, perhaps even forgotten how.

In that regard this particular manifestation of libertarianism is extreme precisely because it violates one of the prime tenets of classic conservatism: reform and 'progress' are best achieved with deliberation and caution, gradually not precipitously, and with the least manageable disruption to their lives and peace-of-mind for the bulk of people. A libertarian realist would have to acknowledge that undoing the modern anti-libertarian edifice that has been constructed over generations will require yet more generations. The idea that it could be dismantled overnight by winning an election or two is a fantasy.

Even beyond that inadequate individual commitment to libertarian principle among the general populace, libertarianism suffers from the broader cultural foundation on which it must now stand. The political libertarianism of our forefathers was sustained by a rich cultural tradition of religious and civic duty, personal honor, and community bonds. That environment was not a part of libertarian political philosophy, per se, but, within such a social/cultural matrix, expansive political liberty could not significantly weaken social stability and civility, nor could it undermine to any great degree the ethic of personal responsibility for the welfare of neighbor and community that allowed civil society to function well. That is, although people of that era were free, politically, to behave in ways that would be socially and morally corrosive, widely-accepted cultural and ethical constraints generally inhibited them from doing so.

The same may not be said for our modern 'liberal' society with its narcissistic popular culture, its social philosophy of entitlement without accountability, and its politicization of civil and social duty. And so, social stability, civility, and civic responsibility are now more often imposed politically through regulation and taxation than expected culturally of individual citizens. Libertarian proposals that depend on the original expectation may be noble and desirable but seem, to many, also naive and unreasonable, especially over any time-frame shorter than generations. And, in policy discussions, the utter disregard libertarians generally show both for social considerations and for social implications, and for indirect effects of those social considerations and implications on individual welfare -- their failure to consider "society" as an entity distinct from its individual members, asserting its own practical imperatives and constraints and providing its own benefits — is another source for the perception of libertarianism as extreme.

Libertarian critics and analysts, though not necessarily the theorists or the true believers in the trenches, tend to be more practical. Libertarian principles have as much basis in the jaundiced 'pragmatic conservative' view of human nature as they do in moral theory, and much of libertarian analysis and prescription at the policy level, while thoroughly grounded in the defense of liberty, falls into the category of "necessary compromise leading in the right direction" rather than the absolute enforcement of ideological purity.

But most people don't hear that. To most people, the primary exposure to libertarianism as an identifiable entity is the crackpot who's run for Congress as the Libertarian Party candidate six times in a row on a platform of abolishing the IRS, OSHA, the EPA, the SEC, the ATF, the FBI, and the Federal Reserve, closing public schools, canceling welfare, Medicaid, and Social Security, eliminating zoning and building codes, privatizing the Army, Air Force, Navy, and the police and fire departments, and either building a wall around America to shut the rest of the world out or utterly dissolving borders to let it come rushing in — and whose only articulable philosophical principle seems to be "Government is evil!"

To most people that sounds like a prescription for turning their lives upside-down — for taking away their life-jackets, tossing them into the sea, and loosing the sharks. And that feels extreme.

Fascism

Fascism — and its most famous specific instance, Nazism — is a political philosophy rooted in both socialism and nationalism. As with Marxist socialism (and other forms) Fascism asserts that the good of society supersedes the individual's right to liberty and prescribes authoritarian (and often totalitarian) mechanisms of state power over individuals to achieve that social good. But, unlike Marxism, Fascism identifies the unity, prosperity, and glory of "the nation," rather than economic egalitarianism, as the overriding social good. And it therefore, unlike Marxism, generally includes a pragmatic embrace of a "crony Capitalism" in which favored individuals are allowed to control capital and profit from production as long as such production serves the Fascist vision of the national good. In the specific cases of Nazism and Apartheid and some of their cousins on the political fringe in the United States (and in the recently recognized Islamic variant), "the nation" is defined primarily by race and religion and only secondarily by geography or social homogeneity.

Fortunately, Fascism is rare and marginal in American political culture. Unfortunately, despite that rarity, the term is thrown about loosely by people on the political "left" as a vague but barbed epithet aimed at the political "right," and there is a general belief that Fascism is, somehow, merely the logically extreme version of 'conservatism.' The most recent and blatant examples of this are the explicit juxtaposition of George W. Bush with Adolph Hitler in campaign advertisements,[1] but those merely made public what has been commonly whispered in private about 'conservatism' in general. I suspect it is a rare 'conservative' of my generation that has not, at least once, been called a "fascist" by one of his or her 'liberal' peers (and has not, in turn, similarly and automatically — and equally unfairly — denounced that peer with the label "communist" in the simple spirit of payback).

It may be fairly said that Fascists are often conservative in the classic sense — that Fascism, as a political movement, is typically an idiosyncratic defensive reaction to 'liberal' changes in society that are perceived to have undermined social cohesion and 'national' identity. But saying that Fascism is an idiosyncratic and conservative reaction to particular forms of liberal transformation is in no way the same as extrapolating from traditional, and particularly from American, 'conservative' values to Fascism as if it were the normal progression of political thought.

The fundamental nature of government — that it requires coercive authority to fulfill its function — implies that the very existence of government will bring with it some authoritarian aspects: police and the judiciary have the power of arrest and imprisonment; the taxing authorities have the power of confiscation; regulatory bodies proscribe various freedoms of action (and collect "fees" and impose fines) in the name of economic or social or cultural justice; the military authorities, in times of national peril, are granted the power of conscription and are exempted, within a war zone, from some of the normal precepts of moral behavior. To an uninformed observer, the very formation of a government — the transition away from anarchy toward a civil order maintained by coercion — could appear as a first step toward Fascism, at least insofar as it imposes constraints on liberty toward some notion of the "common good." That forming a government could also appear as a first step toward Marxism is significant: the difference between the two lies in the ultimate intent and use of authority, not in the mechanisms of authority themselves.

---

1 The more recent instances, at Tea Party rallies, of the same comparison involving President Obama were considered so bizarre by the popular press and political leadership that they were dismissed immediately as a mere sign of racism-induced paranoia.

And intent is critical. In any advocacy of government action, whether 'liberal' or 'conservative,' we can identify authoritarian elements. That is the nature and purpose of government. As we noted before, the traditional American 'conservative' view of government, asserted in the American *Declaration of Independence*, is that the proper purpose of government authority is to secure individual liberty — that the authoritarian powers of government exist to blunt the excesses of anarchy, which make individual liberty practically unattainable. Although different strains of 'conservatism' may emphasize other values like social stability above this one, there is general agreement that government must have enough coercive authority to protect liberty but not enough to enervate it.

Exactly where the boundary is, however, between not enough authority and too much is not rationally determinable. It is a matter of judgment. When authority is exercised directly to protect citizens against the depredations of their peers or their enemies — to enforce criminal laws against theft and murder and to thwart foreign invasion — the boundary is not generally disputable or disputed. When questions turn from defusing direct conflict to modulating social and economic environments, or from national survival to national interest, or from addressing immediate concerns to managing long-term trends, the boundary blurs.

But disagreement over the proper placement of the boundary is different in kind than disagreement over whether the boundary should exist at all.

It is true that moving the boundary farther toward government authority brings it closer in the practice to socialism of one form or another — toward Fascism or Marxism or theocracy or some other variant, depending on the nature and purpose of the adjustment. And, by those incremental adjustments, the boundary can inadvertently end up where few would have purposely moved it in one leap. Thus, ideological purists defend the current boundary by extreme claims, arguing, for instance, that any moderation in freedom of speech amounts to censorship, that any erosion in the rights of the accused amounts to a Star Court, that any regulation of gun ownership amounts to an abolition of the right to self-defense and self-determination, or that any constraint on abortion amounts to sexual serfdom. But these are rhetorical devices designed to remind us of the genuine dangers of incrementalism. They are not moral arguments over the very existence of the boundary.

And the one thing agreed pretty well universally by mainstream 'liberals' and mainstream 'conservatives' is that such a boundary should exist — that individuals and individual liberty matter as much or more than the abstract "society." That does not mean we should simply acquiesce to any and all proposals for increasing government authority just because we grant the proponents honorable intent. To the contrary, often intent does not determine outcome, and caution and loyal opposition are prudent and honorable. But, even if we believe that a particular proposal or series of proposals moves the boundary too far, that does not by itself make such proposals "fascist" (or, to be fair, "socialist").

It is wrong to the point of irresponsibility to assert that the libertarian strains of 'conservatism' could be, in any way, a precursor to Fascism — they are its antithesis. Even for strains of 'conservatism' concerned primarily with social and cultural cohesion, the only way an extrapolation from 'conservatism' could lead to Fascism is in the extreme of an utter disregard for individual liberty — an extrapolation simply not to be found in mainstream American political debate. The same extrapolation from 'liberalism' leads to Marxism, and it is just as irrelevant to our actual leaders and to our actual politics. Accusations to the contrary may stir emotions at election time, but they add no substance to campaigns and the polarization they provoke detracts from governance in the aftermath.

Capitalism

American 'conservatism' is closely identified with Capitalism, so much so that to many people the word "Capitalism" itself seems to have been redefined, unmoored from its narrow foundations in economic theory to serve merely as a synonym for whatever policies some vocal American 'conservatives' are advocating — or, as often as not, whatever policies some popular American or European 'liberals' fantasize 'conservatives' are advocating.

In part, fantastic notions of what Capitalism is and implies come from a conflation of Capitalism with the range of unfortunate economic and social conditions we find within our nominally Capitalistic society. If poverty exists within a Capitalist economy, we imagine that Capitalism is at best indifferent to poverty and at worst embraces it. We fail to see that poverty is the natural human condition, that the most remarkable aspect of Capitalism is the degree to which it *reduces* poverty generally, by creating wealth, rather than the degree to which it allows some residual poverty to remain. If Capitalist societies are sometimes tribal and violent, we imagine that Capitalism evokes tribalism and aggression rather than acknowledging that tribalism and aggression are a part of human nature that Capitalism cannot entirely tame. And, to the extent that our version of Capitalism actually *is* merely "nominal" — to the extent that our government both "helps" and "hinders" the operation of the free market rather than allowing it to function freely — many of the problems that are blamed on Capitalism may actually be more accurately ascribed to a *lack* of Capitalism.

At times this reimagining of what Capitalism is becomes so extreme that it more resembles a caricature than a characterization. We hear, for example, claims that the real and primary purpose of the American invasion of Iraq was to serve the interests of Halliburton specifically and of the American oil industry generally; that the involvement and self-interest of industry is the definitional framework of Capitalism; that, therefore, the war in Iraq was self-evidently a "Capitalist" war and that "Capitalism" must be equivalent to a kind of larcenous imperialism; and, moreover, that, if this particular war is a "Capitalist" war, then we must conclude that "Capitalism" and "capitalists" generally embrace such wars in the pursuit of profit: that "Capitalist warmonger" is a tautology.

Often, however, confusion over the meaning and implications of Capitalism results from an honest, but nonetheless inaccurate, guilt by association: an association of Capitalism with other ideas and policies advocated by people who describe themselves as Capitalists. People who admire Capitalism are likely to be as confused as those who fear it. The confusion is exacerbated by the fact that its admirers often invoke Capitalism reflexively but speciously as a general-purpose justification for a wide range of policy preferences and bad behavior that have broadly to do with business and taxation but that have little to do with the economic fundaments of Capitalism.

Hence, in the modern political lexicon, Capitalism is considered to be synonymous with the law of the jungle camouflaged as Laissez Faire, with Social Darwinism, with trade and markets free not only of coercion but of rules and scruples, with supply-side economics, with low taxes and the Laffer Curve, with greed and the God of the Profits, with corporate welfare, with corporate and governmental corruption, with war and imperialism abroad, with the surveillance state at home, and so on. And Capitalism is considered to be antonymous with any kind of regulation, with corporate responsibility, with ethics, with liberty, with environmental stewardship, with the welfare of the middle class, with the social safety net, and with social conscience in general.

But, in reality, what is Capitalism and what is it not?

To understand what Capitalism is, we must start at the root, with *capital*. In the broadest sense, capital is the means of production — that is, capital is the stuff we can use to create more stuff. Capital is the seeds we use to plant crops; it is the tractors we use to till the soil and the combines we use to reap the grain; it is the irrigation systems and fertilizers we use to feed the plants; it is the granaries in which we store the harvest so that it doesn't rot before we can use it and the trucks and trains we use to transport it to markets. Various economic theories of capital make technical distinctions concerning the ways that raw materials, labor, and ephemeral goods like knowledge and skills fit into that broad outline. However, in all cases capital is distinguished by the fact that it is applied to maintain and increase future economic output rather than merely consumed to sustain life and to pursue happiness.

In a modern economy we assume capital exists within a market and may be bought or sold as it is needed. Hence, we typically think about capital in terms of the medium of exchange — in terms of money that may be invested — rather than in terms of what that money can buy. But that way of thinking reflects our particular modern economic engine, not the fundamental nature of capital. You can convert money to capital by using it to buy means of production; but, regardless of how much money you have, you have no capital if there are no means of production available for sale. Money allows you to buy capital and to reallocate it from one use to another, but money, in itself, is not capital. If you doubt that, ask yourself how much capital a wealthy farmer really has available to put more fields into production if there is a shortage of seed and it has already all been planted. You can't magically create capital by printing money. It can only be created by producing tangible and useful stuff.

Capitalism is the name for a range of related economic theories which describe how individual owners of capital — capitalists — manage and use their capital to optimize the production of goods and services. By extension, Capitalism is also the name given to the general class of real-world economic systems which operate in the manners and by the mechanisms described by those theories.

A crucial and fundamental point to note about capital is that *resources we consume and resources which become capital are interchangeable and, therefore, indistinguishable* — that any decision about how to allocate capital resources must flow from a prior decision to use those resources as capital in the first place rather than to consume them. A bushel of corn may feed the hungry or may feed cattle and pigs and poultry or may become seed stock for growing more corn; a decision to grow new corn, rather than to feed cows, necessarily assumes a previous decision to produce more goods from the bushel, rather than to eat it. Even decisions of what to produce in the first place — more corn or more combines — express a preference for consumption or capital. Hence, *any mechanism for allocating capital is fundamentally inseparable from the mechanism for allocating goods.* Any attempt to control the allocation of capital *must also* control the allocation of goods that people consume.

A second point to note is that Capitalism is a theory and a system of *production*, not of *consumption*. It has relatively little to say about what or how much we ought to consume. And, other than the recognition that the mechanisms for allocating capital and consumption are inseparable, it has relatively little to say about the pattern of consumption, about how the goods we consume should be dispersed throughout society. It merely describes how the capital we choose to accrue can be put to the most productive use.

That said, the very existence of capital depends on a general willingness to shift resources away from satisfying current needs and desires and toward anticipating and planning for future ones. Hence, capitalists concern themselves a great deal with the balance between goods and capital even if theories of Capitalism do not.

A third point to note is that capital generated from prior production may or may not be in a form that is useful for future production. Surplus from this year's corn harvest may provide the seed for next year's crop but it does not provide the fertilizers and tractors and other equipment used in tilling and harvesting, or the gasoline to run them; neither does it provide the seed for a wheat crop if, in the future, we would be better off growing wheat than corn.

In general, no individual enterprise can be expected to produce exactly, entirely, and proportionately what it requires for its own capital needs. And hence, Capitalist theory presupposes that capital will usually need to be disaggregated, exchanged, and aggregated before being put to use. That is, capital is dynamic, not static, and Capitalism concerns itself as much with the *movement* of capital as it does with the *employment* of capital.

The fourth, and perhaps the most important, point of note is that *the source of all growth in production and all improvements in living standards is profit.* Most of us view — and perhaps demonize — profit in a narrow and immediate sense as the amount of money left over after a company has sold what is has produced and paid for the costs of production. Those with a focus on consumption rather than on production might describe profit pejoratively as "that which has been extracted unnecessarily from the consumer." Those whose focus is on labor rather than on capital might describe it pejoratively as "that which has been withheld unnecessarily from the workers." Both, in large part, miss the point.

Individual workers profit from their labor to the extent that their wages exceed their effort — to the extent that the wage their employer pays them exceeds the value of what they could have produced for their own use with the same amount of work. If, for instance, they can buy more food out of their wages than they could have grown in their own garden by working the same amount of time then they have become better off — they have made a profit — by working for wages. They have invested the same amount of time in work and have more food (or clothes or iPods) to enjoy.

Similarly, we presume that consumers buy goods because they get more benefit from the goods they buy than from the money they pay. They would rather buy than not buy because buying makes them better off; if it didn't, they would keep their money instead of spending it. From the consumer's standpoint, that excess benefit is also profit.

Consequently, it is wrong to assert that employers and merchants extract profit at the expense of workers and consumers. Rather, profits are split to some greater or lesser degree between workers and employers and between consumers and merchants.

Whether you view that split as fair or foul, it is an accounting view of profit, not a functional one. As an economic concept, profit represents surplus production. At the level of the economy as a whole, to whom the profit accrues is a minor detail in an important story: profit provides both the goods necessary to improve our standard of living and the capital necessary to keep producing in the future.

None of this should be controversial. It defines the background in which any theory of capital must operate. Karl Marx himself recognized the role and mechanisms of capital even as he criticized various perceived adverse effects of Capitalism and sought ways to tame them.

Theories of Capitalism, then, are concerned with how capital is and should be allocated. Where they generate contention, at least in modern discussion, is in particular conclusions they draw based on moral premises and on practical analyses: that resources, both consumer goods and capital, should be privately owned and exchanged by individuals; that decisions about how resources are to be allocated and about what/how much to consume and how much to save and invest should be made by those individuals in a decentralized manner; and that the best mechanism for disaggregating/exchanging/aggregating capital and for distributing goods for consumption is free exchange in a free market. Along with moral premises about individual autonomy and individual rights, those conclusions are based on several other underlying theories and presumptions, about how we value goods and about how we acquire and use information concerning the ways in which they may be put to use.

To make decisions about how best to allocate a resource you must first figure out all the things it could be used for and the value you would get from each of them. A Capitalist model presumes that *value is not inherent in the resource itself but emerges from the utility the resource can provide to someone who makes use of it.* The value in an apple is that someone can eat it and be nourished; *and* that it can provide seed stock for producing more apples; *and* that it could provide nourishment to livestock; *and* perhaps, to some lesser extent, that it is decorative; *and* that it can decompose and fertilize other plants; *and* that it is a part of the miracle of life. A common rock containing Hematite may be useful in building a wall but not generally more useful than one without the hematite; it is, therefore, of relatively low value to someone without a means to smelt and forge iron but of higher value to someone with those means and of greater value to someone with a more efficient smelter. If the rock happens to contain gold as well as Hematite, it may or may not be of more value to a gold smelter than to an iron smelter. Gold itself is useful as an excellent corrosion-free conductor in the construction of electronic circuits but its beauty and its scarcity recommend it even more for other uses, so most electronic devices make do with lesser substitutes like copper or aluminum or tin. And, for those who believe that the value of a resource derives, at least in part, from the amount of labor invested into its production, I would submit that a thousand pink lace doilies hand-embroidered with the likenesses of George W. Bush and Dick Cheney are probably very nearly worthless, notwithstanding the man-years of a skilled craftsman's labor that may have been squandered in their creation.

In addition to purely monetary calculations, judgments about utility will likely hinge on predictions about what people are going to want in the future, after the resource has been used, and how vehemently they will want it. Those predictions are necessarily ambiguous. Moreover, it will depend on idiosyncratic assessments of non-monetary values — whether lacy images of Bush and Cheney amount to art or eyesore; whether swords or plowshares are more important for our future well-being; whether there is some spiritual or moral benefit or cost to cutting down a primeval forest to create a farm. Hence, those judgments can be neither undisputed nor entirely objective. They reflect individual prejudices and preferences as much as impartial fact.

Furthermore, information about utility does not naturally exist as an integrated summary at some central location where it may be read and acted upon. It is inherently distributed among all the people who want to use the resource.

One might imagine some "valuation authority" who went about quizzing all the possible resource producers and users on their plans — or simply presuming such plans based on his/her own knowledge and imagination — and then collating and analyzing the result to make an aggregated judgment and decision about how "best" the resource could be allocated. That is the vision of central planning.

But one might also imagine that process to be protracted, expensive, contentious, politicized, and prone to errors of omission — how does the authority know it has identified all possible resource users or all possible uses? — errors of commission — each resource user has an incentive to overstate the value of his own use to make it more likely that his use will be chosen — and errors of subjectivity — in a dangerous and chaotic world what *is* the best balance between swords and plowshares; and to what extent does the planner's judgment on that supplant the judgments of "the people" he is nominally representing?

And, if one then imagined extending that process to every possible use of every possible resource in every possible place by every possible agent across the entire economy and at myriad instants in time over days and months and years, one might reckon the task to be beyond human comprehension and beyond the capacity of any human system. Certainly the well-known and disastrous practical experiments with such processes in places like the Soviet Union, Maoist China, Castro's Cuba, and North Korea give us good reason to doubt their efficacy.

Given that, and given the legitimate question of who could assume the moral authority to assign and enforce such decisions upon everyone, a Capitalist model presumes that the only legitimate judges of a resource's value are those who wish to make use of it; that the only reasonable value that may be assigned to the resource is the price they are willing to pay for its use, worked out in a marketplace by negotiation between all possible sellers and buyers and mediated by opposing self-interest, by buyers acting to push the price down and sellers acting to push the price up; and that, *under the reasonable and moral constraint that buyers and sellers refrain from bullying each other or stealing from each other or swindling each other*, the incentive of self-interested reward will maximize the amount of economic good that such commerce can extract from the resource. In this model, the negotiation — the free market of buyers and sellers contending with each other for the best possible individual outcomes — is the mechanism by which the information is exchanged and aggregated; the price is the centralized collation and summary of what all that information signifies; and the choice as to the best use (or mix of uses) of the resource is made individual by individual when they decide to purchase the resource or not at the market price.

All that is, of course, based on an underlying structural and mathematical model of how markets operate, including the "law of supply and demand," so Capitalism and the market theories of economics are inextricably intertwined. However, the general framework of Capitalism rests on the broad base of economic mechanisms, not on the details argued incessantly among economists about to what degree markets are or aren't efficient and whether certain pricing processes are or aren't applicable to markets for certain goods.

That, then, is Capitalism. All else is detail.

But what of that detail? What of all those other things that we presume to be inextricably intertwined with Capitalism and, therefore, synonymous with or antithetical to it? *What of...*

...Corporations?

Aren't corporations the heart and soul of Capitalism? What does Capitalist theory say about them? Nothing in particular.

A corporation is a legal fiction chartered and sanctioned by the government to facilitate dealing with our legal system when aggregating capital from a large number of individuals. It would be unwieldy to require individual negotiation and authorization from each investor — say from the current owners of all 10 billion shares of General Electric — every time a large enterprise approved a new contract, or hired or fired an employee, or bought or sold goods, or dealt with some regulatory agency, or represented itself in public, or indeed every time any individual investor opted to take back his capital or to provide more. Instead the government allows those investors to create a legal entity, the corporation, which can act as their collective agent under law for those purposes.

As a beneficial consequence, a corporation also has a legal existence that transcends any individual shareholder or group of shareholders — the corporate shareholders today may not be the same individuals as the corporate shareholders of yesterday but the corporation endures. Nonetheless, a corporation is, at root, nothing more than the sum of its current investors, chartered to act as a single entity on their behalf. From the standpoint of the market, there is no distinction between an individual and a corporation. They have the same standing as buyers and sellers, as producers and consumers.

Hence, other than the practical consequence that it makes the conduct of large-scale business flow more smoothly and increases the amount of capital that can be allocated to a given enterprise, the existence and operation of corporations has nothing to do with Capitalist theory.

...Laissez Faire?

Doesn't Laissez Faire mean "anything goes?" "No rules"? Isn't "Laissez Faire Capitalism" the law of the jungle in fancy dress? Not exactly.

Certainly the idea of Laissez Faire is now used widely to summarize the philosophical, rather than the economic, basis of Capitalism and, specifically, of the Capitalist attitude toward the proper relationship between government and the economy. The term is attributed, at least apocryphally, to a French merchant of the late 1600s who responded, when asked by a government minister what the government could do for business, "Laissez nous faire" ("Leave us be"). In that telling, the original meaning was more along the lines of "don't try to help" than "don't interfere," a rejection of corporate welfare and a government "industrial policy" more than of government oversight of the market. So much for business subsidies and incentive tax breaks and corporate bailouts and business-oriented foreign policies and the like — there is nothing Laissez Faire about those and nothing that solicits them (and much that rejects them) in any theory of Capitalism.

But, even interpreted in the latter sense, "Laissez Faire" represents a philosophy, not a prescription, and does not imply that the free market should be free of all the normal rules of social and legal commerce. "Laissez Faire" presumes that buyers and sellers in a free market should be allowed to negotiate prices and obligations with each other of their own free will — "leave us be" — and without some outside entity like the government compelling concurrence, dictating the terms, or awarding one side an advantage enforced by police powers. It does *not* imply that the government should abdicate its responsibility to define the basic rules by which individuals interact and create agreements, to adjudicate disputes, to support the terms of contracts with legal sanction, to intervene on behalf of individual rights when they have been usurped through fraud or coercion, or to act on behalf of the public interest when market transactions entangle public resources either directly or indirectly. And it does *not* imply that the market is some sacrosanct space that should be shielded from the ordinary obligations of our legal system or of citizenship in our society, and especially not from the fundamental moral tenets of our civilization.

In particular, a "Free Market" is "free" in a very specifically constrained moral sense, not in an expansive and anarchistic one. The "freedom" of the free market is defined by the right to offer freely to others packages of linked rewards and obligations (for example, an offer to provide some goods in return for a payment), and to choose freely whether or not to accept packages of linked rewards and obligations that have been offered by others (i.e. whether or not to buy those goods at the requested price). But it is bound by the responsibility to fulfill rewards and obligations that have been offered and accepted (to deliver what you promised); it is bound by the responsibility to allow others their freedom to make their choices about what to accept or reject without coercion or deception (that is, don't force people to buy what you are selling or sell what you are buying, and don't trick them into doing so); and it is bound by the general responsibility to respect the property rights of all market participants (not to steal what you want).

In other words, inherent in the principle of "Laissez Faire" is the charge to play fair. Those who defraud others, or take what they want by force, or default on their obligations, or usurp control of others' property — including public property — are violators of free market principles, not participants in a free market and not adherents of Laissez Faire.

...The Commons?

Aren't some resources inherently communal and, therefore, best managed as a public trust rather than by private enterprise? Isn't Capitalism incompatible with such a public trust? Not entirely.

Certainly a Capitalist system cannot function if all resources are held in common. If no one can assert a right to control over a resource it cannot be traded and no pricing mechanism can operate to determine how the resource should be best allocated; and if all resources are similarly encumbered, or if they are all controlled monopolistically by the same person or collective, then no market is possible. But Capitalism can operate adequately, if perhaps not at optimal productivity, when some subset of resources is held in common. Whether the relationship between Capitalism and the commons is harmonious or discordant depends on the nature of the commons and, more importantly, on how it is managed.

It is clear that certain useful resources — for example, oceans and rivers and the global atmosphere — comprise a natural commons and have been treated historically as such. The air moves where it will, beyond human control, and is consumed and befouled and replenished by all living things. The oceans are too vast for any government to enforce sovereignty over more than some small portion of them and, as with air, the resources oceans provide respect no boundaries but migrate and exhaust and replenish themselves according to their own cycles. Universal and unfettered access to these vast resources had been established in tradition and practice long before governments, or even civilization itself, arose to assert sovereign cultural or political or economic claims on them.

Societies have often augmented these "natural" commons with others to support various societal goals. Many small New England towns have some grassy area at the center, still referred to as "the Common," which was once a secure communal grazing area for the citizens' livestock. Modern governments maintain public parks and road networks, and provide "free" (meaning freely-accessible) public services like police and fire protection, schools, and various economic programs to alleviate poverty or to "promote the general welfare." Aside from those discrete public services, government itself, in fulfilling its fundamental moral obligation to protect the rights of its citizens, operates as a form of political commons with all entitled to its protections in equal measure. So, too, society may be considered a cultural commons to which all contribute and from which all may take benefit as they see fit.

In 1968 ecologist Garrett Hardin published his influential article, *The Tragedy of the Commons*, in which he described the inevitable long-term negative consequences arising from the use of unregulated commons — that is, the kind of commons described above in which individuals' access to the public resource is widespread, unrestricted, and available for no or modest payment. Those negative consequences result from the fact that any *costs* generated by a specific use of such commons — say the incremental depletion of a fishery created by one additional fisherman, or the incremental cost of providing medical care at a public hospital for one additional patient — are distributed across everyone equally; whereas the *benefit* from a specific use of the commons accrues wholly to the individual user (the new fisherman or the new patient) and wholly at the individual user's discretion (it's their choice, not ours). In economic terms this is a classic "externality" — some part of an economic transaction (the cost associated with an individual's use of the commons) is transferred to someone else that isn't involved in the transaction (the public). Thus, from any individual's standpoint, the marginal benefit of using the commons is relatively large and the marginal cost is relatively small. That creates a general incentive to use as much of the common resource as possible and very little incentive to conserve it.

Further, in the case of the commons, the externality works in the other direction as well. Small as the cost may be when distributed so widely, an individual pays for use of the commons not only when *he* uses it but whenever *anyone* does so. That means an individual cannot avoid the cost by being conservative himself if others are not, and the less conservative others are, the more cost he accrues. An individual not only misses out on any gain but actually incurs a loss by curtailing use of the commons if others will not, because he is then paying for their use without benefitting from his own.

The net result of these perverse incentives is that resources available as unregulated commons are inevitably used wastefully and to excess, and are ultimately depleted more quickly and more thoroughly than resources traded in a market. With no market to price the resource, with no mechanism to signal which uses are more and less beneficial, the resource is allocated indiscriminately to all, allocated both inefficiently in the short term and ruinously in the long term.

We might presume that we can avoid this overuse and degradation of the commons by a general call for moderation — by an appeal to "environmental consciousness" or "social conscience" or "good stewardship." But in practice, the response to such requests will always be predictably human, with some taking those appeals more or less to heart and others merely taking advantage.

Under such circumstances, those inclined toward "bad" behavior (overusing the commons) will end up rewarded with an extra share of the proceeds while those inclined toward "good" behavior (conserving the commons) will end up penalized with an extra share of the costs. Hence, Hardin concluded that an appeal to conscience as a means of mitigating the effects of perverse incentives, although it might be somewhat effective in the short-term, would not ultimately prevent the degradation of the commons; and worse, over time it would create an evolutionary process that would breed conscience out of society by systematically awarding an economic advantage to those with without one. Appeals to conscience, then, would not only fail to save the commons but would ultimately corrode our moral culture and make future appeals to conscience, for that or for any other purpose, less effective.

It is worth noting that, although Hardin was an ecologist and was, in particular, concerned with the effects of population growth on the earth's carrying capacity, much of the argument he made in his essay derived from the same observations of human nature and human behavior as do the various market theories of economics. In effect, Hardin concluded that any unregulated commons, notwithstanding its communal and seemingly anti-Capitalistic nature, would ultimately fall victim to market forces, to the consequences of people making individual choices in pursuit of their own economic interests.

The tendency of people to overuse and, thereby, to destroy the commons had been observed and noted long before Hardin's essay was published. Hardin's contribution was to illuminate and codify the reasons for that behavior in a way that was comprehensible to policymakers and the public. He gave it a label — "Tragedy," in the ancient Greek and Shakespearean sense of misfortune that grows not from chance or malice but inevitably from intrinsic human hubris and frailty — that allowed it to be discussed as a problem with a pragmatic basis rather than a moral one. Hence, he set the stage for discussing practical ways to mitigate the adverse effects of holding commons rather than merely condemning those effects as the product of unnatural avarice and sloth provoked by an evil Capitalist culture.

By tradition, commons, like the sea and the sky, held common owing to their vastness and unruliness, were not managed as a public resource but were, rather, not managed at all. They simply existed as a state of nature from which everyone could take as they saw fit. They were not considered subject to a tragedy of the commons because, at least until relatively recently in human history, they appeared inexhaustible. When societies began creating synthetic commons, like parks and public services and roads, they were often treated in the same way, with essentially unlimited rights of use. However, unlike the boundless bounty of the natural commons, these man-made commons were often prone to over-use and provided the examples from which Hardin generalized his conclusion. And, of course, Hardin's original motivation in addressing his topic was our dawning realization that even the "boundless bounty" of the natural commons was far from boundless and was, in fact, quickly approaching the point of tragedy that Hardin envisioned.

The obvious and Capitalistic approach to solving the problems associated with an unregulated commons would be to eliminate it — that is, to transfer it to private ownership and control, to make it no longer a commons. In most instances, however, how to carry out that "obvious" plan is, in practice, neither obvious nor easy. Nonetheless, there are many clever schemes for implementing such a change even for those "natural" commons that would seem impossible to privatize.

An example of such a scheme that has been recently on the national agenda is to create a property right to some unit mass of air pollution and to auction deeds to a fixed supply of such units (our "national pollution budget") to individual polluters. Once they were in private hands, the deeds would be tradable. People who could easily and inexpensively reduce the amount of pollution they generate could sell their excess units (and thus be rewarded for their "good" behavior) while people who could not do so would need to buy supplemental units (and thus be penalized for their "bad" behavior). Over time, people would have an immediate and realizable financial incentive to reduce the amount of pollution they generated, allowing them to sell some of their units or to avoid buying new ones; and, at any time, the government (or anyone else) could reduce the overall amount of air pollution allowed by buying and retiring air pollution units in the open market at a price which reflected the real economic cost of eliminating that pollution.

Many of these schemes, however, still founder on what, if any, realistic mechanisms are available for enforcing — and more to the point, for constraining — those property rights. It is easy to observe who is occupying and using a particular piece of land or driving a particular car or wearing a particular piece of jewelry or clothing. Use of those properties is both exclusive and visible. But how do you identify, find, catch, and penalize people who continue to pollute without holding a pollution deed — who are, in effect, pollution trespassers or pollution thieves? How do you measure how much pollution a particular person or enterprise is generating so that you may compare it to the allotment that they own? What kind of regulatory surveillance state does that require, and at what cost to our pocketbooks and to our liberty?[1]

Further, for many people, who are at best uncomfortable with Capitalism and at worst revile it, the notion of allowing someone to get away with "bad" behavior (like polluting) *merely by paying for it* seems morally repugnant. Similarly, they perceive a great unfairness — and moral harm — in allowing "the rich" greater access to some "public" resource than "the poor." For such people, the economic and practical benefits of these schemes cannot outweigh their perceived moral shortcomings.

For all those reasons, although some schemes like the one described may be attempted, many commons will not be privatized in this manner and we must find another way to mitigate the problems associated with them.

If we cannot solve the problem of unregulated commons by making them not common, then the alternative is to make them not unregulated — that is, to regulate access to them. The operation of a regulated commons is based, not on the traditional and expansive notion of the commons as a vast resource shared equally by all individual members of the public, but on a more constrained notion of the commons as a limited resource held in trust for the benefit of the public *en bloc*. There are two fundamental models for such regulation. The difference between them is the management mechanisms employed to restrict access, not the underlying paradigm of stewardship.

From the standpoint of a Capitalist economic system, the fact that ownership of some large resource is held as a public stewardship, rather than distributed, is not vastly different in principle than having the resource held by a corporation or by some wealthy individual. The steward managing the resource — either a government or some quasi-public entity like a conservation trust — represents the collective interest of the "shareholders" and can make the resource available to the market or withhold it based on that interest just as any other market participant would.

Provided ownership of the resource does not create a monopoly on access (and sometimes even if it does) — that is, provided some alternative reserve of that particular kind of resource is available elsewhere (and sometimes even if it isn't) — a market for the resource can exist and the public steward can be a market participant, buying or selling based on the market price

---

1 A generalized "carbon tax" offers an alternative that is not quite as effective but has the advantage that it requires much less regulatory scrutiny. It is less effective because it only rewards people for using less fuel as an input, not for reducing the amount of pollution that a given amount of fuel generates. Hence, it does nothing to encourage development of pollution control technologies. On the other hand, it only requires regulatory monitoring of a few key energy suppliers, rather than monitoring of the much larger and more dispersed population of energy users.

and the internal tradeoffs between utilizing and preserving the resource "in the public interest." For example, the government each year sells a certain amount of mineral ore from public lands, and it rents the radio frequency spectra to radio stations, television stations, and mobile phone companies.

Notwithstanding the ability of a public steward to be a market participant, the distinction between such a steward and a typical corporation or individual bears on the efficiency with which that steward can operate in the market. Although the public steward trades in the market based on its assessment of the "interest" of the public it represents, the way it comes to its conclusion about "interest" is different than the way a corporation or individual would do so.

For an individual, that assessment is, of course, straightforward: he compares his "costs" (monetary and otherwise) against his "benefits" (monetary and otherwise) and tries to make his "profit" (monetary and otherwise) as large as he can.

For a corporation the process is both simpler and somewhat more complicated: more complicated because it must aggregate the interests of all its individual shareholders; but simpler because its specific and legally-constrained objective is strictly and compellingly fiduciary and, therefore, easy to account. The fundamental premise of the way a corporation is structured is that costs, benefits, and authority over the decisions of the corporation are all aligned in proportion to ownership, such that those with the most to gain or lose by a corporate decision also have the most say over what that decision should be. Hence, a majority of corporate shares corresponds directly with the majority fiduciary interest and a vote of the shares is a determinative expression of the aggregate interest of the shareholders.

A public stewardship, by contrast, is almost always designed with some degree of disconnect between the amount of interest a particular "shareholder" has in the outcome of a steward's decision and the amount of authority that "shareholder" exercises over the decision. In particular, decisions about what to do with the commons managed by the steward commonly result in an uneven distribution of costs and benefits among individual members of the public, both because the economic interests of those individuals tend to be disparate and because of the assumption that non-monetary considerations, assessment of which are highly idiosyncratic and volatile, should be paramount in making such decisions. On the other hand, authority over the decisions of the steward are almost always either distributed equally — one man/one vote — or delegated to some panel of "experts" over which the public has very little authority at all.

The result is that the amount of control an individual "shareholder" exercises over the use of a public resource is rarely correlated with the effect that use will have on him or her. It is likely that the "public interest" asserted in the marketplace by a public steward is not equivalent to the economically efficient interest that would be asserted if the individual "shareholders" were allowed to operate in the market exercising individual control over their "share" of the public resource.

There is, of course, another model of stewardship for a public commons which avoids the market entirely in favor of regulatory management. In that model the steward, having used some internal process of valuation to decide how much of the resource should be allocated, and to what purpose, either restricts or awards access to selected individuals directly through some regulatory mechanism, or he takes on use of the resource as an internal project. Since the resource is never offered to the market, it is never priced; and, since it is never offered to the market, no one may buy it. Access (or non-access) to the resource is determined by some non-market mechanism — typically a political one. For all the reasons given in the general description of Capitalism, the allocation of resources in such a scheme is unlikely to be efficient in economic terms. And, because of the discrepancy, described above, between authority over decisions and interest in them, such a system is also not certain to arrive at an unassailable and well-founded assessment of what the public interest actually is, despite it being nominally "democratic."

...Economic Efficiency?

Don't Capitalists and free market economists justify all manner of unfair and anti-social policies by invoking that narrow practical goal? Aren't they willing to sacrifice all other values to its cold, rational, inhuman demands? Not as such.

Efficiency is the ratio of output to input, a measure of how much you get compared to how much you had to give. A high efficiency in some activity implies that you got a lot without having to give much — and, therefore, that you ended up pretty well off for having done it.

Economic efficiency, or "market efficiency," is exactly that. It is a measure of how much wealth the economy creates versus how much it consumes in the process. Higher economic efficiency means we create more for a given amount of consumption and that, as a society, we end up materially better off and with a higher standard of living. So, yes, all other things being equal Capitalists and free market economists place a high value on optimum economic efficiency because, in aggregate, it generates the most good for the least cost. And, all other things being equal and regardless of the ultimate policy goals, they will favor policies that result in higher economic efficiency over those that result in lower economic efficiency because they leave society as a whole with more wealth to use in support of its goals.

But assessments of economic efficiency are based on this presumption: we already plan to expend some amount of resource to pursue some policy goal — that is, we have already decided that the goal, in and of itself, is a worthwhile pursuit. Given that, there is no reason *not* to make that expenditure as efficient as possible. It would be stupid to do otherwise.

But, having examined the economic efficiencies, we may also conclude that we simply cannot achieve that goal for any reasonable cost. We may conclude we should cancel our plan, not because the goal is not worthwhile but because it's just too expensive.

Unless the policy goal in question is purely economic, that judgment is, of course, subjective. There is no objective economic scale for assessing non-economic benefits, and no argument based on economic efficiency can identify whether or not those non-economic benefits outweigh the economic costs. But an attention to economic efficiency can, at least, tell you what those costs will be.

...Business Subsidies?

Aren't incentive tax breaks and price supports and protective tariffs and other policies aimed at "encouraging" or "supporting" business the government's way of protecting and expanding Capitalism? Most emphatically not!

"Business" is not a synonym for "Capitalism." Capitalism is about private ownership and the free exchange of resources in a market. It is about the *flow* of wealth as a way of allocating it most usefully. Business — from multi-national corporations to individual employees selling their services to the highest bidder, and consumers shopping around for the lowest prices — is about *accumulating* wealth.

Capitalist theory posits that accumulating wealth within the context of a free market — without resort to coercion or fraud — requires *creating* wealth. If a business does not produce more wealth in goods than it consumes in capital, then it will soon be no longer in business. If a business does not offer its workers more wealth in wages than they could grow in their own gardens, then it will have no workers to produce its goods. If a business does not offer its customers more wealth in goods than it asks for in payment, then customers will choose not to buy. Hence, a business operating in a free market serves the interest of its investors and its workers and its customers by improving their standards of living, and serves the interest of society generally by creating new wealth that can be made available for new consumption and/or as new capital. Capitalist theory describes how that happens — how the self-serving strivings of businesses and of their customers and of their workers is transformed by the free market — as if by magic (or by Adam Smith's "invisible hand") but, in reality, by implacable logic — into a general prosperity.

But free trade in a free market is not the only *or the easiest* way to accumulate wealth. One could, for instance, simply steal it, by force or by fraud. One could happen upon it by accident, say by winning a lottery or by holding a supply of some commodity that becomes suddenly and unexpectedly scarce or suddenly and unexpectedly desirable. One could manipulate the scarcity and/or desirability of some commodity by monopolizing it or subsidizing it or taxing it or mandating or prohibiting its purchase, an activity made much easier and more likely with the consent and collusion of some political authority. Or one could simply use the political authority of government to expropriate wealth directly from the general citizenry through taxation.

All of those may serve the interest of "business," or at least of individual businesses. None of those represent the activities of a free market and none of them advance the cause of Capitalism.

All the various forms of government "support" for business — or for "labor" and "consumers," which are merely labels for business transacted at the individual level — amount, in the end, to the same thing: using the power of the state to forcibly transfer wealth from one place to another, either from taxpayers to business generally or from some set of disfavored businesses or individuals to some other set of favored businesses or individuals.

Businesses and individuals who are on the receiving end of that will, of course, tend to endorse and encourage such "support." Why would they not? They are capitalists, not Capitalists, wielders of capital, not advocates of Capitalism. That is true of people who run businesses, but it is also true of workers and the unions that represent them, and of consumers and the consumer advocates that agitate on their behalf. They are neither philosophers nor philanthropists. Their purpose is to maximize their own benefit, to accumulate wealth. If the government wants to make that easier for them at the expense of someone else, they are generally happy to go along for the ride.

Politicians and economists and businessmen who advocate such policies often claim to do so in the name of Capitalism, in the name of "helping" the free market to function "better" in some way. But what such policies really reflect is not encouragement for Capitalism but a lack of faith in Capitalism, not support for the free market but a conviction that the market must be made, somehow, less free in order to "improve" the outcomes it produces.

That neither protects nor expands Capitalism. It undermines it.

What it almost always *does* protect and expand, however, is the power wielded by those in government who choose the winners and losers, and the incentives for the winners and losers to game the system to their advantage by influencing (or corrupting) those who wield such power.

...Regulation?

Doesn't regulation fetter the free market? Isn't regulation the opposite of Laissez Faire and anathema to Capitalism? Yes, but no.

In the idealized agrarian vision of a free market in some rural village it is true that regulation — or, at least, formal regulation — would be mostly superfluous and, therefore, mostly undesirable. Transactions in such a marketplace generally take place through face-to-face negotiation between two individuals who know each other and share social and cultural referents. Both live in the same small and insular society and have an interest in preserving their good names and a general sense of harmony within that society; both are likely to depend on an ongoing trading relationship with each other and with others in their immediate social group; their dealings are likely to be simple and unambiguous; their honesty or dishonesty in their dealings can be observed directly by others with whom they might deal in the future; their ownership of property and resources is established and acknowledged through a combination of tradition and possession; their projects are likely to proceed over a fairly short time horizon within a relatively stable economic environment; the scope of their commerce is not likely so large as to be catastrophic if, for some reason, the terms are not fulfilled; and costs they impose on the commons will be noticed and punished, both socially and economically, by their neighbors. All these factors give market participants strong incentives to deal fairly with each other, to fulfill the terms of their agreements, and to preserve social and economic harmony by being conscientious about the use of commons and by forgiving isolated instances of default tied to misfortune. That is, they are nudged by informal mechanisms of regulation, by cultural mores, social scrutiny, and economic self-interest — by "market discipline" — to honor their commitments to each other and to the community as a whole.

In a modern, large-scale, finance-based market economy, however, a great deal of commerce takes place in relative anonymity and among people who do not necessarily share direct social or even cultural or political ties. Information about the background and outcome of commercial activities is obscured by distance, time, political barriers, cultural barriers, and a lack of direct personal experience with commercial partners. Many of the goods exchanged are more ephemeral than physical, comprising credit and debt, contracts for futures and insurance, and other such promises. In that milieu, the social and cultural incentives that are robust in a simple, rural economy become dilute. Hence, more formal institutions are required to regulate — or, perhaps more appropriately, to *regularize* — market transactions.

As we've said before, those primal and necessary regulatory institutions include a system for identifying, establishing, tracing, and abiding by ownership of property and resources; a basic structure of legally enforceable personal and property rights that provides recourse against coercion, theft, fraud, and default; a stable and universal currency to facilitate exchange in the market; and a legal framework for negotiating contracts and for adjudicating disputes over contract terms and obligations.

In addition, for public markets to function efficiently and with minimal opportunity for fraud, information about economic transactions and contractual terms should be generally available to market participants, accurate, and presented in a comprehensible manner. Hence, regulations promoting standard contract formalisms, standard reporting practices, and other supports for information transparency can be helpful and justified. Conversely, markets operate inefficiently (and arguably unjustly) in the presence of externalities — when participants have the opportunity to reap the benefits of an activity while shifting associated costs onto others, including onto the commons — and regulations aimed at controlling externalities and realigning costs with benefits are appropriate. Environmental regulations, for example, which are designed to redirect the widely dispersed and public costs of pollution back onto those who benefit from the act of polluting, may be fully justified in economic terms and are consistent with Laissez Faire.

Finally, since corporations are legal constructs chartered to represent the interests of their shareholders, various legal strictures controlling how they deal with shareholders, report information, and interact with individuals, with the legal system, and with each other are well within the reasonable scope of the chartering process. The rules controlling corporate behavior under their charters is a purely legal matter and, while specific rules may or may not be economically wise, the corporation is at root a creature of the law and it is not unreasonable for it to be bound by law. Nonetheless, given the core economic purpose of a corporation, it would be counterproductive to impose rules on corporations which significantly hampered their functioning as market participants.

The fact that Laissez Faire does not, on its face, preclude prudent regulation of markets does not mean, however, that any and all regulation is consistent with the spirit of Laissez Faire. Regulation which regularizes market operation is generally inoffensive, if not always useful. Regulation which constrains bad actors, holding them to account for their promises and punishing coercion, fraud, and theft is an indisputable good on both economic and ethical grounds. Regulation that constrains the exploitation of externalities reinforces, rather than hinders, both the moral element of free choice and the economic basis of market efficiency. It makes the market more, rather than less, "free."

But all those types of regulation respect the underlying premises of the market economy: the rights of property and contract, the freedom to judge for yourself what is best for you, and the presumption that the aggregation of those choices in the market will lead to the best (though not perfect) economic outcome.

Regulations which violate those premises are as often a problem as a solution. Regulation that interferes with pricing mechanisms usurps some degree of freedom to contract and decreases economic output by pushing the market away from its optimal resource allocation. Regulation that selects and elevates favored market participants or favored resource uses based on political or social or moral goals does likewise. Regulation that disconnects costs from benefits in market transactions perverts the incentives that allow markets to function either efficiently or fairly. Regulation that expropriates private property to public use is little better than formalized theft. Regulation that prescribes what products shall and shall not be available in the marketplace, or that prohibits participation by some while allowing participation by others, or that specifies the terms of market transactions denies individuals the right to make decisions about their own interests. Regulation that specifies the processes by which regulatory goals are to be pursued, rather than specifying the goals themselves, precludes any possibility of innovation and often renders the goals themselves unachievable.

In addition, much of an industrial economy operates on time-scales of years or decades and involves enormous capital investments in fixed infrastructure. In that environment, regulatory instability — a constant updating and reversing and piling on of rules and constraints and costs as political goals and priorities change — dramatically increases the risk associated with long-term investment and, consequently, dramatically decreases the productivity of that investment. In general, the *stability* of regulation over time is often as important to efficient operation of the modern market as the *content* of regulation.

Further, one of the premises of 'conservatism' described earlier is that an economy — or any other human enterprise — works best by exploiting and/or redirecting natural human tendencies than by trying to reform and/or deny them. If people are self-interested, then arrange the economic system to channel self-interest into productive avenues rather than trying to metamorphose self-interest into selflessness.

The same principle applies to regulation. People respond to incentives and tend to resist coercion. Regulations which arrange external incentives to encourage people to prefer the regulator's desired outcome over other alternatives are far more likely to be effective than regulations which command that outcome under threat of penalty. And, because of the natural tendency to resist coercion, enforcing coercive regulation requires that regulators have the authority to scrutinize what people are doing in great detail.

The need for such scrutiny not only invites non-compliance and adds enormous compliance costs, both for regulators and for those regulated, but also requires a regulatory surveillance infrastructure and capability that becomes available — and will almost inevitably be turned toward — regulatory scrutiny of activities that have nothing to do with economics. If you doubt that, remember that New York Governor Eliot Spitzer's slide from grace started not because someone actually observed him hiring a prostitute but because a bank was required to report his payments to federal investigators as a pattern of "suspicious" financial transactions.

Finally, regulation should be honest about what it is trying to achieve and at what cost. Contrary to popular mythology, there is no such thing as painless regulation. But the costs of regulation are generally hard to assess, both in terms of how large they are and in terms of who will pay them, because they so often apply indirectly or as the result of a complex chain of consequences. The costs and benefits of regulation are almost always distributed unevenly, such that a great many people can perceive, correctly, that their own benefits will be high while their own costs — or at least their direct and observable costs — will be fairly low. All of which makes it easy to pretend that the costs of regulation are smaller than they actually are, or even that they don't exist.

But pretending that costs of regulation don't exist doesn't make them disappear. It just means we have no way of knowing whether the cost of regulation is worth the benefit — assuming we have even bothered to measure the benefit. For that reason, cost/benefit assessment should be part of the regulatory process, not only before regulations are imposed but on an ongoing basis when the indirect costs and chains of consequences can be observed rather than merely hypothesized. And, to support those assessments, regulations themselves should be specifically designed to facilitate measuring both the costs they impose and the benefits they bestow.

It is currently fashionable, as a tactic to deflect any criticism about regulatory costs, to insist that certain kinds of regulations — those protecting the environment, for instance, or those which protect human life and health — should not be subject to any cost/benefit assessment at all because the regulatory goals are either not quantifiable in economic terms or are simply too important to be burdened with mere material concerns. That sounds noble, but when pressed we all intuitively understand it to be nonsense.

If saving lives was always worth whatever it cost, we would save about 20,000 lives per year on the nation's highways by instituting and enforcing a universal 25 mph speed limit. But we don't do that, not because of some philosophical opposition to speed limits but because we can all imagine how large the cost would be. We can all imagine economic losses in the transportation of goods. We can all imagine displacements in jobs and homes caused by increased commute times. We can all imagine paying for the number of extra traffic cops that would be required to force us to comply, and the general diminishment of liberty that enforcement would bring. We can all imagine the amount of personal time wasted, and the amount of sheer frustration on the roads. And we all realize those costs could not be shunted off onto a few corporations or "rich" people but would, instead, be borne by all of us.

We know the cost of such a regulation would not be worth the gain, despite the fact that the potential benefit is self-evidently enormous and that both the benefits and some of the costs are non-monetary. We know it so implicitly and so universally that it has never been proposed and need not be debated.

One particular kind of regulation that is common, and often controversial, involves imposing constraints on certain uses of private resources which are perceived to degrade a commons. For example, pollution controls impose constraints on emissions from private factories and power plants and automobiles which foul the regional atmosphere or water table. Proposals to control greenhouse gases in defense of the global climate are based on similar reasoning. In principle these kinds of regulations are well within the spirit of Laissez Faire, intended to prevent a party in a market transaction from deriving benefit by imposing a cost on those (in this case the general public) who are not direct participants in the transaction and who have no control over its terms. We may oppose specific regulations — because they have a poor cost/benefit tradeoff, or because they operate by coercion rather than by incentive, or because they lack a specific legal authorization, or for any other practical reason — without disputing that some kind of regulation may be appropriate in these cases.

Where such regulation becomes a particular problem — and where such regulations have become increasingly popular — is when the commons in question has been recently created or recognized, where no such commons was previously understood to exist. For example, consider a city which has declared a public interest in preserving "open space" and proposed regulations on private uses of property to further that interest.

Prior to that declaration, some "open space" existed by default, because many property owners had not exercised their rights to develop their property in ways that "closed" it. But "open space" had been neither identified as a discrete and controllable good nor understood to be anything over which the public had any claim. "Open space" belonged to the property owner until he or she decided to "close" it.

After that declaration, "open space" became, in effect, public property — a commons — over which the public asserted a right of management.

When property owners bought their properties, before the new regulation was imposed, part of the price they paid was for the right to do things that might "close" the property: perhaps to build a house; perhaps to run a business; perhaps to cut down trees for lumber or in order to clear a field for a horse paddock. After the new regulation was imposed, those uses became no longer available to them. Hence, the declaration of a public interest in preserving open space generated a transfer of property rights — the rights to do things that "close" the property — from the private owners to the public. The public appropriated something of value — the new open space commons — from its previous owners without paying for it.

Taking our example further into specifics, suppose the city's new regulations prohibit, henceforth, any building within a designated "open-space zone." The public has gained something of value, the guarantee of open-space in perpetuity. We know that guarantee has value because, if it didn't, there would have been no reason to impose the regulation.

On the other hand, given that the value of a resource derives from the uses to which it can be put, the people who own property within the new open-space zone have lost something of value: they can no longer use their property for anything that requires building on it. As a consequence, the property is less useful to them than it once was, and the market value of the property, should they try to sell it, is lower than it would have been, without the regulation, because it will also be less useful to any buyer.

It may be true, as various courts have found, that this is not a "taking" in the strictest sense traditionally understood under the legal doctrine of eminent domain because, although there has been a transfer of *value*, no actual transfer of *title* has occurred. The owners still retain possession of the property and some limited right to its use.

Nonetheless, the public has gotten something for nothing while the property owners within the open-space zone have been stuck with a very real and tangible bill.

The nature of this injustice becomes clearer if you consider the analogous case of "mineral rights" which exist in many states rich in mineral deposits. In places where mineral rights are recognized, ownership of a piece of property confers rights to specific usage rather than a generalized right to control. Title to the right of occupation and utilization of the land's surface is separate from title to the right of mineral extraction below the surface. The two may be owned by different people and bought or sold independently of each other.

To those unfamiliar with it, this arrangement might seem odd and unfair, a materialistic triumph of commercial over individual interests. Yet the arrangement actually allows a beneficial balance between the two, paving the way for mixed usage — houses co-existing with oil wells. More importantly to homeowners, it ensures that people primarily interested in owning a home do not have to pay an inflated price for it based on its potential value as a future source of mineral wealth. In other words, *it keeps the price of houses low enough that people can afford to buy them.*

Extending this model to the "open-space zone," one might imagine the city doing something similar, creating separate titles for rights to uses which require buildings and rights to uses which do not, and then transferring the title for the building uses from the property owners to the public. In that case there would be no ambiguity about whether or not this constituted a "taking." A title transfer would have occurred and the transfer would have identified the specific usage rights — and therefore an identifiable value — that had been taken and should be compensated.

The issue here is not whether the public has the right to designate a new commons. There is certainly debate on that proposition but it is a fundamental philosophical debate, outside the scope of economic theory.

But, granting the point, we all recognize that a private profit derived from a public cost is unfair — that taking a gain and sticking the public with the bill is both unjust and the farthest thing from the ideal of Laissez Faire. We should, then, recognize also that a public profit derived from a private cost is equally unfair — that if the public wants a benefit then the public should be willing to step up and pay for it.

...Greed?

Isn't "Greed is good!" the Capitalists' creed? Isn't Capitalism all about getting mine at your expense? Well, yes — but no.

There are those who advocate greed — meaning merely a healthy focus on self-interest, not a rapacious avarice — as a moral principle, an assertion and affirmation of the individual's status as a self-justified moral being. If the individual has moral value and human dignity, then there should be no shame, but rather an equivalent moral dignity, in fulfilling that individual's needs and desires. But, although people who agree with that assertion may most often also advocate Capitalism, there is nothing in Capitalist theory per se that passes judgment on the morality of greed.

From a Capitalist perspective, "greed is good" is a statement of *utility*, not of *morality*. Greed is useful, not virtuous.

Morals aside, self-interest (enlightened or otherwise) is human nature and is the way people behave when they engage each other in commerce. Any human economic system must accommodate that behavior. Theories of the free market — and thousands of years of observation of human behavior (and a bit of honest introspection) — tell us that people will do what they can to get the most of what they want at the least possible cost. It also tells us that allowing them to do so within a "well-regulated" market — meaning constrained by moral principle, acting without resort to coercion or fraud — will lead to optimum, or at least near optimum, economic production overall. In a Capitalist economic system, then, self-interest — the "profit motive" — is good because it is productive, because it satisfies individual appetites and because it unwittingly serves the general welfare by driving markets toward economic efficiency and producing wealth.

More to the point, a free market is a two-way street. In a free market, exchanges happen because both the buyer and the seller feel they will be better off after the exchange than they were before it. Otherwise the buyer would not buy or the seller would not sell. Hence, although one may profit more than the other, neither's benefit may be said to come at the other's expense. Both benefit. Both come away wealthier, having satisfied some need or desire that would remain unrequited but for the opportunity for exchange that the market provided.

When people assert that one or the other side of an exchange has been "greedy" — that (typically) the merchant or the employer has profited at the consumer's or employee's expense — what they are really asserting is one of two propositions: 1) the most fervent version of distributive justice, that any outcome which is unequal must be ipso-facto unfair and, therefore, unjust; or 2) a moral judgment that one participant (typically the consumer or the employee) is somehow more deserving than the other and therefore has a greater moral claim on the total benefit that the exchange produces. That is, they claim aggrievement not because the exchange resulted in any actual loss or victimization but because the gain failed to fulfill some external expectation for a "just" outcome. Moreover, it is probably accurate to say that even the failure to fulfill their moral expectation is nearly always presumed, not demonstrated: for the most part people making such claims have no idea how much either party actually profited and only some ineffable notion of what a morally proper allocation of profit might be.

But the free market is, if nothing else, free. People get to choose for themselves which "injustices" are worth enduring for the sake of gaining some benefit and which aren't. Perhaps it seems unjust that Apple collects millions of dollars from people who buy iPhones, while those purchasers each end up with their wallets several hundred dollars lighter. If you count only their cash they have become "poorer." But they don't *feel* poor. They feel happy because they have an iPhone, and they would rather have the phone than the money.

If we were to throw over the free market in favor of some other method for distributing the goods of society, whose expectations of justice would prevail? By what moral authority would they be imposed on others who disagreed? Or, more prosaically, who is in a better position than I to decide whether I am better off with my iPhone or with my money? And what gives them the right?

And, if the pursuit of such notions of justice eliminated the original opportunity for gain, if it reduced the tangible economic benefits available to everyone, would that trade of a substantive material comfort for an elusive moral comfort make us better or worse off? Capitalists — and iPhone enthusiasts — would answer with an emphatic "Worse! Much worse!"

But, again, what of greed? Not of enlightened self-interest but of actual rapacious avarice? Capitalism offers no moral opinion on it, although even many Capitalists would find it unseemly or repugnant on other grounds. But, *provided it is channeled into commerce in a free market*, avarice is no less and no more beneficial than its milder cousin. Free exchange in the market enriches everyone involved, and if the avaricious are rewarded with great wealth it is only because they have provided great wealth to others in return.

But doesn't it sometimes run amok? Don't we hear often of capitalists without conscience, of greed-driven market excess, and of evil businessmen endangering the public in their relentless pursuit of profit? Yes, but no. Such things exist, but events frequently cited as justification for condemning the free market on the basis of its support for unchecked greed are almost always examples, rather, of individuals breaking faith with the free market, using coercion or fraud or exploiting an unguarded externality to interfere with free choice and/or to default on freely accepted obligations. That certainly represents a market failure, but it is a failure of the market to be fully free, not a failure of the free market.

...Supply-Side Economics?

Isn't "Supply-Side Economics" a synonym for Capitalism? Again, no.

"Supply-Side Economics" is a label not for a Capitalistic economic theory but for a particular government economic policy. The debate over "Supply-Side" or "Demand-Side" economics is really a debate over how the government should match its taxing policies to the way the economy behaves — that is, it is a debate over methods, not principles.

Supporters of Supply-Side policies presume that demand for goods is robust — that people can and want to buy stuff — and that, therefore, governments' tax and monetary policies should support an equally robust supply by helping business to produce. The assumption is that supporting business will benefit consumers by forcing supplies up and prices down, and by increasing opportunities to earn money through employment.

Supporters of Demand-Side policies presume that the supply of goods is robust — that business can and does produce plenty of stuff — and that, therefore, governments' tax and monetary policies should support an equally robust demand by helping consumers to spend. The assumption, in this case, is that supporting consumers will benefit businesses by expanding the demand for their goods.

No theory of Capitalism — nor of 'conservatism' for that matter — explains which, if either, is right. But note that *neither* policy adheres to the ideal of Laissez Faire. Rather, they both presume that governments intervene in the market — either by design, because that is a function they ought to perform, or merely as an unintended consequence, because they have grown so large that they rival the private economy in economic power. But they disagree on the form that intervention does or should take.

In particular, adherents of both the Supply-Side and Demand-Side theories consider government spending and taxation to be *economic* policies rather than *political* ones. Both consider government spending and taxation to be instruments for effecting desirable changes in the evolution of the economy rather than merely as mechanisms for funding the essential functions of government. Neither has anything to do with Capitalism.

...Small Government and Low Taxes?

Are small government and low taxes not the political mien of Capitalism? Not specifically.

There is nothing in any theory of Capitalism that defines how big or small the government should be or how much or little it should collect in taxes. Those are political questions to be answered based on political considerations, based on what responsibilities government needs to assume and on how much revenue is required to fulfill those responsibilities. To the extent that both Capitalism and civil society rely on government to sustain the stable political, economic, legal, and social environments in which markets can operate freely, Capitalism must sanction both government and the taxes collected to support it. It would be nice if that social infrastructure would sustain itself without a need for government. Perhaps, if everyone were equally intelligent, equally ethical, and equally enthusiastic about the benefits of the market, that would happen. But they are not and it will not.

Certainly there is a well-founded presumption in Capitalist theory that a free market is a more economically efficient mechanism for allocating resources than government. Certainly Capitalism is built around the philosophical idea that personal happiness and well-being is better served by individualized personal choices than by some collective choice that everyone must then live with. Certainly the ideal of Laissez Faire implies that the economic affairs of the nation function best with as little governmental interference as is practically and reasonably possible. And all of these, by identifying responsibilities the government should *not* assume, imply a smaller government than would be necessary otherwise. Hence, *relatively* smaller government is a natural consequence of adhering to Capitalist principles.

A generally smaller government will demand less revenue than a generally larger one. And certainly, even within government, a Capitalistic attention to optimizing resource allocation would minimize the revenue required to perform a given governmental function. Thus, relatively lower taxation, like relatively smaller government, is a natural consequence of adhering to Capitalist principles.

Moreover, money collected in taxes and spent by the government is a resource that has been allocated by political fiat rather than by the market and therefore has, according to Capitalist theory, most likely not been allocated as efficiently or as beneficially as the market would have done. Economic models of the market predict that taxes imposed on market activity will move it away from its most efficient point and reduce the amount of wealth that exchange in the market can produce. That is, tax-supported government spending reduces the wealth an economy can create, not because government is necessarily worse than individuals at making rational choices within the market (though that often seems to be so) but because it operates through coercion and pursues communal goals. Hence, all other things being equal, Capitalism asserts there are sound economic reasons for favoring lower taxes to higher taxes.

But all of those reasons for limited government reflect pragmatic considerations. They suggest government should be as small as is *practical* — meaning, it is true, a lot smaller than those enamored of government benevolence and hostile to markets would desire. They are not a philosophical rationale for "small government" or "low taxes" in any absolute sense.

And what of the "Laffer Curve"? It is frequently invoked by 'conservatives' as a justification for cutting taxes and frequently derided by 'liberals' as a mendacious bit of voodoo. How does it fit into Capitalist theory? Nearly invisibly.

The Laffer Curve itself (popularized but not invented by the economist Arthur Laffer) undoubtedly describes a real effect. It can be derived mathematically from basic economic principles, but originates in a commonsense observation: at some point, revenue obtained from taxes on economic activity will no longer rise — and will actually fall — as the tax rate is increased. That may seem counter-intuitive but consider the two extremes.

At a tax rate of zero, tax revenue will be zero and, as the rate rises above zero, revenue will clearly increase. That is, at very low tax rates, increasing the tax rate will increase the amount of tax revenue collected. That is obvious. It's just math.

On the other hand, at a tax rate of 100%, tax revenue will also be zero, or very close to it, *because most people will no longer produce anything on which to collect a tax* — why bother to produce anything if it will only be taken away from you; why bother to work if you don't get to keep any of your pay? That is psychology, not math, but it's no less true. As tax rates are lowered from 100%, and people begin to be able to keep some of what they produce, they start working and producing again and tax revenues rise. In other words, at very high tax rates, *decreasing* the tax rate will increase the tax revenue collected.

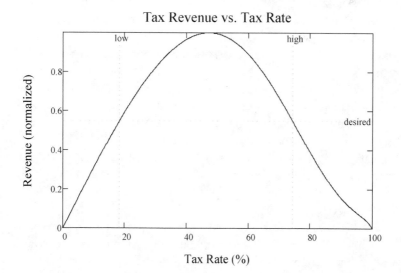

The result is the "Laffer Curve" (the figure shows one of many possible examples[1]): an inverted 'U' with tax revenues low at both very high and very low tax rates (right and left ends of the curve) and with tax revenues maximized at some point in between. The shape implies that to collect any desired amount of tax revenue there are two possible tax rates that could be imposed, one on the upward-sloping ("low") side of the curve and one on the downward sloping ("high") side of the curve.

The only way high and low tax rates can generate the same amount of revenue is if the amount of economic activity being taxed is smaller at the high tax rate than it is at the lower tax rate — that is, the shape of the curve suggests that a government operating on the high-tax end of the curve must be stifling economic activity. It must be making society overall poorer than it otherwise could be. That shouldn't be a surprise, because it is a re-statement of the original premise: if you take away too much of what people produce they won't bother to produce it any more.

Quite aside, then, from the personal financial discomfort associated with paying taxes, all good Capitalists would prefer to operate on the upward slope, at the lowest possible tax rate for a given level of revenue, because it has the least deleterious effect on productivity.

It seems natural that anyone, Capitalist or not, would want that since it implies greater wealth for society as a whole. But 'conservatives' harbor a suspicion that the progressive aspect of the higher tax rate — the fact that it equalizes incomes by taking more money away from "rich" people (presumably to be given in some fashion to "poor" people) than would a lower tax rate — appeals to the redistributionist yearnings of some 'liberals.' And 'conservatives' also harbor a suspicion that the punitive aspect of the higher tax rate — the fact that it takes away more money from rich people who didn't "deserve" in the first place — appeals to the egalitarian yearnings of some 'liberals.'

The real policy question, though, is, "Which side of the curve are we actually on?" The empirical evidence to date is spotty but suggests that, in general, we are on the upward-sloping side of the curve — that invoking the Laffer Curve to justify decreasing tax rates is not justified at current rates — but that we may not have been so at times in the past when tax rates were much higher.

Further, the Laffer Curve applies to individuals as much as to the economy as a whole. Where a particular person falls on the curve depends on his or her individual circumstance — on the marginal tax rate applied to his/her income and on his/her perception of the incremental benefits and costs of

---

1 This is a "real" example, derived mathematically from linear supply and demand curves for a single item, and some assumptions about fixed and variable costs for production.

working harder to increase that income. It is quite possible for a graduated income tax structure like ours to place those in the lowest and highest tax brackets on different sides of the Laffer Curve.

Finally, it is generally accepted that decreasing tax rates would result in some increase in economic output — that it would "stimulate the economy" by some amount — even if that increase would not be sufficient to increase overall tax revenue. Hence, there is an argument to be made, independent of the Laffer Curve, that tax rates should be cut to stimulate a lethargic economy. In fairness, there is also an argument to be made — Capitalists would say a misguided one — that a tax *increase* which, on its face, depressed the economy but which increased government revenue could also serve to stimulate the economy, provided the increased government revenue was inserted back into the economy through judicious government spending. Capitalists would argue that the assumption such spending would be judicious is the root of the problem with this line of reasoning, that government spending will never be judicious enough to compensate for the deleterious effect of extracting productive capital from the economy in the first place. We will probably still be debating the question of which — if either — would be a more effective economic stimulus a millennium from now.

But, all that said, the argument over the Laffer Curve and other tax vs. stimulation policies, as with arguments over Supply Side economics, is an argument about *how* the government should manage its interference in the economy. Such arguments are based on the details and assumptions of mathematical economic models, and more fundamentally on a primary presumption that the government *should* interfere. They are not supported by any theory of Capitalism or any ideal of Laissez Faire.

...Social Darwinism?

Isn't Capitalism all about "sink or swim"? Isn't Capitalism opposed in principle to any form of social safety net? No.

Theories of Capitalism are silent on the question of whether or not there should be a social safety net — they presume that is a question for individuals to answer and that their answers will be reflected in the way they value the various uses of resources. If individuals value a social safety net then they will value uses of resources that promote a social safety net — employment opportunities, insurance, mutual-aid societies, charities, and so on — above those that do not and that valuation will be reflected in the market. No Capitalist would second-guess those preferences on the basis of economic theory.

Nor does Capitalism, per se, necessarily oppose a degree of government involvement in providing a social safety net, although it offers strong opinions on the likely costs and effectiveness of such involvement in its variety of possible forms. The American *Declaration of Independence* declares that the purpose of government is to secure the inalienable rights of man; the American Constitution elaborates on that purpose with specific responsibilities: to "...establish justice, ensure domestic tranquility, provide for the common defense, promote the general welfare, and secure the blessings of liberty..."; and we have already described the practical role government must play in regularizing the conditions in which a free market can flourish and in enforcing market-related responsibilities on those who would evade them. If fulfilling those functions arguably requires some amount of protection for those unable to protect themselves, some amount of support for social and institutional stability, and some amount of intervention when cultural or political forces threaten to exclude classes of people from the opportunities the free market provides, then Capitalists should support that effort as citizens of a democratic nation.

The extent to which government should involve itself in providing a social safety net is both an economic question and political one. By definition such government support entails a coercive reallocation of resources from personal to public use — if coercion were not required then neither would be government. The same philosophical support for individual liberty and property rights that motivates Capitalist economic theories suggests that, for purely non-economic reasons, such coercion should be minimized. Further, economic theories of the free market predict that the redirection of resources from market transactions into political transactions — the allocation of resources according to some autocratic or collective desire rather than according to individual desire, and by force of law rather than by mutual negotiation and agreement — will reduce the aggregate wealth that the economic system can create. Hence, such theories predict that any attempt by government to coerce society into being economically more uniform will also make society overall economically poorer.

However, *there are no postulates in any economic theory to tell us whether or not that is a good tradeoff.* It is a moral question, not an economic one. But — in light of that tradeoff — as a foundation for economic security Capitalists generally favor market-based mechanisms over public programs supported by taxation and implemented through collective decision-making or autocratic decree.

Those market-based mechanisms include a dynamic marketplace with high capital mobility to encourage economic activity and entrepreneurship; high rates of individual savings coupled to investment diversification to provide a buffer against hard times; mutual-aid pacts (including both family ties and more formal and public arrangements) and insurance policies to protect against chance catastrophes; and charities to catch those in a free-fall to the bottom — all of which involve individuals taking some responsibility for their own protection, individuals taking some responsibility for the protection of others, and individuals choosing individually the mechanisms that best serve their individual and communal needs.

To the extent that political society believes government action is required to encourage economic security, Capitalists would argue that government should point its legal and regulatory mechanisms primarily toward aligning individual incentives with the use of those market-oriented supports.

If the political judgment of society is that government should, as well, provide some amount of direct support for economic security, then Capitalism, as a theory of economics not of politics and not of social responsibility, can predict the degree to which society will be impoverished by that effort but, again, does not provide a philosophical basis for rejecting it. However, theories of Capitalism do suggest that methods of providing such support which involve government interference in market operation will generally result in lower economic output and higher economic volatility than simply extracting and redirecting resources in general from the economy through broad-based taxation. Examples abound: taxes on specific types of market transactions rather than on economic activity in general; subsidies for certain industries or companies; demands for specific transaction terms like wage rates or commodity prices; rules that favor one side over another in economic negotiations; policies that create a disconnect between work and recompense, or between risk and reward, or that artificially discourage or encourage market participation; socialization of entrepreneurial risks; artificial externalities that push private costs from the market onto the commons. If government must extract resources to provide for a social safety net, Capitalists would favor market-neutral broad-based taxation and public insurance programs to a hodgepodge of market distortions aimed at "fixing" some array of perceived market inequities.

Such direct taxation and redistribution of resources also offers the advantage that it is clear and honest about the costs it imposes: often the indirect market-distorting mechanisms for "protecting the less fortunate" find favor as much because they are nearly impossible to account — and therefore nearly impossible to oppose on a cost/benefit basis — as because they are particularly effective.

...Non-Material Values? Non-Monetizable Resources?

How can a market value the aesthetic value of a wilderness or of art, or the moral value of generosity and stewardship, or the spiritual value of quiet and solitude, or the holistic value of biodiversity? The answer is that *people* value those things and people create the market.

Even if the things themselves seem to be non-material, people are very good at making judgments about how much of some economic resource they are willing to trade for them and those judgments set a monetary valuation. Can the market value a wilderness? Ducks Unlimited and The Nature Conservancy and other such groups purchase tracts of wilderness either in their entirety or in the form of conservation easements — essentially packets of development rights — in order to conserve them in a wild state. The market has no problem defining a price for those tracts based on the competing values that the property owners and potential developers and the conservationists place on them. When the conservationists place a higher value on them than the owners and developers, then they are conserved. And where do the conservationists get the money to pay for conservation? People who value conserving the wilderness over some other use of their money choose, within a market of competing uses, to contribute to the cause.

Can the market value generosity? It happens all the time. People with money to spend have a choice between buying things to make their lives easier or happier and donating that money to charity to help others who are less fortunate. And every year an enormous amount of that money is donated to charity because those people value charity more highly than what they would have bought otherwise with that money. Similarly, every year various businesses donate some amount of money to charity either because their officers and shareholders feel some responsibility to society or because they believe the goodwill such donations elicit will attract customers to their products. Why? Because they believe their customers value charity enough to be willing to pay extra — either directly in price or indirectly in brand loyalty — to support it through their purchases in the marketplace.

Can the market value quiet and solitude? People who greatly desire quiet and solitude will allocate more of their wealth than others who do not value them to buying larger pieces of property or homes in quieter neighborhoods, or to vacationing in the woods rather than in the city, or to frequenting a library or a park rather than a concert, or to eating out in a traditional and quiet restaurant rather than in a chic and noisy one. And others will cater to those tastes by providing superior access to quiet and solitude at a price which equals the value placed upon them.

The market is actually very good at valuing things, even "non-material" things, provided that those things are clearly defined entities that can be traded and that the rights to them are clearly delineated and transferable. Perceived failures of the market to value "non-material" resources "correctly" or "sufficiently" almost always either result from the resources being untradeable (because ownership of them is either ambiguous or held in-common — see the discussion of "the commons") or reflect a market valuation that falls below someone's (meaning someone who has no intention of paying for it) ephemeral notion of what it "ought" to be.

Certainly there are mechanisms, well-described by market economic theories, which can distort market pricing and therefore cause a mis-valuation of resources. Such mechanisms typically involve some sort of coercion, some sort of externality, or a vague and/or defective conception of property rights to the resource. The latter problem is particularly acute when considering property rights to recently-considered and novel holistic characteristics of otherwise tangible property, like "biodiversity" — characteristics that apply to and depend upon, for example, an ecosystem operating as an integrated whole and which cannot, therefore, be infinitely subdivided and consumed or conserved in discrete parcels. Such characteristics — and property rights to them — have never before been codified and assigned in any systematic fashion. Perhaps they can't be. We don't know, because we haven't tried. Hence, such resources have never been valued by a market and cannot be valued unless and until they become tradable in and of themselves, rather than merely as the unintended byproduct of trading in some other aspect of the wilderness to which they are attached.

And certainly disparities of wealth can distort the valuation placed on scarce resources that are prized highly. Two people may value a piece of art or a rare gem or a pristine wilderness equally, but only the one with a bank account to back the valuation will actually have an opportunity to purchase it and, so, his or her valuation will be the only one the market recognizes.

It is relatively easy and inconsequential to inflate your valuation of something you cannot pay for. It is just as easy to claim you would be willing to pay a million dollars as a thousand dollars for a painting or a plot of wilderness if you cannot pay more than a hundred and know, therefore, you will never have to pay anything. For that reason, such valuations are suspect on their face, more statements of aspiration than real economic judgments.

Nonetheless, the valuation of a scarce item is always limited by the resources potential purchasers bring to the table; and, therefore, the opinions of those with money to spend count more than the opinions of those without in valuing such items. That means scarce resources are inevitably distributed unequally and, perhaps, unfairly. Fairness and equity are non-material values that the market has not accounted for.

That argument is often used as the subtext to justify supplanting the market pricing mechanism with some more "democratic" one — typically some coercive mechanism of government asserting authority to act "in the public interest" — in allocating resources like wilderness areas or radio spectrum bandwidth. The rejoinder is to note that such "democratic" allocations depend for their justification on the fact that they represent the will of the "majority." But, if that is so, then government coercion should not be necessary because the "majority" can choose to bring a great deal of resources to bear in the marketplace: a barest majority of the 300 million people in the United States, each contributing a mere $10, could collectively bring $1.5 billion dollars to a market transaction — more than most individuals and even most corporations could muster.

That is, of course, often used as a *justification* for such government expenditures: it's *only* $10 per citizen; surely it's worth that for such a huge "good." But if the citizens really want it, if they were sufficiently motivated and organized — as opposed to merely acceding to it because someone in power proposed it — they could make it happen even without the participation of government. Isn't that what the Sierra Club and the ACLU and the United Way and the Red Cross and Goodwill Industries and hundreds of other such organizations do? The interest of "the public" is not excluded from consideration in the market unless "the public" is so apathetic as to be unwilling to put up even a modicum of money or effort to defend that interest. Where purchasing power exists, regulation is superfluous.

Further, and critically, the pricing of a scarce resource in the market is not an intellectual exercise designed to satisfy some moral criterion. It is the mechanism by which scarce resources are rationed — a high price serves to suppress demand to the point that it matches the supply available.

If some political mechanism was employed to depress the price artificially, the resource would still need to be rationed, and more so than before because a lower price would both increase the number of consumers who want to buy it and reduce the incentive for producers to create more of it. However, without the mechanism of price to manage that rationing, some other means — a lottery, or a social competition to prove greater "need" or "merit," or a political competition to assert greater power, or corruption and graft, or a black market, or perhaps merely the chaos of a mob — would supplant it, if not by intention then by default. It is not obvious that any of those other mechanisms would necessarily and consistently generate a "better" outcome, by whatever criterion you might choose to measure it, than the market would.

We can always envision some extraordinary circumstance in which the result created by a market would seem to defy common sense or violate our notions of fairness or decency. Imagine, for instance, that a fierce hurricane in the Caribbean surprises forecasters by making a sudden and swift turn toward Florida, endangering the entire coastline from Miami to Jacksonville. The people along the Florida coast suddenly begin demanding great quantities of plywood to board up windows and doors on their homes as protection against the winds and rain. But, due to the suddenness of the danger, there is no time to import plywood from other places and the demand will probably outstrip the supply available.

In a free market, the price of plywood will rise, effectively rationing the limited supply to those most willing to pay for it. Following a rational economic model, those with the most to lose — that is, those with the most expensive houses or with houses in the most exposed areas — will be willing to pay more than those at a lesser risk and the market will, therefore, allocate the limited supply to those people.

We note, with a great deal of sympathy, that this puts poor people at a disadvantage with respect to rich people: rich people can more easily afford to pay the higher prices. But the real problem is the *storm*, not the *market*.

Both the poor and the rich are going to lose something to the storm's fury, and those losses will weigh more heavily on the poor than on the rich because the losses will represent a larger fraction of their personal wealth. That is unfair.

But the unfairness has nothing to do with the market for plywood. The pricing of plywood neither generates nor exacerbates the loss; it merely mediates the form the loss will take: cash out the door now or storm damage later.

If a poor person must spend $500 now to prevent $1000 in damage later, that is still a bargain for him. The $500 may be a painful amount to spend — there is no dispute about that — but it is the least painful alternative *given the reality, completely unrelated to the market, that the storm is coming*. The market is not causing his loss. It is ranking the magnitude of his loss against all the other losses that are just as inevitable as his.

We might still object to that result on the grounds that the poorest people would be the most likely to lose their property while the wealthiest people, able to protect their property, would lose only the money they spent on plywood. We might judge that disparity to be unfair from the perspective of social equity or justice. We might assert that allowing everyone a bit of protection would be better than having some well-protected and others unprotected; or we might assert that deciding who was protected and who was not should be left to chance so that no one could be said to have taken any advantage from another.

But, from a material standpoint, the market outcome would be both reasonable and optimal: by preferentially protecting the most valuable and the most at risk properties it would minimize the overall material loss. And, as a consequence, when the storm was over and the time came to rebuild, the rebuilding effort could be both more rapid and less costly than it might have been otherwise. Society overall would be, arguably, better off than had the distribution of plywood been "fairer" according to some non-material criterion. We might legitimately ask ourselves, then, whether such "fairness" is really to be desired.

Now imagine that Bill Gates owns a greenhouse full of exotic plants somewhere along the Florida coastline which is also threatened by the storm. Following a rational economic model, Mr. Gates would be willing to spend some amount of money, perhaps up to the full value of the building and plants, on plywood to protect his investment. If, in the scarcity-driven market, enough plywood to wrap up the greenhouse costs less than that amount he will buy it; otherwise he will not because protecting his investment will cost more than replacing it. He will be a market participant like any others and his economic needs — his inevitable losses — will factor into the market in the same way as theirs will, admittedly with less angst on his part about paying the inflated price.

But what if Mr. Gates has a strong — and "irrational" — emotional attachment to the plants in his greenhouse? What if he has hand-raised them himself from seeds or finds them particularly beautiful or fragrant? What if he attaches an extreme emotional — that is, "non-material" — value to their survival?

In that case, and because the value of the greenhouse is such a small fraction of the resources available to him, the amount he would be willing to pay for the plywood to protect his plants might be higher than the "rational" economic value of the greenhouse. It could, in fact, be much higher. He is, after all, Bill Gates. He has billions of dollars at his disposal. He can bid the price of plywood up high enough to guarantee he gets what he needs. He can, in short, subvert the economic efficiency of the market, using his great wealth to protect himself by placing at risk a "value" of others' property much higher than the "value" of his own.[1]

Those who are concerned with a presumed inability of the market to value non-material goods should take heart, for in this hypothetical instance that is exactly what it did. Mr. Gates placed the non-material value of his love for the plants into the market and it came up with a price.

Most people, however, would consider this to be a market failure. If Bill Gates has used more plywood than he needed to mitigate his economic losses, then he has left less plywood available to mitigate everyone else's. By any but the most idiosyncratic of criteria, the economic loss created by the

---

1 I don't mean to imply Bill Gates *would* do that; his public record of philanthropy makes me fairly sure he would not. He just happens to be one of modern America's most recognizable icons of extreme wealth and, therefore, the obvious choice as a symbol of affluence for my parable.

storm would have ended up greater than it might otherwise have been and would have been more unfairly distributed.

Is this, then, a reason to mistrust the market? Only if you believe that kind of scenario is common or likely. But it is neither. Such scenarios are built upon acute and idiosyncratic "irrationality" by someone with a particularly large reserve of available resources operating in an environment of extreme scarcity and on an emergency timeline. They are, as we said when we introduced our example, *extra*ordinary and, therefore, not a reasonable basis for rejecting the market as a valuation mechanism under ordinary circumstances.

Finally, if we are concerned that a market is unable properly to assess non-material values and non-monetizable resources and should, therefore, not be allowed to do so, we must ask what alternative mechanism should be used in its place. By what means are we to determine the value of resources and how they should be allocated among competing uses if not by allowing users to bid for them? Do we really believe that a democratic vote can make that determination more accurately? Can democracy adjudge depth of preference in the way a market can? Does the fact that a majority can be convinced to vote for something — and especially for something that evokes their self-interest without imposing an obvious cost because the cost has been politically impressed upon some minority — make their choice necessarily wise or correct? Should we leave it, instead, in the hands of "experts"? Which ones? How are they chosen? What is their expertise? And, even presuming (a huge presumption) they are both wise and beneficent, can they possibly gather and analyze enough information about all the various resources that make up our economy and all the various uses to which they can be put to make timely and consistently valid judgments?

Even if you believe that the market is untrustworthy in this regard it may merely mean that, as Winston Churchill said about Democracy,[1] the free market is the worst form of economic system — except for all the others that have been tried from time to time.

And, finally, what of...

...Accountability?

Many who favor government over the market as the arbiter and enforcer of some abstract sense of the "public good" do so out of a conviction that a democratic government is accountable to its citizens in a way that a market cannot be.

---

1 Speech to the House of Commons, 11 November 1947. Recorded in *The Official Report, The House Of Commons* (5th *Series*), 11 November 1947, vol. 444

The market is, after all, run by immense and impersonal corporate titans controlled by robber barons, with exploitation as their means, greed as their motive, and our own implacable human needs and desires as their opportunity. They are self-selected and self-interested. They operate beyond our control and with no care for our wishes or for our well-being, dictating the terms of our commerce with them.

Whereas, democratic government is run by people dedicated to public service and selected by us to represent our interests. It is run by people whose goal is the general welfare and whose incentive is to please us, that we may select them again in the future. Democratic government is accountable because we choose it, and if it does not reflect our desires we can choose differently. Democratic government is accountable because it is government "of the people, by the people, and for the people."

But, in a fundamental sense, those views of government and of the market are not only distorted but exactly backward.

A free market is not run by faceless corporate titans because it is not run by anyone. Or, more accurately, it is run by everyone. It is run by us. No one in a free market forces us to buy or sell any particular thing or at any particular price, and even less does anyone force us to buy from a particular merchant or sell to a particular customer. Every choice, to buy or to sell or to do neither, is a vote for or against a particular product, for or against a particular price, and for or against a particular buyer or seller.

Those votes, aggregated across all of us and all of our purchases, create the market and set the terms of market transactions. And buyers and sellers alike, far from being aloof from our desires and demands, adjust to accommodate those desires and demands, as expressed by the goods we choose to exchange or hold and the prices we choose to accept or reject.

We may object that the price is "too high" for something we feel we need, or that the wages are "too low" for some labor we can provide. The market cannot (nor can government) transcend ultimate limitations on what resources are available or on the utility to be gained from them.

But if we agree to buy at that price or to work for those wages it is because we have decided it will make us better off than if we hadn't — perhaps not as well off as we might want, but better off than we were before. And, should we decide we would not be better off, we will not agree to the transaction and those selling us goods or buying our labor will lose their opportunity to become better off, in turn, by dealing with us.

Others may or may not offer us better terms; and others may or may not make the same choices we do. We buy from the vendors who fulfill our needs and desires and spurn those vendors who don't, largely independently of the choices that others make. If enough people are left unfulfilled then entrepreneurs will create new companies and new products to meet their needs. And if enough people don't like a company's prices, or its products, or its practices, or its philosophy they will choose not to buy what it has to sell or to sell what it wants to buy, and it will either change those prices or products or practices or philosophy or it will go out of business. Accommodate your customers and your vendors or die. That is accountability stripped to its core.

The market is the ultimate democracy, a democracy in which you get to vote ten or a hundred or a thousand times a day and in which your vote has both immediate personal consequences and indirect collective ones. It is a democracy in which you get to vote individually on every preference and in which your vote can count in proportion to the vehemence of that preference, as measured by how much you are willing to spend on it. It is a democracy that can accommodate the individual along with the communal, in which the will of the majority defines the norm without proscribing the extreme, and in which a willing buyer and a willing seller determine the bounds of what is possible, regardless of what most people find reasonable or pleasing or advantageous.

The accountability provided by democratic government, on the other hand, is dilute under the best of circumstances and seems often unachievable in practice. It is true that, in the traditional New England town meeting, participants get to vote individually on every line-item in the local budget; and the famously clumsy and oft-abused ballot initiative process in California places a few major policy choices per year directly into the hands of voters. But those are the rare exceptions in American governance. In most cases, and in all questions of federal authority, you do not get to choose directly which goals or policies or practices you prefer of government. Instead, you get to proffer a preference as to who should represent your interests — intermingled with the competing and possibly contradictory interests of a great many other people — when those choices are to be made.

If your preference for representation happens to coincide with the preferences of the majority of your fellow citizens, then it is honored. If not, then it is discounted. In that case you may hope that, even if your representative does not speak up for your minority preference, a roughly proportional minority of others' representatives will. But there is no guarantee that will happen. Under the most common and equitable of conditions it very well may not and, in practice, the electoral system is often twisted by the partisan application of political power to ensure it won't.

Further, in making your choice for representation you are likely to have different preferences on different issues. On some issues you may agree with one candidate, on some issues with another; on some issues you may agree with several candidates; on some you may agree with none.

But ultimately you must choose one candidate for a given office, with the full package of positions he or she espouses. And your choice must be made in the context of what others may choose: you may prefer a candidate who advocates for gay rights yet dislike his anti-Capitalist bias, but if you vote for one you get the other by default. If you find his stance on gay rights more important to you than his stance on economics, you still may not get your choice if most of your fellow citizens care little about either issue and a great deal about abortion, or universal health care, or something else.

And, when your preference has been noted and your representative makes choices on your behalf — or even if you got to make the choice yourself at town meeting — those choices will not be individualized but aggregated. You get what most people want, not necessarily what you want. That is the nature of government: it is a collective and acts collectively, with one policy for everyone and on behalf of everyone, one policy designed to accommodate some collective notion of the "common good" with negligible accommodation for the unusual or the idiosyncratic or the personal.

Further, the final form of that policy will be influenced as much by compromise and backroom dealing and special pleading required to cobble together a consensus, and by the unrelated individual imperative for the various representatives to be re-elected, as by what the mass of constituent citizens actually want or need.

And, finally, never forget that people in government are still people, that they can be as self-interested and self-serving as anyone in any private enterprise. The titular goal of democratic government may be "the public interest" but the practice of government is undertaken by people no less driven by personal ambition (and often more driven by an attraction to power if not to money) than their non-government counterparts.

In light of this contrast between the market and the government, it is worth asking: what do we mean by "accountability"? And in what fashion do either market or government provide it?

At root, being "accountable" means taking responsibility for the consequences of your actions and, in particular (since few would bother to avoid responsibility for positives), for any negative consequences. And, because it is human nature to evade such responsibility when possible, "accountability" implies some means for inducing people to take responsibility when they would rather not — that is, to "hold them accountable." Accountability is justice, in the 'conservative' sense of the word. It means suffering the consequences of behaving badly in proportion to how bad the behavior was; and it means using the potential for those consequences to discourage bad behavior in the future.

But accountability is actually somewhat less than that definition would imply, for not all "bad" behavior requires an accounting. We are, specifically, accountable *for* — and only for — the ways in which our behavior harms others and are, therefore, accountable *to* — and only to — those we have harmed.

We may hold people or companies in a free market accountable for what we consider bad behavior by refusing to buy from them or sell to them — by starving them of revenue and/or of opportunities for revenue. Since anyone's — even individual workers' and consumers' — purpose in the market is to profit, reducing or eliminating profit by refusing to deal with them is a punishment; and in the extreme, if enough people choose to hold them to account, it can drive them into bankruptcy — the market equivalent of a death sentence. That is "market discipline."

However, a "free market" is "free" only if it is free of coercion — either by force or by deception — and must honor society's broader ethical frameworks. Market discipline can only work if the market is actually functioning according to its own rules and constraints, if it is "free" in practice and not merely in rhetoric. Hence, government is the enforcer of choice for disciplining thieves and thugs, those who will not honor such constraints or commitments either within the market or without it. That is, in fact, among the primary reasons for government to exist: as America's founding document and statement of moral purpose declares, "...to secure these rights, Governments are instituted among Men...."[1]

Similarly, within reasonable bounds, government regulation aimed at regularizing market operations and guarding against the exploitation of externalities is appropriate and sometimes necessary. If we collectively pay the cost of industrial pollution in the commons then companies which profit by polluting the commons are doing so at our expense and, arguably, without our assent; if we choose, through our government, to recover the costs they have imposed (or to prevent the imposition in the first place) then we are merely asserting our right to participate in that transaction, restoring a coercive market to some imperfect semblance of a "free" one.

And the tort system, with proceedings mediated by government and with verdicts assigned the force of law, is the forum of last resort for adjudging responsibility for damage done through negligence or malfeasance — including through breach of contract — and for eliciting compensation. One may decry the erosion and distortion of standards for culpability and

---

1 From the American Declaration of Independence.

the growing laxity of process within the tort system without denying its fundamental and valid role in securing accountability in dealings between and among citizens.

In short, if a market is truly free, then its participants are accountable, in a direct and substantial way, to other market participants. But government is, and generally must be, the agent of accountability for offenses against freedom itself — including offenses against market freedom — and for offenses against the legal code. No one defending market theory could or should posit otherwise.

In addition, it is worth noting here that all of the examples discussed above have social as well as individual aspects. Offenses against market freedom harm those who lose their money but they also undermine the general trust that allows a market to operate. Indirectly, they harm the market itself and all those who utilize it. A robbery or a mugging or a murder harms the victim but it also undermines the social compact that allows people to live their lives free of fear, that allows them to accept and trust strangers — "the others" — in their midst. Hence, it is not only the immediate victim but society overall which demands an accounting for such misconduct. Government is the designated political authority for protecting liberty and justice but it is also the designated social authority for "ensuring domestic tranquility," for protecting the social fabric from injury by anti-social predators.

There is no honest Capitalist who would dispute any of that. If individuals or corporations cheat people or intentionally harm people the government may and should hold them to account for that under the law. If they cause harm through negligence or recklessness the government may and should hold them to account for that through civil actions and enforcement of torts. For lesser offenses, customers and suppliers extract accountability financially through an unwillingness to deal with the miscreants. Where, then, is the controversy? In what ways is that approach to accountability insufficient?

When someone claims the market is not "accountable" he or she will often add, either explicitly or by implication, the ancillary phrase, "to the will of The People" or, merely, "to The People." That is, the complaint is not necessarily that the market (or some ill-favored market participant) has behaved immorally or maliciously, let alone illegally. Rather, their complaint is that the market has not done what "The People" wanted it to do; or, more broadly, has behaved in a fashion that serves its own interest rather than serving the "public interest."

Even assuming such critics have accurately interpreted what "The People" want or accurately determined what is or is not in the public interest, they confuse being *accountable* with being *responsive* or *benevolent*; and they presume that the market ought to be democratic in the same sense that our government is democratic, ruled by the principle of one-man-one-vote and with all votes having equal weight.

But that is not what a market is or does. The democracy of the market is weighted by *enthusiasm*, not by mere *attendance*, by the price you are willing to pay, not merely by your desire to buy; and its decisions are binding on "The Public" only to the extent that alternatives are uneconomical in spite of that enthusiasm — to the extent that "The Public" wants something it is not willing to pay for.

In such cases, then, what the accusation of being "unaccountable" often really means is that the accuser has been unable to persuade "The Public" to make choices in the market that he would prefer: had he been able to do so, had the public at large been persuaded to take affront, it would have expressed its displeasure by withholding its business and the offender would either repent or go bankrupt.

On occasions when that doesn't happen, despite a genuine public outrage, one will generally find that the market has failed to be accountable (or, rather, responsive) precisely to the extent that it has failed to be free. That is, market discipline will fail because someone has been, somehow, protected from its judgment.

In almost every case, such protection derives from government policy that has distorted the functioning of the market to subvert its normal feedback mechanisms, to enforce some advantage or disadvantage by political means, or to create opportunities for socializing costs while privatizing rewards. It may (or may not) be true that, in the passion of the moment of the latest financial crisis, the government had no choice but to bail out the banks to prevent a general panic and an economic crash. But it is also true that the government's past promises that it *would* bail them out if things went wrong, not explicit but implied by its history of prior dealings with faltering economic giants, probably skewed the bankers' assessments of the risk they were taking on; and the eventual fact of a government bailout insulated them from the flogging the market would otherwise have given to those whose judgment of risk was so outrageously unrealistic. We can't really complain that the market failed to provide accountability when the government intervened specifically to prevent it from doing so.

But, as illustrated by the banking crisis, many who decry a lack of accountability in the market do so because their definitions of "harm," of "punishment" — and, in particular, of culpability — differ from more conventional notions. We are accountable specifically for behavior that harms others, but what do we mean by "harm"? What repercussion is required in order to say someone has been "held to account"? How direct must the connection be between action and consequence before we may say that the one caused the other? How much foreknowledge is necessary in order to assign not only causality but responsibility for those consequences? And to what extent does the moral agency of those harmed affect that assignment?

The answers to those questions may seem obvious, and they *are* more or less obvious when there is clear malicious intent, demonstrable bad faith, and measurable economic cost. But such situations are not the ones in which accusations of a "lack of accountability" are typically asserted.

What was the "harm" in the recent banking crisis, and who were the victims? One might posit that shareholders of companies like Bear-Stearns and Lehman Brothers were certainly harmed by direct financial losses, as were various individuals and companies that bought mortgage-backed securities at what turned out to be inflated prices. Arguably, the country as a whole was harmed by the economic freeze that followed the great devaluation of the real-estate market as credit became scarce and people and businesses became suddenly anxious and, therefore, cautious, choosing to preserve their resources rather than either to enjoy or to cultivate them. Many individuals lost a great deal of equity in their homes — their mortgages went "underwater" — as housing prices collapsed. And many people lost their homes entirely as unemployment left them unable to pay those mortgages, "underwater" or not.

Of course, those demanding "accountability" don't generally mention shareholders and investors, and for good reason: their risks, though apparently little understood or appreciated, were nonetheless undertaken voluntarily, were under their control; they chose to invest because they saw an opportunity for an outsized return and their ignorance or recklessness about the risks that entailed was a consequence of their own action (or inaction), not of any kind of duplicity. There were probably some instances in which investors were misled or were, at least, left uninformed about the quality of the investments they were being asked to make. But in the vast majority of cases, these types of investments were sold to people and institutions that were in a position to assess that risk for themselves. Notwithstanding a few cases wending their way through the legal system in which highly sophisticated investors are claiming to have been otherwise, these were wild-eyed optimists, not dupes. And besides — and this, perhaps, is the primary reason for a lack of sympathy — these were *rich* people. They may have lost money but who could imagine that they actually *suffered*?

In other words, although these people clearly endured harm, there is general consensus that they were not "harmed" — that is, whatever misfortune they bore was not imposed upon them by the action of some other moral agent and was, in any case, tolerable. A self-inflicted wound is a wound, but the infliction of the wound was not an assault.

As for various mortgage-holders, who *have* been declared victims by the accountability police, what makes them fundamentally different from investors? Did someone force them to buy a house and take on the associated mortgage debt? Did someone give them a guarantee that house prices would never fall or that the economy would never stumble? Did their employers promise them lifetime tenure in their jobs?

It is unfortunate for them that things worked out badly, and we can (and, really, I do) sympathize with their plight. Under other circumstances and with somewhat poorer planning, it is possible I could have been among them. A recession hurts people. There is no doubt and no dispute about that.

But one can't have opportunity without risk. They thought they would win the game of real-estate roulette and so they played. They made their decisions to invest in their houses in the expectation, widely held within and without both economic and political circles, that things would just keep on getting better forever, or at least for as far into the future as the typically short time-horizon of the typically short-sighted American extends. In the end, that didn't happen — or, at least, that outcome has been indefinitely delayed.

But no one dragged them into a bank and forced them to take out a loan. No one dragged them into a real-estate office to start a search for the perfect house-as-nest-egg. If they were duped, they were duped by the talking heads on television who proclaimed the glorious ascent of the "new economy," and by their elected representatives (on both the right and the left) who declared that owning a house was some kind of natural right, and by the endless news reports about the soaring real-estate market, and by the artificially low interest rates maintained by Federal Reserve monetary policy. If they fell for come-ons by banks and mortgage companies urging them to get into the game, it was only because they'd already been primed by their cultural and political leaders to believe that the game was rigged in their favor. So although, again, we can acknowledge they suffered a harm we may legitimately dispute the question of whether or not they were "harmed" and by whom.

And it is ironic that the accountability police seem to reserve a special ire on behalf of those who were allowed to buy houses despite the fact that they clearly couldn't afford them, coaxed in with offers of zero down-payments and/or down-payments financed by secondary loans. It is said that banks were grossly irresponsible to have lent them the money and that is true, though arguably the irresponsibility was with respect to the well-being of their shareholders, not their customers. But the rules under which the mortgage market operated — rules created by the federal government specifically to *encourage* the extension of credit to those of marginal creditworthiness — created perverse incentives that rewarded such irresponsibility.

Leaving that aside, what of the mortgage holders, themselves? Perhaps some have "lost their homes," meaning they can no longer live in the houses they "purchased." But what have they actually lost? *Pretty much nothing*: having committed no resources as down-payments, *they had no significant equity to lose.* They had to move, but the same would have been true had they stopped paying their rent instead of their mortgages. Perhaps they have been spending somewhat more in a mortgage payment for a few years than they would have in rent, but they have also been living in their own house under better conditions than they might otherwise have done as tenants. By any reasonable accounting of economic gains and losses, *they have come out very nearly even.*

The point here is not that people have not suffered. They *have* suffered.

The point is that claims of a "lack of accountability" are based on a radical philosophical assumption — that because big banks were *involved*, and because they have lots of money (and power), they must be *culpable* — which goes beyond any traditional understanding of how moral responsibility is to be apportioned. It is an assumption based on a particularly condescending view of the broad American populace — that they are ignorant and incompetent; that, therefore, they must be taken care of and anything bad that happens to them must be someone else's fault; and that, therefore, America's elite, including in particular those who accumulate wealth, have some special and ineffable responsibility to protect them from themselves.

Or, more succinctly, it is an assumption that, if something bad happens to someone who is not rich, there must be some rich person who is responsible either for causing it *or for not preventing it* and who, therefore, must be "held accountable." Q.E.D.

In reality, what did those captains of finance do? Fundamentally, there were two faults here: some were reckless with their shareholders' money, committing to excessive leverage based on myopic assessments of the risks they were taking on; while others, more prudent in their risk assessments, facilitated and encouraged that leverage by taking the other side of those risky bets. That is, some of them were "negligent" for not recognizing their folly; while others were "malicious" for helping them indulge in that folly.

All of that created a bubble fueled in part by investor and homeowner greed, in part by federal housing policies that encouraged lax credit standards and subsidized risk in support of expanded home ownership, and in part by artificially and unjustifiably low borrowing costs underwritten by Fed monetary policy; and the ill effects of the (in hindsight) inevitable bursting of the bubble were immensely amplified by federal regulatory accounting rules that demanded losses be recognized and redressed immediately rather than after the panic had subsided, creating a momentary liquidity crisis that immobilized credit markets. There were probably pockets of actual malfeasance but they appear to have affected the overall market only at the margins.

It is undeniable that the entire country suffered harm as the consequences of that burst bubble, and especially of the credit freeze, spread throughout the economy. And it is undeniable that a great many of the people who suffered the most — who lost jobs or whose savings became suddenly much less valuable — had no part in creating the crisis. They were, truly, innocent victims.

But, were they "harmed"? That is, was there someone who "did it to them" in any direct and meaningful way? Was their misfortune the result of malice and negligence or was it more like the "perfect storm," a cascade of small factors that happened to align in a particular way and at a particular moment to create an effect that was both seemingly disproportionate and beyond any reasonable expectation of prediction and control?

In the traditional understanding of accountability, that question is the heart of the matter and, perhaps, we should investigate the causes of the crisis to determine the answer. Maybe someone did "do it to them"; or maybe not. To the new accountability police, however, that question appears to be irrelevant. "Someone suffered. Therefore, someone must pay." For them, that is both the beginning and the end of the discussion.

And, finally, what of that "payment"? If someone is to be held accountable, how are they to settle their account? In a gross sense, the market has already extracted its accountability on some of the players. Shareholders in various companies that were over-leveraged have lost some or all of their investments. Various executives of those companies have lost their jobs. Had the market been allowed to function without intervention by the government, more shareholders and executives would have been punished in the same way or to a greater extent. It is true that the ways in which financial executives are compensated favors short-term over long-term performance and, so, many of the people who engineered the crisis through their short-sighted risk assessments also walked away with some of their rewards intact, collected and secured during the run-up and, therefore, largely immune to the effects of the crash. That is an unfortunate quirk of corporate pay structures that we might hope future shareholders will insist on reforming. But, for the most part, companies and executives that were reckless have paid some price for that recklessness and those who were more prudent have weathered the storm.

Those who decry the "lack of accountability" are not satisfied, in part, because they hold those who were prudent — those who "knew" that mortgage-based securities were over-valued and yet participated in the trades anyway on the contrary side — to be as (or more) culpable as those who were blinded to the risk, culpable precisely because they "took advantage" of the blindness instead of trying to cure it. They, of course, assume in hindsight that such "knowledge" was certain, not an educated guess, and therefore came with a "responsibility to protect"; and they ignore the fact that, in a financial market, taking the contrary side of a trade is precisely the mechanism that communicates such "knowledge," precisely the way in which you tell the world that you think everyone else is blind and that it is you who can see.

But the major complaint about "accountability" coming from the financial crisis is not about *who* was punished, but *how*. It is not that the *wrong* people have been held accountable but that *no one* has, because "no one has gone to jail." Never mind any financial or professional consequences. Never mind whether or not anyone has actually broken the law. Bad outcomes should be illegal as a matter of course, so if something bad happens then someone must have committed a crime. And a crime requires prosecution.

In a way, that is the crux of the objection by people who claim that the market is not accountable. It is not that the market can't punish people; it is that the market's punishments are not public spectacles imposed under some rubric of collective social condemnation. In this view, it is not enough for someone to receive punishment; they must be "punished." Accountability requires active participation by the aggrieved. It requires attention. It requires acknowledgement. It requires some sort of satisfaction. It requires shame.

If that is your criterion for what is required by accountability then we will have to admit: the market cannot provide it. But then, if that is your criterion for what is required by accountability you should stop calling it "accountability" and refer to it by its proper name: "retribution."

Social Responsibility

The question of civic and moral responsibility for "social justice" is often considered a primary issue which divides 'liberals' and 'conservatives' in modern America. The popular presumption is that 'liberals' embrace that responsibility with an egalitarian idealism, while 'conservatives' reject it in favor of a natural hierarchy of privilege; and that, as a consequence, 'liberals' advocate governmental structures and policies which direct public resources toward fulfilling that responsibility, while 'conservatives' oppose such projects.

That view has become so common it is almost a political definition in campaign reporting: 'liberals' are compassionate and 'conservatives' are callous; 'liberals' represent "the People" while 'conservatives' represent "the Rich" (who, it would appear, are not people). When, as the Republican presidential candidate, George W. Bush asserted a vision of "compassionate conservatism," it was considered by reporters and the 'liberal' political establishment not as a credible policy approach, worthy of critical examination, but as a self-evident oxymoron. That a 'conservative' might be compassionate was an idea simply too incredible to conceive as anything other than a campaign ploy. Their skepticism was reflexive, not analytic, based on preconception and not on an honest examination of evidence or of possibilities.

In hindsight, it was also not fair. The Bush years saw no significant attempts to dismantle support systems for the poor and saw several significant initiatives to expand it, including the Medicare prescription drug benefit, an expansion of federal funding for local medical clinics, a commitment to AIDS treatment and economic development in Africa, a sincere but abortive, and perhaps ill-considered, attempt to put Social Security on a firmer financial footing for the future, and an honest, if not completely successful, effort to improve the educational opportunities for children in America's worst schools.

But President Bush was given very little credit for any of that, and the most recent debates in Congress over the federal budget reinforce the stereotype of the conservative Grinch stealing Christmas from the poor.

Are 'conservatives' really — and necessarily — opposed to "social justice" or even a social safety net? Must 'conservatism' mean "every man for himself," without regard to the vagaries of fortune and fate and without regard to empathy or compassion?

To be fair, the perception of 'conservatism' as inherently hostile to "social justice" lies partly in a disagreement between 'liberals' and 'conservatives' over what "justice" means. 'Conservatives' don't typically believe that inequality in circumstance is inherently unjust because fairness encompasses a moral element: it depends on what one has earned (or will earn) by his/her behavior and not merely on what one has in hand at the moment. They are not troubled in principle by evidence that some have more property or more power or more moral esteem than others, because they presume that some have done more than others — materially or socially or morally — to have warranted them. They trust that people who currently have less than they want can do better through personal effort, through a commitment to do more in the future — materially, socially, and morally — to earn what they desire.

Hence, 'conservatives' are more likely, for example, to view "poverty" as a condition of extreme privation rather than merely of comparative economic deficit, to believe that being "poorer" than someone else does not automatically make you "poor." They are more likely to view persistent and widespread poverty — at least in wealthy and entrepreneurial America — as predominantly the *result* of antisocial or imprudent behavior rather than the *cause*. As a result, they are more likely to assume that poverty must be addressed by demanding better behavior and personal responsibility as much as by disbursing money. And, as a result, they are more likely to assume that a comparative economic deficit represents a problem of skill, or opportunity, or ambition, or conduct, and not merely a problem of distribution.

From a 'liberal' viewpoint, this may be the very definition of "callousness," of "blaming the victim" and of "indifference to those in need." And, if so, the 'liberal' view of 'conservatives' as "callous" may be at least partially accurate — and largely a matter of conceit. It may be that 'liberals' simply can't recognize a 'conservative' enthusiasm for "social justice" when they see it because the 'liberal' and 'conservative' conceptions of what "social justice" means and requires of us are so different.

So let us stipulate: a society in which everyone is wealthy is to be desired; and lacking that, a society in which no one is poor would be a lesser, but satisfactory, substitute. Pretty much any 'conservative' would agree with that wholeheartedly. The questions are: "Is it possible? If so, how do we best get there — or at least get closer to it? And how much are we willing to sacrifice to that cause?"

We say 'conservatives' would agree with that wholeheartedly, but they sometimes suspect 'liberals' would not, or at least not with the lesser substitute. It seems that, to many 'liberals,' disparity looms larger than poverty in the pantheon of evils and that they would therefore prefer a society that is poor but equal to one that is wealthy but unequal. In other words, a great many 'conservatives' perceive that the 'liberal' answer to the question of how much we are willing to sacrifice is "a great deal" — that 'liberals,' on the whole, would willingly and perhaps enthusiastically sacrifice both prosperity and liberty on the altar of egalitarianism.

That perception is reinforced by the populist rhetoric that accompanies so much 'liberal' scolding on "social justice," rhetoric that seems to be as much or more concerned with tearing down "the rich" and "the powerful" as it is with lifting up the poor and the dispossessed. Finley Peter Dunne, writing as his alter-ego Mr. Dooley, asserted that the newspaper (among other things the press does) "comforts th' afflicted, afflicts th' comfortable..."[1] His original intent was both satirical and a warning against placing too much trust in the pronouncements of reporters, editors, and others who presumed to tell you what to think, so it is ironic that this statement of effect seems to have been adopted as a guiding principle by many modern journalists and much of the modern 'liberal' political class. It is as if they believe "comforting the afflicted" and "afflicting the comfortable" are endeavors of equal moral merit and equally to be desired; as if they believe a state of comfort is, in and of itself, some kind of moral affront.

As a result, there often *is* a reflexive quality in 'conservative' opposition to 'liberal' proposals for alleviating poverty and inequality. But that reflex is a response much more to the quixotic, self-righteous, demagogic, anti-capitalist, communitarian, and authoritarian undercurrents in those proposals, and in the language used to promote them, than it is to the humanitarian purposes they are intended to fulfill.

The suspicion that 'liberals' are more concerned with equalizing well-being than with expanding it is reinforced by a purely pragmatic observation about the government's social safety net. In one chapter of his book, *Parliament of Whores*, P.J. O'Rourke "proved" that poverty doesn't exist in America[2] by comparing the amount of money government had spent on the "War on Poverty" — on various poverty relief programs at the Federal level — and the "income deficit" of those in poverty — the difference between their actual incomes and the incomes they would need in order to live above the poverty line. Since, by his accounting, we had spent vastly more on anti-poverty programs than what would have been necessary to make up that income deficit he concluded — satirically! –we must have solved the poverty problem.

---

1 "Th' newspaper does ivrything fr us. It runs th' polis foorce an' th' banks, commands th' milishy, controls th' ligislachure, baptizes th' young, marries th' foolish, comforts th' afflicted, afflicts th' comfortable, buries th' dead an' roasts thim aftherward," Finley Peter Dunne, *Observations by Mr. Dooley*, Finley Thomas Dunne (Harper & Brothers, 1902)

2 *Parliament of Whores*, P.J. O'Rourke (Atlantic Monthly Press, 1991), in a chapter titled, "Poverty Policy: How to endow privation"

What was true in 1991 seemed still true nearly two decades later. According to a Census Bureau report from September of 2010[1] there were almost 40 million people living below the poverty line[2] in 2008 (the year of President Bush's last budget). Based on some simplifying assumptions[3] likely to cause an *over*-estimate of the problem, it would have taken about $624 billion dollars per year, distributed directly to those poor people, to lift them all out of poverty.[4] Compare that to the approximately $533 billion the federal government actually allocated in its 2008 budget to anti-poverty entitlements of various sorts,[5] and the additional billions contributed in non-entitlement programs like SNAP (i.e., "Food Stamps") and WIC, by Social Security and Medicare, and by state and local governments and non-governmental charities on top of that.

Yet, people are still poor. Not merely moderately poor. Not merely poor relative to the "excess" of the fortunate rich. People still live in privation and desperation.

All matters of ideology aside, then, most 'conservatives' conclude from such exercises that a sufficient argument against continuing to fund anti-poverty programs — at least as we have envisioned and practiced them since the start of the "Great Society" — is purely practical: they are a colossal waste of resources *because they don't work*. Or rather, since they clearly *do* provide some relief to a great many poor people, they don't work nearly well enough to justify the vast sums they consume; and claims that they fail principally because we underfund them are baseless and irrational.

Yet, raising such objections has traditionally elicited from the "left" swift and unequivocal defenses of those programs, without any reservations, along with accusations that the "real conservative agenda" is not to improve those programs but to destroy them. The absolute refusal even to consider that they might be improved in any way other than by shoveling more money into them seems, to 'conservatives,' equally baseless and irrational.

Or, perhaps, not so irrational if we assume a noteworthy but undeclared secondary goal of such programs is to knock down the wealthy rather than

---

1 *Poverty: 2008 and 2009*, U.S. Census Bureau, September 2010
2 Defined at the time as $10,400 for an individual
3 We ignore the fact that some among that population are transiently poor and therefore require only modest help from society as they are industriously helping themselves; simplify by assuming all poor people live alone rather than in families or with roommates (and therefore get no collective advantage from communal living); further simplify by assuming all poor people have no income at all; and stipulate that the government estimate of the "poverty line" is too low by half.
4 To provide an income 50% above the official poverty level: about $15.6K for an individual, about $31K for a couple, or about $62K for a family of four.
5 *Excluding* Social Security and Medicare, which spent nearly a trillion dollars by themselves; and excluding programs, like food stamps and WIC, that come from the discretionary budget and are not identified as "entitlements."

to raise up the poor. If the goal is equality, rather than prosperity, it is just as effective — and in many ways easier — to impoverish the rich as to enrich the impoverished. No doubt that is not an explicit or even conscious policy goal for most 'liberals.' But it may be an implicit and emotional one.

"Soak the rich!" is a rallying cry of the modern 'liberal.' It may not solve the problem, but it feels good. It feels fair. It feels just. It feels "progressive" and must, therefore, represent progress. And, if the rich protest, it is easy and virtuous to dismiss their protestations as merely the selfish whining of those who have more than they "need" or "deserve."

Although it may not seem obvious at first blush, 'conservatives' see a direct relationship between the practical observation that traditional anti-poverty programs don't work well and the theoretical debate over the nature of justice — and therefore over the nature of poverty. As P.J. O'Rourke put it in concluding his thought experiment, "You can't get rid of poverty by giving people money." Why? Because poverty is not predominantly *about* money. It is predominantly about behavior.

To be sure, there are people who are simply unlucky, who are victims either of circumstance or of actual malevolence. For them, poverty is decidedly not about behavior and they deserve both our sympathy and our help. A car accident or an illness or a general economic malaise — or, yes, an unreasoning and unjust prejudice that places barriers between the individual and his aspirations — may be beyond individual control and could befall any of us regardless of our talents or our skills or our personal integrity or our diligence or our prudence. And, if an individual is temporarily impoverished because he is down on his luck, then temporarily giving him money to see him through the crisis does, indeed, solve his problem.

But, excepting those few whose misfortune has left them profoundly and irrevocably disabled, people who are truly just down on their luck, people who are victims only of misfortune, tend not to stay down on their luck after such help is provided (and often even if it is not) because *they are not poor;* they are merely temporarily impoverished.

The truly poor, on the other hand, tend to be persistently and habitually poor because they behave in ways that keep them that way. Theodore Dalrymple, the pen name for an English psychiatrist who made a career of treating the poor and the incarcerated in British slums and prisons (as well as working, for a time, in sub-Saharan Africa and in Latin America), subtitled a book about his experiences, "The Worldview That Makes the Underclass."[1] He described the most common condition among the English and American

---

[1] *Life at the Bottom: The Worldview That Makes the Underclass*, Theodore Dalrymple (Ivan R. Dee, 2001)

underclasses not as "poverty" but as "squalor," a squalor largely brought by individuals upon themselves through behavior that is self-indulgent, self-gratifying, self-deluding, self-defeating, and lacking in either foresight or self-control. We routinely see the signs of that in snapshots of poverty that pop up in news reports and in popular culture: alcoholics and drug addicts, high-school dropouts, teenage mothers and deadbeat fathers, neighborhoods infested with street gangs, housing projects littered with garbage that no one has bothered to clean up, and cultural norms that glorify bravado and violence, that disdain education, that revel in grievance, and that disparage work.

Those are, of course, the extremes, not the norm, lifted as exhibits from (typically) the worst urban islands of despair. But even in places like rural New Hampshire one can see cousins to those attitudes at play, imposing their own self-limits on peoples' prospects and aspirations.

Contrary to the nightmares "the left" has about "the right," recognizing such self-limiting behavior as a root cause of poverty is not an automatic step away from assigning its victims the sole blame and responsibility for it. It is likely many people behave in such ways because they were never taught how to do otherwise, because it is such an ingrained part of the impoverished culture in which they have spent their lives as to be invisible to them and, therefore, nearly inescapable. But that makes it no less real and makes it, perhaps, more important that we acknowledge it, grapple with it, and find a way to overcome it. There is a small irony in the fact that so many 'liberals' endorse all manner of government efforts to protect us from ourselves by modifying what they deem to be our self-destructive personal behaviors — New York mayor Michael Bloomberg's wars on the consumption of trans-fats and soft-drinks come immediately to mind — and yet, perversely, find the suggestion that we might encourage the self-destructive poor to shed their self-destructive *economic* habits "demeaning" and "intrusive" and "judgmental."

The kind of contingent and episodic poverty that results from sudden misfortune is the model that advocates of anti-poverty programs like to present to us to engage our empathy — and a bit of self-interest — when they want to enlist our cooperation. "There, but for the grace of God, go I." It could happen to anyone because it is the result of ill-fate and circumstance, not of any personal failing; and so we should help out, not only as a matter of conscience — simply because someone is in need — but also as a matter of insurance, because what we provide in help today may come back to us tomorrow if we should find ourselves on the raw end of misfortune.

But, in general, that is not the kind of poverty targeted by our anti-poverty programs. In fact, other than unemployment insurance, it is often quite difficult for someone only temporarily impoverished, for someone who needs only a leg up, to access those programs at all.

Why? Because, notwithstanding the way they are marketed to the public to solicit funding, for the most part government anti-poverty programs are designed to help and support people whose poverty is not episodic but persistent, not contingent but habitual.

Which presents a problem: if we debate the proper form and funding of anti-poverty programs in the language of contingent poverty but design and operate them as instruments of habitual poverty then we cannot help but design and operate them badly.

To illustrate the gap between the stereotypical 'conservative' and 'liberal' understandings of poverty and how we should deal with it, let us re-imagine the old proverb about giving a man a fish versus teaching him to fish. To start:

> Stereotypical 'liberals' see three men, one who is hungry because his fishing pole is broken so he *can't* fish, one who is hungry because he *doesn't know how* to fish, and one who is hungry because he *won't* fish. They perceive that all three men have the same problem: they are hungry *because they have no fish*.[1]

> Stereotypical 'conservatives' see three men, one who is hungry because his fishing pole is broken so he *can't* fish, one who is hungry because he *doesn't know how* to fish, and one who is hungry because he *won't* fish. They perceive all three men have the same problem: they are hungry *because they are not fishing*.

Here's a news flash: *they're both right!* But only in part and only superficially. As a result of that partial and superficial understanding, their prescriptions for how to solve the problem are also partial and superficial:

> Stereotypical 'liberals' see a man hungry today and want to give him a fish. But, of course, then they will still need to give him another fish tomorrow, and another the day after, and another the day after, and so on for as long as he depends on free fish for his meals. They may talk about helping him to have fish over the long term, but what they

---

1 There is, of course, a more extreme variant of the 'liberal' view, epitomized by the likes of Michael Moore and Ralph Nader (and now Bernie Sanders and Elizabeth Warren), which presumes that people are hungry because "the rich" (or "the 1%") have *stolen* all the fish. While that view appears to be popular at the moment, it doesn't have much to do with traditional anti-poverty projects.

mean is to do so by making other fishermen share the fish they have, not by prompting him to catch fish for himself.

Stereotypical 'conservatives' see a man hungry today and want to get him to start fishing. But, of course, he will still be hungry today, and he will still be hungry tomorrow, and he will still be hungry the day after, and so on until (and assuming) he becomes skilled and diligent enough to catch fish. They may talk about helping him with his hunger but they mean next month or next year, not today, and they require that he be up to the task of helping himself.

Neither really addresses the underlying problems consistently because neither really differentiates between the three cases. For the first man, the problem can be solved quickly and permanently by getting him a fishing pole so he can resume fishing; for the second, it can be solved permanently, but only over time, by teaching him to fish (and, perhaps, also getting him a fishing pole) but, in the interim, he will also need fish; and for the last, it can only be solved permanently by forcing him take on the responsibility of fishing for himself, which may actually require, at some point, refusing to give him any more fish.

Which brings us to the superficiality of the discussion about what to do about poverty:

'Liberals' listen to 'conservatives' talking about teaching a man to fish (and/or forcing a reluctant man to fish), but what they hear is, "It's his own fault! He's hungry because he doesn't fish!" Then they accuse those 'conservatives' of "blaming the victim."

'Conservatives' listen to' liberals' talking about giving a man a fish, but what they hear is, "Those who have fish are greedy! We should confiscate fish from the hard-working fishermen and give it to those who couldn't be bothered to fish!" Then they accuse those 'liberals' of being socialists.

At root, it comes down to a 'liberal' over-generalization: If people *can* fish for themselves then they *will*; if people *don't* fish for themselves it must be because they *can't*, so providing them with fish is a matter of common decency and justice.

And then again, at root, it comes down to a 'conservative' over-generalization: Not only *should* people fish for themselves, they *can*; if people *don't* fish for themselves it must be because they *won't* and we should, therefore, *force* them to. Merely handing out fish, free for the asking, will ultimately discourage people from fishing and encourage them to depend on others to do it for them.

In philosophical terms, a 'conservative' might say that the ultimate solution to the problem of poverty is economic liberty: give people the opportunity, the tools, and the freedom to generate wealth and then demand that they do so. A 'liberal' might say that the ultimate solution to the problem of poverty is economic equity: some people are lucky enough to accumulate wealth and some people aren't, so those who have wealth should share with those who do not.

My use of that particular language — *demand that they do so* and *lucky enough to accumulate wealth* — was substantive, not merely a rhetorical flourish, because behind that divide is a fundamental difference of opinion on agency: 'conservatives' tend to assume people can be and are the agents of their own fates; whereas 'liberals' tend to assume that people's fates are thrust upon them by outside agents and irresistible forces beyond their control. As a consequence, the prototypical 'conservative' approach to poverty is to urge the poor to become active participants in determining their own fates, whereas the prototypical 'liberal' approach to poverty is to demand redress for the inequitable effects of a fate that is ungovernable.

And, again, the news flash: *It's not one or the other!* Yes, there are ungovernable external forces and random chance imposing themselves on our lives, and at some times and for some people those are truly overwhelming. But for a great many people, perhaps most, how they are affected depends as much on the way they respond to and manage those forces and vagaries as on the forces and vagaries themselves.

We might suspect, therefore, that the true causes of — and the true solutions to — the problem of poverty lie somewhere between those two extremes. We might suspect that solving that problem requires different approaches to different types of poverty. And we might suspect that, until we can get past the disconnect in the language with which we discuss it and actually listen to each other, we will never get to a credible and comprehensive — and harmonious — solution.

Notwithstanding all that, it would be unfair to say the argument over the form poverty programs should take is limited to the terms of a disagreement over cause and effect. There are also fundamental philosophical and practical issues concerning remedies on which 'liberals' and 'conservatives' would clash even if they could agree on what problem they were trying to solve.

At the forefront of those is a pair of moral questions: What is anyone's moral duty to help others who are less fortunate? And, presuming such a moral duty exists, by what moral authority does the government enforce that duty by taking from one person to give to another?

Although many 'liberals' would assume otherwise, there really isn't a lot of disagreement between most 'liberals' and most 'conservatives' on the first question: though there are a few lonely voices who assert otherwise, there is a general consensus that we do have a moral duty to the less fortunate. That is why charities exist and thrive. That is why we have the concept of *Noblesse Oblige*. A duty to the poor was at the heart of the teachings of Christ and is, therefore, both a moral and a spiritual obligation to many in this predominantly Christian nation. Christ's teachings were, themselves, rooted in the *Torah*, and the duty to provide charity is part of *Koran* and part of the tenets of many other religions, so that is not a uniquely Christian obligation.

There *is* debate, however, over how far that obligation extends. To whom do we owe this duty? What does it mean to be "less fortunate"? Does it mean merely that someone has less than we do? What if they have less because they chose not to work or chose to spend all their money on alcohol or drugs or gambling, or on a flashy car and faddish sneakers? What is my obligation to the *undeserving* poor? Is that term valid or invalid? If it is valid, what is *their* obligation to *me*, their benefactor? May I demand that they stop behaving badly or that they do more to help themselves as a condition of helping them?

For the *deserving* poor, those whose poverty is largely beyond their own control, how much "less fortunate" must they be to elicit that obligation? Or, reciprocally, when we help them, at what point are we allowed to stop? Must we impoverish ourselves? Are we bound to give to the point of utter equality? If not, how much "less fortunate" can we leave them; or, more prosaically, how much more fortunate may we leave ourselves?

This is not an esoteric topic. A great deal of political rhetoric has been expended in the last few elections in exhorting "the rich" to "contribute" their "fair share" to the betterment of society. No one, however, actually specifies what that "fair share" might be, nor does anyone offer any explanation, moral or otherwise, for how that share might be determined. For the most part, "your fair share" appears to be a synonym for "much more than you are contributing now" and "as much we can get a majority of people to vote for." That is, it appears that what anyone's "fair share" might be in a 'liberal' world would be determined not by some moral principle or practical constraint but purely by political power.

'Conservatives,' however, generally believe that moral judgment is a personal prerogative, not a social one, that the nature of moral obligations must be evaluated by each individual, not defined and enforced by some social consensus. And so, they are understandably uncomfortable with the open-ended nature of a politically enforced mandate to "contribute" and a politically-determined level of contribution that is deemed to be "fair."

The other side of the question of moral obligation is moral claim: if I have an obligation to the "less fortunate," is the converse true? Can the "less fortunate" assert a moral claim on me? Do they have a right, in effect, to enslave me: do they claim the right to extract a certain proportion of my knowledge and my labor — to make some limited use of my mind and my body — in order to produce something for their own consumption? And, if so, does that right exist by simple virtue of the fact that I have already produced something for myself and am, therefore, "more fortunate" than they? Does producing something for myself automatically beget a moral obligation to produce something for someone else?

The language we use to talk about our anti-poverty assistance — and the behavior of many who receive that assistance and those who advocate on their behalf — would suggest they believe the answer to those questions is, "Yes!" We call such assistance "entitlements" and tell people that they are, in fact, entitled to them. We hear claims that people have "rights" to things like food and health care that must be produced by someone else. 'Liberal' partisans talk about tax cuts as "gifts to the rich" rather than as reductions in what is to be taken away from them, as if any money we earn through our own effort belongs by default to society, by way of the government, and that the government, as an act of benevolence, may (or may not) grant us the privilege of keeping some of it.

All of which brings us back to the second of the questions we started with: by what moral authority does the government take from one person to give to another? The answer from the left, it would appear, is precisely what we asked and answered above: indeed, others — whether as individuals or as "members of society" — have an enforceable moral claim on your mind and your body, a claim that comes magically into being the moment you produce enough for yourself that you become "more fortunate" than they. For rather obvious reasons, 'conservatives' find that a bleak prospect.

If you doubt that conclusion about what 'liberals' believe concerning social obligations, turn again to the language they use to talk about it and compare it to the language of charity.

A charity appeals to your better nature and treats a donation as a moral positive. It assumes the best of you, acknowledges your sacrifice, and affirms that you are a good person because of that sacrifice. It asks politely for generosity, and it makes a point of thanking you when you respond. It makes you feel good and virtuous.

'Liberal' government and its advocates, on the other hand, shame you for your base nature and demand that you fulfill a duty. They treat your contribution as, at best, a moral neutral. They assume the worst about you, declare that you didn't "need" or "deserve" what they've taken, and emphasize that you would be a callous person but for the fact that you paid up, that you probably still are a callous person because you haven't actually yet paid your "fair share." They do their best to make you feel bad about yourself, the better to extort from you more guilt money. When was the last time a politician or an activist advocating higher taxes to support more poverty programs (or to support anything else) used either the word "please" or the words "thank you"? Those aren't in their vocabulary. Instead, they substitute other words, like "demand" and "obligation." And they apply labels like "greed" and "excess" and "unfair" and "stingy."

That attitude creates a spiritual problem as well, for it denies people the gift of giving on the one hand and the gift of receiving on the other. Recipients of aid are told it comes as a right, so they have no reason to feel gratitude, and it comes anonymously, so they have no one to feel grateful to — and, therefore, they have no opportunity to observe and be blessed by basic human kindness. Givers of aid are told it is in payment of an obligation, so they have no reason to feel virtuous, and its distribution is out of their control, so they can only hope it will eventually emerge in some inchoate form of general "good." They have no chance to direct their "donation" to any particular act of grace, to connect it with any particular life saved or need fulfilled.

And, from both ends, there is no opportunity for fellowship or empathy between donor and recipient and, instead, every opportunity for resentment of those who take without gratitude and those who give without enthusiasm. I've often wondered what attitudes toward poverty programs might be, among poor and rich alike, if each recipient had to send a thank-you note to a taxpayer every time they received a check.

And, finally, there are practical questions about what kind of society and polity we create with such policies. Does an "entitlement" to a certain level of support undermine the culture of self-reliance that makes our society and our economy so dynamic? Does it undermine self-respect and ambition and a sense of responsibility in those who depend on it, create a "culture of dependency"? Does it undermine incentives to entrepreneurship? Does it foment, rather than alleviate, a class-based schism in our culture, a schism not between rich and poor but between makers and users, between givers and takers? Does it lead, ultimately, to a system in which government can no longer be effectively controlled because a majority of citizens depend directly upon government for their livelihoods, in which the majority is free simply to take from the minority because they have the political power to do so? What other mischief can and will the authority to transfer wealth from one use to another be applied to? And can we constrain that authority once it has been granted?

'Conservatives' believe the answers to those questions are an important part of the debate. But it is hard to get to those answers, or even to discuss them, because, to most 'liberals,' even asking the questions is tantamount to cruelty, tantamount to a suggestion that we eliminate the social safety net entirely. Even asking the questions elicits a flood of condemnation and effectively shuts down any further conversation.

There is, actually, a 'conservative' argument, rarely articulated, for supporting government social programs. It can be summed up in a simple, traditionally conservative statement:

> *That which can be overcome with resolve or made tolerable by reform will not be overthrown by revolution.*

In other words, if excessive economic and social stratification is socially destabilizing (which it is), then ensuring that stratification does not become excessive is necessary in order to maintain a stable social and economic order. Hence, conservatives who value stability, either as an inherent good or as a practical defense against the risks of social upheaval, should support programs that ameliorate that stratification. They might prefer that those initiatives arise privately but, to the extent that does not happen, should concede some must be run by the government. Even stalwart libertarian economists like Milton Friedman[1] and Friedrich Hayek[2] have advocated for some kind of guaranteed minimum income.

Basing support for such programs on a need to promote social stability, rather than on some obligation to equalize individual well-being, provides the distinct advantage that it implies a logical stopping point for allocating resources to them: the right amount to expend is the amount that will maintain stability. And it avoids the philosophical pitfall of enslaving one individual to the needs of another, for the purpose of an individual's contribution is not to serve the needs of some other individual but to enable the defining purpose of government: to secure our liberties against the anarchy of the jungle or of the mob.

In addition, there are several practical reasons why 'conservatives' might support such policies:

- Freed from the baggage of the language of moral obligation, those policies can be viewed without prejudice as a form of insurance against the catastrophic misfortune of social and political upheaval.

---

1 *Capitalism and Freedom*, M. Friedman, University of Chicago Press, 1962
2 *Hayek on Hayek: An Autobiographical Dialogue*, F.A. Hayek (ed. Stephen Kresge and Leif Wenar), University of Chicago Press, 1994

- To the extent that a primary source of economic and social stratification is the distortion of the market by political forces — and many libertarian-minded conservatives, concerned more with individual autonomy and liberty than with stability, would assert that is the case — any policy designed to minimize such stratification would, presumably, also reduce such political interference in the market.

- The detrimental effects of extreme poverty and stratification are likely to be a drag on the economy due to poor health and idleness among the impoverished and excessive friction between the managerial and working classes. Hence, reducing stratification is likely to improve economic productivity along with social concordance.

The focus on stability would also affect the forms that such policies might take. For instance, the primary destabilizing feature of economic stratification is not that there are both wealthy and poor people but the perception that those categories are static — that there is no opportunity for economic advancement. If you can aspire to becoming wealthy, or even merely comfortable and secure, then you are likely to view poverty as a stage you must pass through, rather than a permanent condition, and you will have no particular interest in overthrowing the system that encourages that aspiration. Hence, we might suppose that encouraging and enabling economic mobility — and individual aspiration — would be the best aim of such policies. Perhaps that is a program that 'liberals' and 'conservatives' could agree on.

Finally, a common, orderly, and civil society is a boon to most individuals. Yet, the actions necessary to maintain such a society are often detrimental to the individual in the short term, and are most often so when they are not widely honored and shared among the citizenry. Society is the ultimate commons, and is subject to the tragedy of the commons. We might suppose, therefore, that "social responsibility" extends beyond mere economic concerns, beyond the mere alleviation of poverty, to a more general care for society as an organism.

There is an irony in that, for the 'conservatives' who are considered by 'liberals' to be wholly hostile to "social responsibility" in its economic forms are, at the same time, castigated for pointing out and resisting the detrimental social effects of a great many 'liberal' policies from the last forty years. One of the defining characteristics of modern 'conservatives' has been their intense sense of social responsibility when it comes to family, community, culture, and general social concordance. And one of the defining features of modern 'liberals' has been their disregard for the ways in which their overturning of so many mores and traditions have disrupted family and community, coarsened culture, and fractured social concordance.

On the continuum of human behavior spanning the range from conventional to evil, the boundary between "legal" and "illegal," at least in a democracy concerned with civil rights, must lie somewhere between "depraved" and "intolerable" rather than close to the norm. That means a great deal of bad and anti-social behavior must be regulated through social sanctions rather than through legal ones; and the 'conservative' "values" so often ridiculed by 'liberals' are largely those which govern such social sanctions, which regulate behavior that is not and should not be illegal but is, nevertheless, in some ways troubling or disruptive or socially corrosive.

The "values" cherished by modern 'liberalism,' in contrast, appear to be something like this: "If it is not intolerable, then it shouldn't be illegal; *and if it isn't illegal then it must be conventional.*"[1] In other words, modern 'liberalism' asserts there can be only a single step between "conventional" and "intolerable," and that any recognition of some categories in between or, worse, any attempt to apply social constraints on behavior that falls into those categories is, by definition, "intolerant." Modern 'liberals' appear to reject the notion of social sanction entirely and, instead, advocate minutely detailed and constraining legal sanctions for enforcing their preferred standards of behavior.

Many 'conservatives' believe — perhaps somewhat ironically given the focus on individual liberty and autonomy that underlies so much 'conservative' thought and rhetoric — that "social responsibility" is as much about the individual's responsibility toward society as it is about society's responsibility toward individuals. The economic and cultural concerns at the heart of the 'liberal' conception of "social responsibility" seem generally to be about what we all, collectively as members of society, should do to make our society fair for the individuals and groups who live there. But so-called "cultural conservatives" worry as much, or more, about what we all, as individuals living within society, should do to nourish the moral foundations, social bonds, and cultural institutions that make society itself stable and supportive.

At least to the extent that many modern 'liberal' attitudes and policies seem to undermine social stability and cultural harmony, and especially to the extent that many 'liberals' seem to regard that disruption of stable social institutions as a cause for celebration rather than for regret, it is

---

1 There is, of course, a corollary that both 'liberals' and 'conservatives' appear to agree on: "If I don't like it, then it should be illegal."

'conservatives' who may legitimately ask of 'liberals,' "Where is your sense of social responsibility?"

Conservative Tendencies

When I was growing up my father was generally as 'conservative' as they come, although in the late 1960s and the 1970s the common understanding of 'conservatism' had a different lilt than it does now. There was, for instance, nothing even remotely hinting of the religious about him. He tended to like institutions even as he distrusted authority. He wanted to be left alone to do as he saw fit with what was his, and chafed under restrictions imposed "for the common good" — not because he did not believe in the "common good" but because he did not believe those imposing the restrictions necessarily knew any better than he what the "common good" was, nor that they knew or cared what those restrictions cost him. And, left alone to do as he saw fit, he volunteered his time prodigiously to community organizations like the Boy Scouts, the volunteer fire department, and local and regional planning commissions because he believed in an ethic of service. He was anti-union, not because he thought workers were getting a good deal from employers but because of the frustration that inane union work-rules had caused him in his various jobs, the implied presumption that he and all others were merely interchangeable labor units rather than individuals with unique skills and desires, and the effective monopoly — in practice a protection racket — they imposed on 'union shops.' He thought the primary purpose of government was to protect us from bad guys — either foreign or domestic — and lamented that it seemed to be abdicating that responsibility, instead redirecting an increasing proportion of its resources to supporting lay-abouts and wastrels who had no interest in being productive members of society or even in conforming to civilized norms of behavior; he believed in their freedom to be lazy and repugnant, but not in their freedom from economic hardship and social condemnation for having made that choice — and he did not think he should have to support their irresponsibility. He disliked the activism of judges and regulators who seemed to be changing — or even making up — the rules as they went along to support some personal vision of "social justice."

And yet, this 'conservative' was also, for a while, the local building inspector and, in that capacity, he took great delight, even pride, in imposing increasingly intrusive standards of building codes and zoning restrictions on local property developers. At one time he recounted with satisfaction how, in the name of safety, he had forced developers to install Ground-Fault Interrupter circuits on outlets in their kitchens despite the fact that the building codes at the time did not yet require them — and how the developers had complied with his edict because the cost was moderate and they depended on his continuing goodwill for the smooth completion of their projects.

He is a smart man — he was, in many ways, a visionary when it came to managing the phenomenal rate of growth that was then transforming rural farms and woodlands into suburban housing tracts in northern New England — and the rules he envisioned and enforced were invariably useful (if intrusive) and justifiable (if beyond the scope of his actual authority) in terms of building safety and population growth management.

Nonetheless, he was a contradiction. He despised being told he had to comply with someone else's vision of what was best — but happily imposed his own. He disliked regulatory agencies and judges that assumed legislative authority to extend the rules — but assumed that authority with aplomb when it was available to him. And he found the fact that cooperation with his edicts was the result, not of any legitimate authority, but of his ability to make future dealings arbitrarily difficult an indicator of his own effectiveness rather than a symptom of a minor despotism.

In short, he is human; and his story is the rule rather than the exception.

There is an underlying, if oversimplified, truth to the observation that conservatives are liberals with something to lose and that liberals are conservatives with power. That is not to imply that all, or even most, people merely and consciously serve themselves above all else. But, for most people, political decisions result as much from unconscious attitudes and judgments as from the conscious application of principle. And, in the political realm, costs and benefits typically accrue to different people and in different (and often non-monetary) forms.

Hence, seemingly objective assessments of costs and benefits are inevitably colored by subjective assessments of their magnitudes and of their relative importance. And, since most people consider *themselves* reasonable and moral but *others* less so, forcing others to modify their behavior to your standard is rarely as troubling as being forced to modify your own behavior to theirs. Restrictions on "violent" or "dangerous" or "pornographic" or "racist" or "misogynist" or "hateful" or "offensive" speech seem reasonable and less perilous than restrictions on the expression of "mainstream" social or political ideologies. Yet, students of history and of politics know that most 'progressive' ideas were initially deemed worthless and dangerous; that free speech tends to be a package deal; and that an authority that can regulate speech based on the value of its content will, eventually and inevitably, get around to regulating content you would find valuable.

Similarly, any assessment of our vulnerability to foreign enemies and of strategies required for our protection will depend in large measure on perception of the threat they pose — which depends heavily on our views of human nature. If you believe human nature is primarily generous, that war is caused by misunderstanding, injustice, and singular greed, then you will perceive different risks and propose different strategies than if you believe human nature is primarily selfish, that war is caused by unstable power structures, social and cultural animosity, and ideology in service to megalomania.

Aside from political principle, then, general cultural assumptions and philosophical attitudes can have great influence over the inferences 'liberals' and 'conservatives' draw from their experiences and over the particular policies they actually propose or oppose when they are in and out of power. So it is worthwhile to think about what common cultural assumptions and attitudes 'conservatives' tend to share.

Naturally, no such list can be comprehensive or universal and I am aware of very little social science research to buttress or rebut my anecdotal observations — so any attempt to compound such a list invites criticism. Nonetheless, some observed tendencies are common enough to be worthy of mention.

Perhaps the most fundamental aspect of 'conservative' attitude is an underlying presumption that the world is not fair, that it is full of events unexpected and unpredictable, and that there are some things about it we cannot change. This presumption comes directly from the first two postulates in our list of 'conservative' principles: that there is an external reality to the universe disinterested in human affairs and unaffected by human desires and plans; and that, despite all efforts to coerce or entice them otherwise, large groups of human beings tend to behave according to an ancient nature inextricably embedded in the human psyche and not necessarily well-aligned with our modern civilized ideals.

That doesn't mean that 'conservatives' can't "dream big." It certainly doesn't imply they are more immune than anyone else to being led astray by wishful thinking or by fear. But it does suggest a primal 'conservative' skepticism about idealistic projects intended to align either the world or its inhabitants with some utopian vision. 'Conservatives' can "visualize world peace." In general, however, they don't believe visualizing it has all that much to do with actually achieving it.

Such a skeptical world-view can, of course, appear as pessimism rather than as realism and, to the extent that doubts about our ability to achieve idealistic ends or about the costs incurred in trying is misinterpreted as hostility to those ends themselves, it can also appear as callousness. That appearance is exacerbated by a related 'conservative' assumption: a belief in the inherent corruptibility of human beings and, by extension, of human institutions.

People who disagree often dismiss that assumption as a kind of misanthropic cynicism, or worse as a modern reflection of some Dark Ages doctrine of Original Sin — "people are evil and greedy, altruism is a myth, free will is the downhill path from heaven to hell"; and those who do so also thereby dismiss 'conservatism,' itself, as a selfish, dour and hopeless creed or as merely the moralistic condescension of Christian Fundamentalism.

But, though much of the Judeo-Christian moral tradition does concern the struggle for mastery over that human vulnerability to temptation, the assumption of human corruptibility is not a singularly religious artifact. Neither is it a call to pessimism nor a judgment on individual moral worth. It is rational and pragmatic: the histories of individuals and of societies, and particularly of governments, are largely compendia of ignoble motivations and the corrupting effects of power — and there is no credible evidence that any recent human enlightenment has made the lessons of that history obsolete.

Corruptibility, however, is not the same as corruption. Although it is frequently derided as otherwise, the 'conservative' view is not that human nature is *evil* but that it is *amoral*, egocentric and aggressive yet inclined to both empathy and sympathy — and, therefore, capable both of great cruelty and of great kindness. As an assumption about human nature, not about individuals, that is not disproved by the existence of a Gandhi or a Mother Theresa, nor is it proved by the existence of a Hitler or a Saddam Hussein. Neither does it imply that moral society is impossible, or even unlikely, for, though humans are by nature amoral, their ability to reason makes them both educable and inquisitive, and their capacity for empathy and for sympathy inspires cooperation and opens them to moral contemplation and moral suasion.

But the amoral nature of human beings *does* imply that a moral society is neither inevitable nor effortless. *Lord of the Flies*[1] may have been an exaggeration but it was not a fantasy. Moral society must be created and maintained by innumerable conscious acts of will.

Most self-consistent moral philosophies, whether inspired by religion or by some secular ideal of human dignity, acknowledge this human nature at least implicitly. Precisely because serving your *own* interest is the human norm, their ethical codes are primarily guidelines for when and how to serve others' interests *above* your own; and, to induce such humane behavior, their ethical frameworks seek to engage natural human empathy/sympathy — and to extend its scope — by defining a community of moral, intellectual,

---

1 William Golding, Faber and Faber, 1954

emotional, and spiritual kinships beyond the narrow bounds of the family or the tribe.

That is true even for the most individualistic moral philosophies. The merest mandate to respect others' rights to moral autonomy (to "life, liberty, and the pursuit of happiness") is an injunction against coercion as a method of self-gratification and is rooted in a presumption of moral kinship and mutual sympathy among members of the human species. In this sense, ethical systems are, by nature, social systems (although emphatically not "social constructs") intended specifically to operate in a social environment and to moderate social behavior.

If moral behavior is learned then it must *be* learned; and, therefore, if it is not to be merely the haphazard and egocentric inference from chaotic experience, it must be *taught*. It can also be disregarded, forgotten, or renounced, especially if it is undermined by experiences that seem to contradict moral lessons, like punishments associated with ethical behavior, rewards associated with unethical behavior, or events and actions which alienate the individual from the moral community. Hence, it must also be reinforced over time.

This, too, makes morality, in practice, partly a social phenomenon. Society, as a collective of individuals, will manifest the collective moral sensibilities of its participants; but, conversely, both the need for initial moral education and the need for continuous moral reinforcement imply that the general moral tenor of society will also mold personal moral behavior. Personal and social decadence (and virtue) reinforce each other, and a decadent (or virtuous) society will mold correspondingly decadent (or virtuous) citizens.

Moreover, to the extent that moral education engages us through empathy and sympathy, it will always be in tension with the egocentric impulse — and the egocentric impulse is reinforced by high personal costs for altruism or high personal rewards for selfishness. Similarly, empathy and sympathy themselves tend to wane as the conception of the moral community becomes more abstract: a million faceless and nameless people are harder to identify with than one person whose face and name you know; and a duty to all God's children feels more vague and unsustainable than a duty to God himself on behalf of those children.

Empathy and sympathy can even be corrupting, in and of themselves, if excessive concern for the well-being of a particular group becomes an excuse for otherwise immoral acts aimed at other groups. Tribalism in its various forms incites conflict with "outsiders"; terrorism is almost always rationalized by its perpetrators as an act of protection or of liberation; and the sacrifice of individual lives, liberties, and property has been justified throughout history by claims of benefit to the greater society — by a philosophy of "the needs of the many outweigh the needs of the few" enforced through political power by the few self-designated voices of "the many."

The assumption that humans are corruptible leads to a corollary assumption: that human beings and human institutions are also not socially perfectible — that the egocentric and aggressive nuclei of our nature may be controlled but not eradicated; that attempts to eradicate them, attempts at perfect socialization and a denial of the self, are not only fruitless but dehumanizing. Self-regard and autonomy are as much a part of us as are our social natures and are not matters for shame or lamentation.

This is not "greed is good" or "altruism is bad." It is acknowledgement of the contradiction — and of the immorality — in presuming a higher moral status for others (individually or collectively) than for ourselves. Why should we assume that our own needs and desires have less moral heft than anyone else's? If serving others is noble, and if their service to us is equally noble, then why should serving ourselves be less so? On what basis do we conclude that their needs must necessarily and consistently trump our own?

It is a rejection of the core socialist ideal: the elevation of society and of social man in supremacy over the individual. It is a declaration that the socialist ideal is not merely impractical but inhumane precisely because it is inhuman.

Another attitude that 'conservatives' tend to share, perhaps related to the presumption of corruptibility, is a kind of risk aversion, a preoccupation with minimizing harm rather than with maximizing benefit. That attitude makes sense if you presume any human enterprise is in danger of subversion by corruptible human nature, but it is also descriptively conservative. Social and political changes introduce uncertainty and risk, which is amplified by the potential for error and corruption when changes are enforced by political power. In the absence of imminent upheaval, leaving well enough alone generally keeps things from getting quickly worse.

That is not to say that 'conservatives' must always be hostile to action or even to progress. They are as interested as anyone in fixing what is broken and in improving the human condition. But they refuse to allow starry-eyed visions of progress to blind them to economic or social costs, either demonstrable or potential, and prefer to make changes incrementally precisely because it allows for management and mitigation of those costs before they become catastrophic. If that often makes 'conservatives' over-emphasize the dangers of 'liberalism,' they would legitimately counter that 'liberals' often preach the other extreme, seemingly ignoring those dangers as if they were irrelevant or even illusory. From that perspective, demands for radical change seem — to the extent that the risks and costs of change are typically borne by those who want things to remain as they are — not only risky but genuinely selfish.

The tendency of 'conservatives' to overemphasize the cost of change is accompanied by a tendency to underestimate the benefits. That also should not be surprising. We may presume — either because they find it morally proper, or because they find it materially beneficial, or because it is their nature to conform to social expectations, or because they are so secure and self-confident that they find the social consequences of their non-conformity irrelevant or exhilarating, or because they so lack security and self-confidence that they feel things can only get worse — that 'conservatives' are comfortable with their current arrangements. Otherwise they would not want to preserve them. In all cases, although they may understand intellectually why others would choose different arrangements, they may not connect emotionally with the zeal for change. They can understand that others want more amenable social and political structures without comprehending why it seems so imperative or so urgent.

That does not mean that to be 'conservative' is necessarily to be a congenital conformist — although that might be a fair characterization for some. But, at the least, a 'conservative' respect for the utility of social structures and cultural mores implies a willingness to accede to their strictures under most circumstances, if not because they are personally agreeable then because they serve the goal of social harmony.

That incomprehension of the urgency for change is exacerbated by another aspect of our empathetic natures: the tendency to project our own world view onto others who fall far from our immediate community — to mitigate our ignorance about others by extrapolating from our own experiences and attitudes. If we presume others are "like us" and ought to share our motivations and reasoning, then their aversions to what we appreciate can seem not only inscrutable but irrational; and if they are so inscrutable and irrational then perhaps they are not really like us at all and do not have our best interests at heart. 'Liberals' fall prey to the same delusion and find 'conservative' defenses of stability equally inscrutable and irrational.

All of this fits with a general 'conservative' preoccupation — in some cases excessive — with autonomy and self-reliance. If you believe human institutions are fundamentally corruptible, unreliable, and prone to falling short of their expectations, then depending on them for your well-being is an uncomfortable and imprudent proposition. Further, such a sense of self-reliance calls to mind the traditional American archetype forged from our history as a nation of immigrants and fresh starts: the courageous immigrant or pioneer (or perhaps pejoratively in modern parlance, the cowboy) throwing off the shackles of tradition and community to forge a new and independent life from the harsh but plentiful opportunities of a new land. That both immigrant and pioneer experiences were, in historical fact, often as communal as they were individual — that immigrants and pioneers often depended as much on local social and economic networks as on individual perseverance for survival — does not detract from the individual acts of ego such breaks with tradition and community required. Nor does it detract from the mythology or from the human ideal it embodies: the individual as the noble master of his own destiny. It is an ideal that is traditionally and quintessentially American and embracing that traditional "American Spirit" is quintessentially conservative in an American context.

But there is an ethical basis to that preoccupation as well: such physical autonomy is a logical extension of and companion to moral autonomy. Exercising your physical and moral autonomy does not necessarily preclude either acting in concert with others or accepting (or even requesting) support and succor. People benefit from cooperation and therefore choose to cooperate; people seek security and pay for it with sacrifice and commitment; people value community and will voluntarily exchange a bit of independence for its pleasures; people desire intimacy and willingly bind themselves to friend and family for the comforts it provides. There is no shame in that. Nor is there shame either in weakness or in misfortune.

But all those reflect individual choices in the matter of social participation and include an agreement to give as well as to take. The ethical standard of moral autonomy does imply, at root, a personal responsibility for your own circumstance, a responsibility to contribute to the community if you will receive from it, and a responsibility at the least to provide what you can for yourself before relying on others. And, although accepting what others have freely offered cannot objectively confer on them reciprocal moral claims, most people have an innate and subjective sense of moral accounting that tallies — and accumulates or discharges — such 'debts.' What can be more conservative than balancing your accounts?

Clearly not all communal relationships are so mercenary, even among individualistic 'conservatives.' Families, tribes, friendships, congregations, clubs, neighborhoods, and similar communities-of-interest operate more like risk pools than like markets. As long as each member's contribution is perceived to be reasonably related to their means, the accounts are considered balanced; and emotional ties — an abiding interest in the welfare of the community and its members — reduces even that minimal interest in moral accounting. Within the group, empathy and loyalty and communal welfare eclipse self-reliance and self-determination as moral ideals.

But even within such groups people do not relinquish their own autonomy entirely. How common is the story of the child striking out alone to escape the oppressive conformity of his or her family role; or of a member of the congregation breaking with the faith to find his or her own and individual spiritual path? As often as not, such assertions of individuality and ego are considered 'liberal' rather than 'conservative' rites of passage. Beyond such immediate and intimate communities, expecting that individual autonomy will be consistently subordinated to the needs and the authority of some group — or to the needs and authority of a broader and impersonal "society" — is both unrealistic and unhealthy.

Which demonstrates another and familiar aspect of this preoccupation with self-determination: it is human nature, not merely 'conservative' nature. Most people, 'conservative' or 'liberal,' are uncomfortable with unbridled authority (or at least with unbridled authority over themselves; they rarely find their own authority over others as troubling). That discomfort with authority persists even when they believe the authority has both wisdom and moral virtue. Most people resist being told what to do even when they crave and seek out guidance about what they ought to do. Most people sense keenly the difference between leaders and rulers. They may be willing, perhaps eager, to be led; they are as likely to rebel against being ruled.

A final aspect of this preoccupation with autonomy is a 'conservative' focus on opportunity rather than on status. If you believe that individuals have both primary responsibility for and agency over their circumstance, then your notion of "fairness" and "justice" is likely to emphasize the availability of tools — and a willingness to use those tools — to affect that circumstance in the future, rather than merely the state of that circumstance in the present. That also implies a 'conservative' tendency to hold a dynamic view of status, both economic and social, inasmuch as the availability of such tools — of opportunity — makes social and economic mobility possible.

For that reason, 'conservatives' tend to deemphasize the unfairness or injustice of unequal outcomes — of contrasts between rich and poor or between powerful and powerless — provided they perceive that those contrasts are dynamic, that opportunities for changing those outcomes, for creating success, are available to individuals who choose to take advantage of them. This is in contrast to the common — and typically 'liberal' — view of fairness and justice strictly as an equality of contemporary status, presumed to be relatively static and insensitive to individual effort in the absence of some active intervention and support by "society," generally through the instrument of government.

Which is not to say that 'conservatives' are apathetic about fairness and justice. They simply view unfairness and injustice differently than 'liberals' do. Since the 'conservative' notion of justice is focused on moral balance, the equilibrium between actions and consequences, 'conservatives' tend to be concerned with whether or not people are following the rules and, particularly, with whether they are being rewarded for breaking the rules and/or punished for adhering to them.

And that is not merely a matter of justice. As we said before, 'conservatives' acknowledge the recurrent need to reinforce moral lessons lest the communal moral sense degenerate. Bad behavior which goes unpunished and good behavior which goes unrewarded undermines that reinforcement. Hence, 'conservatives' are concerned not only with the immediate injustice of impunity but also with its long-term systemic effect on society.

As a result, 'conservatives' are much more willing to accept some amount of self-inflicted inequity and even suffering — for example, over-optimistic loan-holders enduring a foreclosure or undocumented immigrants a deportation — than are 'liberals.' 'Liberals' tend to focus on alleviating immediate and unpleasant personal consequences; and they tend to deemphasize (or ignore) both any reckless behaviors that led to those consequences and the long-term moral (and behavioral) costs of rescuing or excusing those behaviors. In the name of minimizing suffering, they tend to dismiss (or ignore) the fundamental unfairness — both to individuals and to society — of providing succor, and even validation, to those who behave irresponsibly, skirt the law, or disregard the social compact at the expense of those who do not.

And, of course, the other side of autonomy is restraint. If you have authority over your own behavior then you must also have the self-discipline to moderate that behavior, particularly if we assume, as conservatives do, that it is human nature to be selfish and aggressive. Hence, 'conservatives' tend toward exacting standards for judging both personal and social conduct.

Recent research[1] has suggested that 'conservatives' generally have a stronger "disgust" impulse than do 'liberals,' which forms a visceral emotional basis for a strong aversion to varieties of libertine activities. 'Conservatives' might consider that a sign of virtue; 'liberals' might consider it prudery. Certainly it suggests that such aversions are emotional, not intellectual, that they fall into the irrational realm of passion rather than into the rational realm of ideology.

But, as we noted earlier, controlling your baser impulses is also the basis and purpose for all ethical systems. Conservative discomfort with socially distasteful behavior is not just about the behavior, per se. It is about what the behavior represents: a narcissistic inability to behave in socially and, therefore, ethically acceptable ways; an injurious dearth of self-discipline; and an anti-social and hedonistic lack of respect for others' needs or desires.

---

1 See *The Righteous Mind*, by Jonathan Haidt, Vintage Books, 2013

Conservatism in Practice

To now, we have been discussing 'conservatism' as a theoretical construct, as an intellectual framework that might, we hope, guide the way we ask and answer questions about political culture and public policy. To be sure, it is nearly impossible to have such a discussion in any accessible way without reference to actual cases, so the discussion has not been devoid of practical and instructive examples. Those examples, however, were chosen for their utility in illustrating some particular principle or assumption, not because they were of interest in and of themselves; that is, they were chosen specifically because they were useful in proving a point. In general, the examples provided in earlier sections were selected through a search for real-world situations that fit the theory, rather than by trying to apply the theory to some pre-determined real-world situations.

The measure of any such intellectual framework, however, is how well or badly it maps onto the real and messy world of actual human behavior. Thus, no discussion of 'conservatism' would be complete without some attempt to show how that mapping might work in some representative cases that were not specifically and narrowly chosen *because* of the fullness of such alignment.

The following discussions are intended to illustrate how conservative principles might apply to a few topics of particular contemporary interest. In general, the arguments are more accurately portrayed as being rooted in 'conservative' philosophy and informed by a 'conservative' viewpoint than as direct arguments from conservative principle. They are intended to be persuasive without being pedantic.

The choice of subjects will be familiar from recent political discussions but is far from exhaustive, and it is not my intent to represent the "official" version of 'conservative' thought on the subjects or to make any claim that they represent the only, or even the most common, 'conservative' viewpoint. As noted early on, the ways that individual 'conservatives' resolve discrepancies and contradictions among the various 'conservative' principles is idiosyncratic, based on their own value judgments and on the perspectives provided by their personal histories.

Hence, these examples represent my personal, and perhaps atypical, ways of looking at the topics; and there will, I am sure, be self-described 'conservatives' who take exception to some of what they might say. Take them, then, for what they are: illustrative forms for how to make arguments from a 'conservative' viewpoint and consistent with 'conservative' principle, not assertions of demonstrable truth.

Same-Sex Marriage

There once was a word which described a particular joyous frame of mind — a state, according to *Webster's*, of being "excited with merriment"; of "manifesting [and inspiring] sportiveness or delight." It had synonyms, of course — words like "carefree," "cheery," "merry," "lively," "fun-loving" — but none of them alone encapsulated the entirety of the concept, the combination of internal ebullience with external inspiration, the combination of joy and exhilaration and passion, in the way that word did. Using that word one could communicate simply and directly the elemental nature of that experience, and the listener would immediately not only have an understanding of the outward form but an archetype of all that it might imply. The word was shorthand for a multitude of emotions and behavior; without it one could only fully describe the concept using an array of other almost-words to surround what it was and fence off what it was not.

The word was "gay." It still exists, of course, and dictionaries still list its old definition for those who might encounter it in an archaic context that requires decoding. But its utility for invoking that peculiarly human state of being is forever lost because, to modern listeners, "gay" evokes an entirely different human experience: that generally of homosexuality and, specifically, of a particular late 20th century homosexual culture and lifestyle.

The concept of "gaiety" also still endures — although not of "gayness" — in part because human nature persists more obdurately than language and in part because that particular noun form was spared when the adjectival form was appropriated for its alternate use. But recognition and appreciation of the concept has been diminished: lacking the language to describe it succinctly, people begin to lose the distinction between that and other, similar notions.

There are other concepts that have been robbed of their precise descriptors by circumstance or ignorance: "niggardly" is forever tainted by its imagined association with that other "N-word"; "balls out," misconstrued as referring to masculine anatomy rather than to rotating machinery, carries a similarly pejorative burden. Synonyms provide approximations but not equivalence, so these, too, diminish both our language and our universe of ideas. But at least they result from accidents of misapprehension, not outright appropriation. Gayness was lost by intent.

Of course, other than my grandmother and my high-school Russian teacher, I've never heard anyone seriously lament the loss. We can appreciate gaiety when we encounter it even without knowing how to name it and, at any rate, it seems somehow generally less applicable to the turn of the 21st century than it did to the turn of the 20th.

But the loss of labels for abstract concepts is not always so benign. George Orwell observed in his classic novels *Animal Farm* and *1984* that language is the instrument of analysis, and to control language is to control thought. The two sides sparring over abortion vie for the right to name what is in contention. Are supporters *pro-choice* — and opponents, therefore, against individual autonomy and in favor of a police state? Are opponents *pro-life* — and supporters, therefore, against protecting the helpless and in favor of murder? Are third-world factories sweatshops or a source of economic opportunity? If high taxes amount to slavery, then what was it that was happening on plantations in the antebellum South? If George W. Bush was a Hitler, then how do we reconcile the vast and indisputable contradictions between the political cultures of modern America and 1930s Germany?

For a long time, advocacy on behalf of same-sex marriage was framed in large part by issues of equity and civil rights: the state sanction of marriage brings with it certain privileges and responsibilities that are denied to same-sex couples in deference to ancient gender roles. On that basis we now have a widespread — though not yet unanimous — acknowledgement, recently formalized by the Supreme Court,[1] that marriage laws, as currently formulated, are discriminatory and ought to be amended to accommodate a more modern concept of what it is to form a committed relationship and a family unit.

Way back in 2004, the Massachusetts Supreme Judicial Court, in its first ruling on the issue, seemed to embody that new spirit and, in response, the Massachusetts legislature offered up civil unions, available to any couple and embodying all the same legal sanction, benefits, and responsibilities as were currently afforded to marriage. At the time, conservative opponents of same-sex unions seemed to be signaling that they might not take up the fight

---

1 U.S. Supreme Court, *Obergefell v. Hodges*, 2015

to oppose that offer; in Massachusetts civil unions seemed an acceptable compromise, and even President Bush declined to take a stand on it.

But courts are not structured to negotiate compromise. It is not in their nature to balance and trade off competing interests but to adjudicate between them, to declare that one interest supersedes the other, to declare a winner and a loser and award the prize. That is precisely why policy controversies are and should be a legislative prerogative, not a judicial one. The original SJC decision acknowledged that and deferred to the legislature, which fostered the compromise that was offered. But the court's follow-on ruling on that offer, foreshadowing the way the issue would evolve nationally over the next decade, precluded compromise and moved the debate out of the legal realm and into the cultural one, for it asserted a claim not just on legal consequences but on the *word*; and nothing short of "marriage" could satisfy that claim.

The institution of marriage is ancient and ubiquitous in human cultures. Throughout its history, in almost all cultural contexts, marriage, in both tradition and law, has consistently had two aspects: *a joining* — whether legal or spiritual — and *gender roles* — husband and wife. This was not the result of an artificial fusion of two disparate traditions; it was an integrated cultural concept, husband and wife joined to form a single social unit. The ubiquity of that combination of factors across human cultures — and the general absence of similar concepts for the joining of husbands with husbands or wives with wives — argues that it is likely an expression of some fundamental human social function rooted in biological imperative. The two aspects have always been united, and the word "marriage" has always embodied that unified abstraction of dual-gender joining.

In that regard same-sex union, although *legally* a mere extension of existing contractual arrangements, is something *culturally* new and distinct. If "marriage" embodies gender, then this is something else.

Yet you would never know that from the rhetoric of its advocates. They declare that their unions are in harmony with the fundamental quality of "marriage" — commitment to each other in a family unit — and that gender is superfluous. They declare that their unions *are* "marriages" in all but law, and that therefore the law should change. The legal point — that the law should be gender neutral as a matter of civil right — is compelling. Fair-minded people grant it without dispute, letting the cultural point pass.

But as a *cultural* matter, and as an intellectual one, declaring marriage to be gender-neutral is hubris. It amounts to the assertion, despite millennia of contrary understanding, that one of the two aspects of marriage is suddenly irrelevant to the concept of what a marriage is, that the abstract concept is not unified but divisible. Further it asserts that advocates of gay marriage have a special insight, denied their opponents, into which sundered aspect — the joining rather than the gender roles — is the more fundamental. And worse, it asserts that the diminution of the lesser aspect would not even fundamentally *alter* the abstract concept of marriage — that the gender distinction is not only irrelevant but actually devoid of meaning — that a gender-neutral marriage is not only *equivalent* in all important ways to a traditional one but is, in fact, *identical*. It is a distortion of history and of culture that obscures the study and understanding of both.

That redefinition of marriage is, of course, the goal. While, for many, the legal benefits of civil unions and the statement of *legal* equality that they imply are sufficient for now, the few who hold out for "marriage" demand more, demand immediate *cultural* equality as well; and, rather than pursuing that goal through persuasion, they would, instead, eradicate by coercion the very language that makes distinguishing between same-sex and mixed-gender unions possible.

But the traditional concept of marriage is valuable in itself, not only because it seems to represent something basic to human experience, and not only because a great many people still find it relevant to their lives, but because it is so fundamental to our history, our heritage, and our ancient cultural foundations. There are no synonyms that truly convey the entirety of the meaning of "marriage," and with the loss of that word to a more all-encompassing ideal we will no longer have the language to discuss and comprehend those facets of our human nature and of our cultural past.

Marriage, both the abstract concept and the word to name it, does not belong to the state. It belongs to the culture. Certainly the state has appropriated the word for its own use because the cultural concept has traditionally aligned well with a particular and narrow state function — that of designating the legal benefits and responsibilities of participants in a family unit — but it is, in that regard, merely borrowed, not owned. And, because the state does not own marriage, it is not a state prerogative to redefine marriage to adhere to an updated consensus on that narrow legal function. It is not appropriate for the state to dictate any definition of "marriage" to the rest of society, whether it be by judicial fiat, by legislative initiative, or by constitutional amendment.

If a state chooses to live up to the more modern understanding of its obligation to fairness and equality under the law by creating a gender-neutral form of civil union, that is certainly just and arguably wise. If a same-sex couple, having been properly joined by such a state-sanctioned civil union, chooses to call themselves "married," no one can or should stop them. If a church chooses to sanctify their union and call it "marriage" in the eyes of God, that is its right. If members of their community choose to honor the union with the same designation, then the communal sense of marriage will begin to evolve. If enough people in enough communities defer to the new usage, as appears to be happening, then the traditional concept of marriage will begin to lose its name and, our ability to conceptualize it thereby undermined, will slowly fade from our cultural memory, just as gayness did decades ago. And we will be culturally poorer for that, even as we are culturally more inclusive.

But that is a transformation that should be decided individual by individual in a cultural dialog over years or generations, in which some are free to preserve the old concepts and others to embrace the new until the weight of cultural consensus removes the last holdouts — or never does. It is not a transformation that should be enforced by political power.

Abortion

The issue of abortion is a perpetual plague on our electoral system. For the last forty years it has been the bogeyman in the shadows, an obsession for a few on both sides of the 'liberal'/'conservative' divide, ignored by the many until politicians need some phantom with which to terrify voters they think are becoming too happy with the opposition. Abortion is universally recognized as divisive and intractable, a subject to be used for advantage among partisans but avoided in polite company, a fuse you can light but cannot control. What makes it so? Why, when we seem able to find common ground on many other contentious issues, does this one belie our belief in the primacy of consensus? And why can we not let it go?

The heart of the answer is that Abortion, the national debate, is not a surgical procedure but a tangible metaphor for philosophical chasms that divide us. It is not one issue, but three, and not one subject, but a proxy for an entire policy debate that reaches into the fundaments of our politics and our society. That the participants in the debate are blind to that complexity only makes the problem more intractable.

The questions at the center of the abortion debate are primal: *what defines 'human life,' endowed with rights that demand protection by the state; and what is the state's obligation in protecting those rights? What is the legitimate function of government in regulating personal and social conduct? What is the proper role of judicial interpretation in construing the meaning of law?* Each faction in the abortion debate focuses almost exclusively on one of these questions and on one answer, which it assumes to be the only moral choice. And, in the realm of moral choices, compromise is impossible, passion is extreme, and civility disappears.

The result is that the factions, for all their argument, never actually engage; they merely talk past each other.

It would be comforting to think that, recognizing this problem, we could redirect the debate to overcome it. But, on this topic, polarization is not an artifact of miscommunication or misunderstanding. The poles exist because they must, because they reflect fundamental differences in interests and values and beliefs. No amount of pushing or coaxing will make them come together. The problem cannot be resolved; our best hope is to make it go away.

And go away it must, for it is corrupting both our civil discourse and our political process. The issues at the core of the abortion debate are important on their own merits — far more important than abortion itself. But, as long as abortion is on the table, debate devolves into argument and argument proceeds only within that narrow context. By focusing the debate so finely on a single manifestation of our philosophical differences, we run the risk of ignoring the broader implications of the choices we must make, to our ultimate detriment. If we are to choose wisely, we must agree to disagree on abortion so we may move beyond it.

Pro-Life: Defending Life

To the pro-life community, there is only one issue and one answer relevant to the debate over abortion: a fetus is a human life that demands protection under the law. In this view, debates about personal liberty or constitutional meaning are irrelevant.

Pro-choice advocates counter that the pregnant woman also has rights deserving of protection, and are incredulous when those rights are dismissed wholesale as beside the point. The fact of a moral tradeoff between the interests of the mother and those of the fetus seem so clear to them, in that limited context, that they cannot imagine how one could view it otherwise. But consider the following scenario.

Imagine a set of conjoined twins, George and Barack, who share enough vital organs that they cannot be separated without killing one of them. One day they go for a bicycle ride and, during the ride, because George misjudges the steering, they hit a rock and crash. George is unhurt, but Barack hits his head and ends up in a coma with no perceptible brain function.

The doctors say there is a small chance that Barack will die within the next three months; otherwise there is a good chance that brain function will resume within that time, and he will awake from his coma within another three months or so — and require years of therapy to fully recover. If brain function never returns, he will certainly die within the year.

During all this waiting for death or recovery, George will be tied to his brother — responsible for caring for him, feeding him, and seeing to his treatment, his activities constrained by their physical connection. On the other hand, if the two were to be surgically separated, then George could live out his life free from that constraint — but at the expense of ensuring that Barack, who is otherwise likely eventually to recover, will die.

Clearly George is facing a sudden, unexpected, enormous, life-altering burden, one that will last for years, and for which he may be unprepared. Separation from his twin would save him from that ordeal; does he have the right to order it?

This situation, while tragic, presents a fairly clear moral choice for most people: Barack's life — however enfeebled and tenuous it may currently be — demands deference, and must take precedence over George's burden. George can't order that they be separated until Barack is dead, by whatever criteria — physical or mental — death may be judged.

If you believe that a human fetus, regardless of age, constitutes 'human life' — however feeble and tenuous it may currently be — this is a realistic and illuminating analogy for an unwanted pregnancy and the choice of abortion: two individual lives physically linked, one independent and one dependent, one exercising free will and one insensate.

In fact, it is a good working analogy even if you don't believe that life begins at conception: whether you think it happens earlier or later, at *some* point a fetus *does* make the transition from mere human embryonic cells to a 'human life.' At that point the mother, under any system which affords human life an innate value and dignity, must lose her status as a wholly free agent with regard to their intertwined fate. In the parlance of law, the state, at that point, acquires a 'compelling interest' in protecting the rights of the individual — and, therefore, a right and a duty to interfere in otherwise personal decisions. I suspect that most rational people, whichever side of the abortion debate they inhabit, could agree at least on that much.

On the question of the "right to life," then, the crux of the issue is not *"does the state have a compelling interest after some point,"* but *"what is that point?"* At the extreme of 'pro-life' are those who contend it occurs at conception; at the extreme of 'pro-choice' are those who contend it occurs at birth. Most people, including most on the pro-choice side, find themselves where the Supreme Court did, somewhere in between, with the first trimester most likely 'embryo,' the third trimester most likely 'human,' and the second trimester hotly debated. But all of those answers — *even those on the pro-choice side* — are based on faith more than on science. The point is, *no one knows, objectively, what constitutes the boundary of 'human life.'* And there is not and will not be — *cannot be* — a consensus on the question.

But if we cannot find a consensus, what is the prudent and moral position for the state to take?

From the pro-life perspective, one would argue that, in the absence of consensus, the safe choice is to assume that life starts at conception and protect it appropriately: in that case, we never run the risk of extinguishing it. On its face, that is perfectly rational. It is, "Err on the side of caution." It is the justification cited for Illinois' moratorium on the death penalty, to ensure there will be no execution of the innocent; it is the "precautionary principle," the rationale used by environmentalists to argue for more regulation of greenhouse gases and industrial chemicals, even absent compelling evidence of their hazard; it is the philosophy enshrined in the Hippocratic oath: "First, do no harm."

As illustrated often in the context of environmental issues, however, regulation is not cost-free and the costs of regulation can sometimes be as harmful as what is being regulated. In the case of abortion, the costs of regulation are borne by pregnant women as a usurpation of their autonomy, and there is an equally reasonable argument that the resulting restrictions on liberty are far too onerous to be justified by 'potential' benefits. In that view, prohibiting abortion to prevent killing a 'potential life' would be like locking up each teenage boy until age 25 to save 'potential victims' from the possibility that he is a budding sociopath: that policy might (and undoubtedly would) save lives, but it is unacceptable in a free society.

From the opposite perspective, one can argue that, in the absence of consensus, the best course is no course at all — let the individual decide based on her own beliefs and her own conscience. That is the mainstream pro-choice position and it is appealing, not only in its promise of protection against a tyranny of a minority, but also in that it acknowledges the fundamentally personal nature of the decision.

But leaving it to individual conscience can also be problematic. Consider that, prior to the Civil War, a great many Americans believed slavery was justified precisely because the Negro was not quite human, at least not in the sense that the term applied to the rights to 'life, liberty, and the pursuit of happiness.' In the absence of consensus on the 'humanity of the Negro,' would it have been a proper and moral choice for the government to have deferred that judgment to the individual, rather than embodying the just choice in law by abolishing slavery? That was, after all, nominally what the Confederacy was established to achieve.

What, then, should we do? The best we can, I suppose, which is what the Supreme Court attempted in 1973. We know from philosophy and theology that, whatever else may make us human, consciousness and self-awareness are consistent themes; we know from science that these reside somewhere within the brain. We routinely use 'brain death' to put a boundary on the far end of life and it seems reasonable to do so on the near end as well. Other than religious dogma, there is no reason to suppose that a small collection of embryonic cells with no discernible nervous system or higher brain function is fully 'human life'; other than its locale, there is no reason to suppose that a wholly formed but yet-unborn fetus with both is not. In between, we just don't know, so we draw a line somewhere plausible: at the start of brain function, or at 'quickening,' or at the point of 'viability,' or at a fixed point in time. Exactly where the line lies depends as much on our ability to measure something as it does on what we measure.

Then, if we are prudent, we do everything we can to ensure we never have to decide a case close to the line.

That is the 'reasonable middle' that chronic negotiators constantly seek and, unsatisfactory as it is, it may be the only position that we, as a divided society, can tolerate. But do not confuse *reasonable* with *comfortable*. This is not a comfortable compromise and, so, it will never be a settled one. Those who believe that a fetus is a human being cannot — and ethically should not — be satisfied with such a result and will forever continue their efforts to undermine it. To the extent that they do so by persuasion, by trying to forge the consensus that eludes us, they should be honored for their moral integrity and commitment even as they are opposed.

Pro-Choice: Defending Liberty

Whereas pro-life advocates cannot see beyond the question of when life begins, the pro-choice community dismisses that question entirely as answered or unanswerable and, in either case, irrelevant. For them, the debate revolves around a different question: *absent* a compelling interest in protecting the rights of the individual human life, what role should — and what role may — the state play in regulating abortion? In the *pro-life* world-view, this question is moot because the compelling interest in protecting human life is assumed to exist; in the *pro-choice* world-view, this question is paramount because the compelling interest in protecting human life is assumed to be absent.

It is easy and satisfying to propose, as pro-choice advocates do, that the state can have no possible claim to jurisdiction in the realm of such private behavior — in the realm of something so *personal*. Indeed, any civil libertarian would wholeheartedly embrace that position, and the general public currently seems to agree. A review of the history of twentieth century political thought, legislation, and jurisprudence, however, lends neither a moral foundation nor a practical support for such a proposition.

The dominant theme in the progression of twentieth and twenty-first century politics and society has been the erosion of autonomy. From the emergence of socialism, to the New Deal and the Great Society, to the modern regulatory state, we have seen the ascendance of government authority and government oversight over ever finer details of our lives.

Today the federal government claims and exercises authority over what foods we may eat, what recreational and medicinal drugs we may ingest, what prices we may charge for our labor or for use of our capital, how much water we can use to flush our toilets, what safety features we must buy in a car, how we must insure our health. Various state and local governments regulate our choices for child care and education, whether we must have fluoride in our drinking water, whether we wear seatbelts in our cars, what our children must be taught about sexuality in school, what immunizations our children must receive, where we may smoke, the color we may paint our houses, how many cars we may have in our yards. Restrictions on personal financial arrangements abound. Public transit advocates want to restrict our choice to drive a car. Advocates of 'multiculturalism' propose speech codes to regulate the expression of 'hateful' ideas, while advocates for the arts propose to use tax money to create art that some find hateful. The religious right wants to require public prayer in the schools; the ACLU wants to abolish public prayer anywhere the government claims even a remote interest. Ralph Nader and John McCain, and many allies, want to prohibit us giving any significant amount of our money to those who would advocate for our political beliefs. Gun control advocates want to prohibit the private possession of firearms. Hard-core feminists join with the religious right to advocate continuation of existing restrictions on prostitution, or creation of broader restrictions on pornography.

Perhaps those regulations are worthwhile. Perhaps they are even worth the corresponding injury to individual liberty. But what can be more *personal* than your choice of what you eat and breathe, or how you value your own labor, or on what you spend your money, or why and with whom you have sex, or what you read and watch in the privacy of your home, or who you permit to view your naked body and under what circumstances, or how you express your pleasure or displeasure to others?

These and myriad other encroachments upon personal liberties exist because legislatures and executives, at the urging of citizens and with the blessing of the judiciary, have determined that some "compelling societal interest" — in order, in fairness, in justice, in safety, in comfort, in security, in morality — is more important than each particular liberty being curtailed. The same argument can be made for abortion: even those who support a woman's right to choose commonly concede that abortion itself is undesirable, that society would be better off if it happened less often. How far is it from that concession to a "compelling societal interest" in regulating it? And, given the endless examples of other behaviors that are fundamentally "personal" and that the government, nonetheless, regulates, what sets abortion apart as something morally beyond its reach?

For now the electorate seems to favor less, rather than more state control, so the pro-choice position seems safe. But the electorate can be fickle, and, in the absence of moral or legal constraints, a change of heart could easily reverse that. If the pro-choice side wants to ensure that a woman's right to choose remains unconstrained, they ought to direct their efforts less toward the specific issue of abortion and more toward a general change in the philosophical attitude about government intervention in *any* aspect of the lives of the citizens. As long as the government is allowed and encouraged to assert authority over *any* personal choices, including economic ones, the right to abortion is at risk.

Strict Construction: Defending the Rule of Law

It is ironic, given the fundamental philosophical questions about the nature of life and the role of government underlying the argument over abortion, that the major battleground in the debate is not in the churches and universities and legislatures, where such things have traditionally been hammered out, but in the high house of practical law, the Supreme Court. It is even more ironic that the debate in the court hinges not on these questions, but on an unrelated question of legal philosophy: what is the proper role of contemporary interpretation in the rule of law?

Imagine you buy a piece of property upon which to build your dream home. Before you build, you carefully research all the zoning laws in the town to make sure your house is in compliance. Yet, when you are finished, the town government declares you in violation of the law and orders you to tear down your house, on the grounds that it is "ugly." There is nothing anywhere in the ordinances regulating ugliness — in fact neither the word nor any of its synonyms appear in the text of the building code. Nonetheless, the zoning department finds that ugliness is forbidden due to "penumbras formed by emanations from specific items in the zoning code which help give them life and substance," penumbras and emanations which, taken together, imply that ugliness is proscribed.

That, roughly speaking, describes the constitutional foundation upon which the 'right' to abortion rests. And the decrepit nature of that foundation is reflected in the tenuous balance of opinion on the Supreme Court that

protects it from being overturned. If you find the language of the example —
"penumbras formed by emanations...that help give them life and substance"
— too bizarre or intangible to be taken seriously as a comfortable basis for
law, then you, too, might overturn the right to abortion: it is precisely those
words[1] that form the basis for the constitutional 'right to privacy' upon
which the right to abortion depends.

In deference to the Court, the point they were making is less esoteric
than the flowery language would imply. There have been many rulings from
the Court in which specific guarantees of the Bill of Rights — for example,
protection of free speech — have been logically extended to apply to other
activities that are not actually mentioned in the text — for example, freedom
of association. In this case the argument is that freedom of speech would be
an empty promise without freedom in the specific *means* of speech, one of
which is "association" with other, like-minded people (the same reasoning,
by the way, is behind the so called "money-equals-speech" decisions by the
court: that the promise of freedom of speech would be an empty promise
without freedom in the specific *means* of speech, one of which is the ability
to pay for publication and/or broadcast of that speech).

These specific, practical applications of a general principle found in the
text are the "emanations from those guarantees that help give them life and
substance."

To the extent that different provisions of the Constitution (and their
"emanations") seem to be specific instances of a more general philosophical
theme — for instance, of a 'right to privacy' — one might presume that a
statement of the general theme could, itself, also be considered a part of the
Bill of Rights. As the 10th amendment to the Constitution reminds us, the
Bill of Rights was never intended as an exhaustive list, was never intended
to imply an automatic grant of government authority over anything and
everything not explicitly proscribed within the text of the Constitution.
Quite the contrary: the intent of the Constitution was that authority
must be explicitly granted to the government, and that anything not so
granted was to be beyond its jurisdiction. Hence, it is not unreasonable to
extrapolate from the specifics identified in the Bill of Rights to the general
themes they represent. Those more general statements of principle are
the "penumbras" of the Griswold opinion, penumbras which become new
constitutional guarantees and creating, in turn, their own new "emanations"
and "penumbras" in an exponential cascade.

Clearly these acts of 'logical extension' are exercises in inductive
reasoning; equally clearly, they require subjective judgment. In legal theory,

---

1 U.S. Supreme Court, *Griswold v. Connecticut*, 1973

this process of logically extending the meaning of a law beyond the actual text is called *construction*.

Limits on the degree to which construction *may* or *should* be applied are ill defined; they are a matter of philosophy, not statute. Those who believe the judiciary should be free to apply construction liberally to situations either unanticipated by the original authors of the law or for which the social and political climate has changed since the law was written, are said to favor *broad construction*. Application of the principle of broad construction enabled the Supreme Court not only to infer a right to privacy from the provisions of the Bill of Rights but to enforce that judgment on the state, as well as the federal, governments. Those who would severely limit — or abolish entirely — the authority of the judiciary to apply construction are said to favor *strict construction*.

Although the progress of American legal theory since the 1930s has seen an enormous shift toward the use of broad construction in both statutory and Constitutional law, the degree to which construction should be the foundation of judicial action is far from settled and is the heart of the constitutional debate over abortion rights.

It may seem obvious to some that judges should be allowed leeway in applying laws to new situations in new times. No legislature can anticipate and accommodate social, political, and technological change even a decade ahead. Laws designed for the horse and carriage may not apply as well to the automobile, much less to the airplane. The law must be *adaptable*. And when the result is the discovery of new 'rights' for the citizens, it seems we all must benefit.

But, as the example of the ugly house shows, such freedom can impose a cost, in both the predictability and the fairness of law. If the meaning of law cannot be discerned from a reasonable reading of its text, how is one to conform to it? And, if the meaning is open to wide interpretation by different judges at different times, how is it to be applied equivalently to everyone? Laws created in the age of horse and carriage may not be well-suited to the age of the automobile and the airplane. But, perhaps, rather than depending on the courts to figure out how to make them apply anyway, we should, instead, demand that the legislature re-write them in a more appropriate fashion.

For *adaptation* — the remaking of law — is a legislative function, not a judicial one, assigned by the Constitution to the legislature and not to the courts. And for good reason: granted authority to decide what the law intends when its text is silent, or to redefine the meaning of that text when it is not, or to hold its provisions unenforceable because they are anachronistic or socially unacceptable, a judge becomes a de-facto legislator — but without the electoral exposure that constrains our actual representatives.

In the case of the Supreme Court, he becomes a *super-legislator*, unconstrained either by electoral exposure or by subsequent judicial or legislative review for, in our system, the nine appointed justices of the Supreme Court get the final word on the meaning of law. As George F. Will asked in his 1995 essay, "Eventful 1965,"[1] "Armed with emanating penumbras, what could the Court *not* do?" Even if you agree with what the Court *has* done with that authority, you may doubt the wisdom of allowing such unfettered power over the content of law by nine appointed individuals with lifetime tenure.

And indeed, what the Court has done with that authority over the last seventy or eighty years has been to vastly expand the scope and power of the federal government over behavior that was previously seen as the purview either of the individual states or of individual citizens. For this reason, the authority to 'legislate from the bench' implied by broad construction is seen by many as the greatest threat to liberty we face today, with the potential to completely undermine the rule of law.

It is, however, also the basis for a great many Supreme Court decisions on which the constitutional legitimacy of the modern regulatory/welfare state rests. Thus, a return to true strict construction, by returning authority for such issues as civil rights and environmental regulation from the federal to the state governments, could threaten a great deal more than just abortion rights.

Which is not to say we should not pursue that path. If liberty is truly at risk, perhaps the policy turmoil that could result, including the return of control over issues of liberty to the state level, is not too high a cost to pay for its preservation. Or perhaps it is. Those tradeoffs are central to the debate.

But those tradeoffs aren't *being* debated. Instead, the choice between broad and strict construction is being made, one judicial appointment at a time, almost entirely on the basis of its implications for the 1973 abortion decision. And those driving the process often seem unconcerned about construction itself, as long as the answer on abortion comes out in their favor.

The ultimate irony for both sides is that, for all the intensity of the fight over the Supreme Court, in the long run neither broad nor strict construction provides any guarantees for the fate of abortion rights. Broad construction, by itself, gives the Justices only the *tool* to protect abortion, not the *mandate*. Future justices could use the principle of broad construction to find different "emanations" and "penumbras" that point to different conclusions, limiting federal authority over state abortion laws, or authorizing the

---

1 Collected in *The Woven Figure*, Touchstone, 1997

federal government to enact its own restrictions, as it consistently and self-righteously does on all other drugs and medical procedures. Even given continued adherence to broad construction, the potential for pro-life or states' rights biases in future justices will ensure that the right to abortion is always just a few votes away from reconsideration.

Conversely, on the pro-life side, even a complete victory for strict construction would only throw abortion back into the individual state legislatures or state court systems, where the battle would continue on fifty fronts instead of just one. And on many of those fronts the legislatures and courts would prove openly and decisively hostile to the pro-life cause.

Incrementalism and Moral Authority

The old Bedouin homily about the camel's nose under the tent is well-known and respected by people and organizations dedicated to the preservation or overthrow of long-standing public policies. The American Civil Liberties Union opposes even modest and popular attempts to regulate speech because they know that each small exception to the basic principle is both a precedent and a starting point for the next assault. The National Rifle Association opposes even modest and popular gun control proposals for the same reason. And on regulation of both speech and guns, proponents propose exactly those modest and popular measures, hoping to gain the precedent and the new starting point for yet further regulation.

Abortion activists perform the same dance, with opponents proposing "common sense" restrictions, proponents reacting with shock and outrage, and each side portraying the other as "extreme." What makes the entire process worse in this case is that many of the actual proposals are empty: for the most part, incremental restrictions on speech or guns really are intended to significantly affect the ability of people to speak or to own guns; the most commonly-proposed incremental restrictions on abortion could, however, be classified more as nuisances than as restrictions, meant only to trim at the margins. In general, the argument is mostly symbolic, rather than substantive.

The primary forms of "common sense" restrictions proposed by pro-life advocates are procedural, and would merely make abortion either a bit more difficult to obtain or a bit more difficult to perform: waiting periods to allow abortion-seekers time to change their minds; 'technique' regulations to limit the use of particular procedures; parental notification requirements for minors. Quite aside from inconveniencing a few abortion seekers and abortion providers, the ultimate goal of these restrictions is to establish the precedent that restrictions, in the abstract, are acceptable. From that point forward, the argument over abortion shifts from *whether* it may be regulated to *how*.

Thus the restrictions proposed are chosen primarily for their appeal to common sense and emotional hot buttons — for their probable popularity. That not only increases the likelihood some restrictions will become law, it also forces the pro-choice community onto the record as opposing something that most people want.

Pro-life advocates try, whenever possible, to portray pro-*choice* advocates as pro-*abortion*, in hopes of enlisting the sympathies of the large pool of people who are generally pro-choice, yet find abortion itself distasteful or even repugnant. Proposals to restrict certain abortion techniques, such as the infamous argument over 'partial-birth' abortion, play upon these sympathies, picking out the most viscerally disturbing images of surgical procedures and proposing to ban those as a proxy for all abortions. These are not logical arguments in any sense; if the moral status of a fetus is such that abortion, itself, is acceptable, then technique ought to be irrelevant. But they are effective in associating 'pro-choice' with 'cruel' and 'extreme' in the minds of those to whom the issue is ambiguous.

To counter this, pro-choice advocates take great pains to describe the emotional nature of abortion for those who choose it, their personal ambivalence, and perhaps even guilt. They emphasize the difficult and wrenching nature of the decision, and use that to argue for leaving the government out of it. Pro-life advocates then call for waiting periods and counseling for those seeking abortion, playing upon precisely that emotional turmoil. They argue that such a difficult and wrenching decision should not be made precipitously or in ignorance, that counseling followed by a waiting period of a few days, far from being too onerous, would allow time for reflection to resolve precisely that ambivalence and guilt. Again, those who would deny such opportunities for reflection are portrayed as interested not in the needs of women in crisis but only in advocating for abortion.

While arguments over technique and timeline are aimed at discomfort with abortion itself, parental notification is an issue that resonates with many people precisely because it has very little to do with abortion and very much to do with governmental abrogation of parental rights.

In general, doctors and nurses cannot provide *any* non-emergency medical care — even aspirin or a cough drop — to a minor without first requesting permission from the parents. Abortion is a surgical procedure, and advocates for abortion insist that it is inextricably bound to the general subject of "women's health." Why then, ask proponents of parental notification requirements, should abortion be excepted from the general rule? Because a young girl might be afraid to go to her parents? The same could be said of a teenage boy in the emergency room because he just wrecked the family car. Because the parents might deny permission? Perhaps they should; perhaps father *does* know best. Are we to second-guess parents on whether their children have jobs, or drive, or attend church, or play sports, or date, or get orthodontia, or on other issues involving their children's welfare? It is precisely the fact that excepting parental involvement for this decision, and *only* for this decision, seems arbitrary and extreme that the issue is in play.

For their part, the pro-choice community has its own "common sense" issue with which they attempt to split the pro-life forces, forcing their own camel's nose under the tent. Faced with a claim that abortion should be outlawed to protect the fetus, they bring up the dual subjects of rape and incest, making the case that only a heartless ideologue could deny a rape or incest victim the opportunity to terminate a resulting pregnancy. Both the woman's status as a victim and the reprehensible nature of the crimes themselves plead the case for compassion; and making the victim carry a fetus to term merely extends the original assault on her body and on her dignity.

The argument is, of course, spurious. *Moral* and *painless* are not synonyms. The fact that an act of human evil has created a painful moral choice does not invalidate morality. Moreover, the circumstance itself, for all its dramatic power, probably accounts for a miniscule proportion of actual abortions; this is an argument about the extreme, not the norm.

Nonetheless, the argument succeeds. Faced with such an ugly consequence to their moral consistency many pro-life supporters, and most of the politicians who pledge allegiance to their cause, falter and compromise, conceding an exception for those circumstances.

And of course, that concession undermines their original moral argument: if these 'lives' may be exempted from protection, perhaps they aren't really 'lives' at all.

Agree to Disagree

An embryo or fetus with the higher cerebral functions not yet engaged — pre-sentient and without the consciousness from which may eventually emerge self-awareness and free will — has the *potential* to become human not the *quintessence* of humanity. In my areligious worldview, with no faith in some revealed and ancient catechism to instruct me on whether or not a soul exists independent of corporeal sentience and on when such a soul might manifest, I cannot justify surrendering to government unfettered authority over a palpable liberty that already exists in the defense of some ineffable essence that may yet come to be.

And yet, I must agree with the religious conservatives — not out of any theological insight but out of a humanist and libertarian respect for human dignity — that such potential for ineffable essence *has value*. And, therefore, I equally cannot countenance the view that discarding such potential is an act utterly without moral import. Nor can I countenance the view, extreme but seemingly common on the far "left" and particularly among the feminist fringe, that such ineffable essence somehow suddenly and miraculously materializes at the emergence from the birth canal and not an instant before.

It seems clear, to me at least, that at some point, *after* the cerebral cortex begins functioning and *prior* to full-term birth, the potential of a human fetus transforms into the quintessence of a human baby. It seems equally clear that by exercising one choice — to carry a pregnancy to that point of quintessence — a woman, herself, circumscribes other choices including, in particular, the choice to have an abortion thereafter.

And, even if you believe that prior to the point of quintessence a fetus or embryo lacks sufficient moral standing to justify what would otherwise be an improper government interference with a woman's autonomy, that does not mean you must believe abortion is either desirable or inconsequential. It certainly doesn't mean you must accept that abortion should be a casual and common act.

As with obnoxious speech, or pornography, or flag burning, or drug use, or sexual appetites, or greed, or smoking, or gun possession, or eating trans-fats, or driving an SUV, we may and should separate the questions of whether and when one ought to engage in a particular behavior from the questions of whether and when the government may assume authority to regulate it. And, as with obnoxious speech, or pornography, or flag burning, or drug use, or sexual appetites, or greed, or smoking, or gun possession, or eating trans-fats, or driving an SUV, how objectionable abortion may be is a matter of degree, a function of how far along the path from human tissue to human being a particular embryo has progressed. Discarding a blastocyst may be a relatively minor thing; discarding a fetus on the cusp of consciousness is almost certainly not, especially given how little we know about the nature and timing of that mysterious transition.

In that sense, the frequently disparaged "moderate" notion that abortion should be "safe, legal, and rare" is not some ugly political compromise but an honest, well-reasoned, and principled statement of humanist values — provided, at least, that an emphasis on rarity over legality advances along with fetal development. It is also fundamentally 'conservative' in the traditional libertarian and cultural senses of 'conservatism': the coupling of legality with rarity implies a reliance on non-binding and apolitical social sanction — on social condemnation and a sense of personal shame and (dare I say it?) a modicum of intolerance — as a legitimate and effective alternative to government regulation for controlling anti-social — or merely disagreeable — behavior.

One of the absurdities of abortion politics is the contradictions inherent in the political alliances it creates. Pro-choice has traditionally been associated with the political left, which consistently advocates for more rather than less government intervention in almost everything — *except* in a woman's right to choose abortion. Pro-life has traditionally been associated with the political right, which claims to favor less government regulation of almost everything — *except* access to abortion. The sad fact is that when it comes to abortion, consistency and logical rigor are rare.

If that was the limit of its effect — that on this one issue we succumb as a society to the lure of the irrational — we might dismiss it as an aberration, even laugh about it, and move on. But instead the effect spreads like a plague over our entire political process.

In the incredibly close election of 2004, between Al Gore and George W. Bush, abortion may well have been the issue that pushed the result into the Supreme Court and ignominy. Again and again during that election I was told by people I knew, and read in opinion pieces and letters in the paper by others — a few of whom even preferred the Republican proposals on almost every other issue — that, as bad as Al Gore was, they would vote for him to prevent George W. Bush from appointing pro-life justices to the Supreme Court. The Democratic Party made that appeal a central part of their campaign strategy. The religious right can be counted on to vote as a bloc against anyone who declares himself pro-choice, regardless of his positions on other issues. The one question that will be asked of any Supreme Court nominee — indirectly, of course — is how he or she would vote on abortion. And the confirmation vote in the Senate will break down almost exclusively along pro-choice/pro-life lines based on the perceived answer to that question.

If this was an issue fundamental to our national survival, or a determinant of the nature of our society, or even something that could be settled once and for all, such emphasis might be justified. But it is none of those. It is a never-ending side-show to the central questions facing us: how much liberty should we trade for security; what is our civic obligation to our fellow citizens; is the individual or the society the fundamental measure of worth; can democracy survive extremes of wealth and poverty; what is law, and how should it be interpreted; what should be our role in the world?

But these questions, debated as they are, too frequently take a back seat to single-issue politics, led by the monomania over abortion.

What are we to do?

The primary thing we can do is to recognize the question will never be resolved. It is with us for the long-term. No election is pivotal, no gain or setback is permanent, and no amount of persuasion will change the minds of the opposition. So don't let it consume you. Agree to disagree. Pay attention to something else for a while.

A corollary to that is that neither side of the issue has a monopoly either on truth or on compassion. The issues are not as black-and-white as they seem to you. You may disagree with your opponents, but they are not villains, and you owe them respect and consideration.

As for the debate itself, focus first on the one thing both sides generally agree on: there should be fewer abortions. Then figure out how to get there within the constraints that exist. For the pro-life community, that may mean giving consideration to better sex-education and better access to contraception. For the pro-choice community, that may mean giving consideration to education in the *morality* of sex, rather than merely in the *mechanics*. For the pro-life community, that may mean supporting an effective economic safety net for the poor. For the pro-choice community, that may mean supporting market strategies to lift the poor out of the safety net into the middle class. For the pro-life community, that may require redefining their understanding of family. For the pro-choice community, that may require redefining their understanding of rights and responsibilities. For the pro-life community, that may mean less reproach and more sympathy. For the pro-choice community, that may mean less sympathy and more judgment. For everyone, that may mean a commitment to create and support realistic alternatives to abortion for women pregnant and unprepared for motherhood.

Beyond that, be consistent. If you don't want the government regulating your body, support the general concept of limits on government authority. If you generally want the government to intervene in private decisions, don't act indignant when they tell you what to do.

And, if nothing else, recognize that other issues matter. Recognize that, in the long run, you are most likely to get an abortion policy you can live with if you elect a government you can live with, with a philosophy that generally respects your values and a consistent policy agenda that fulfills that philosophy. Vote your conscience, certainly, but vote for the long-term and the broad view, and abortion will take care of itself.

Social Security and the Trust Fund

The recurring debate over reform of the Social Security system has taken on all the qualities of an argument between 6-year-olds, reduced in essence to the intellectual content of the classic "Is not!," "Is so!."

In the arena of solutions, that at least has some justification: much of the argument is over values and preference rather than over facts. Privatization is either "*too risky*" or not, reflecting judgment on risk tolerance not on returns; reform of the Cost of Living Adjustment (COLA) formula is either "*a benefit cut*" or not, depending on whether you view projections of benefit level increases as moral pledges of future obligation or merely as neutral accommodations to inflation; extending the payroll tax cutoff upward in income is either "*fair*" or not, depending on whether you view the program as insurance or investment and on how you view the obligations of the "rich" for the welfare of the "poor."

But on the issue of the Social Security trust fund — "*secured investment*" or "*accounting fiction*" — we should be able to avoid those value judgments and look at numbers: will the trust fund provide the resources we need to cover shortfalls or not? Unfortunately, even in that realm value judgments abound, and the shorthand language we use to discuss it — "full faith and credit" vs. "IOUs" — engages the emotions rather than assists the intellect.

I come down on the side of "*accounting fiction*," but rather than merely assert that and assume it is self-evident to every right-thinking person, I want to exhibit my reasoning for anyone to examine.

To begin we must understand why we have a trust fund in the first place. Everyone agrees that, at some time in the next 15 to 25 years, demographics will push spending on Social Security obligations above the revenue raised by the payroll tax that funds them — that expenditures will exceed receipts and that we will need to begin making up the difference somehow. In a world without the trust fund, we would have three options: *decrease spending* (that is, cut benefits or other programs), *borrow money* (that is, run up debt), or *increase taxes* (that is, extract more revenue from the taxpayers and the economy). There is actually a fourth option — devalue the dollar by printing money — but even politicians who have historically flirted with that economically disastrous ploy are probably not foolish enough to use it in this case, if for no other reason than that the COLA provisions ensure that the resulting inflation would drive up the obligations at least as fast as the money supply.

The demographics are sobering: in the foreseeable future the number of workers paying to support each Social Security beneficiary will reach two; that is, every working American will be responsible for, in addition to his own needs and those of his family, *half* of the retirement benefit for someone else. To cover that obligation would require either massive budget cuts elsewhere or massive borrowing or massive increases in the payroll tax collected to fund Social Security.

More than 30 years ago, the Greenspan commission concluded that all these options were untenable — that neither cutting nor borrowing nor taxing at such levels could be sustained. The Social Security trust fund was specifically envisioned as a means to avoid such untenable schemes.

What does the trust fund do? In principle it is an investment account that we can use to fund future obligations. The revenue generated by the current payroll tax is more than we need to fund current Social Security obligations, and the excess is deposited into the trust fund, which invests the money in U.S. Government Bonds; the bonds pay interest, which increases the value of the trust fund over time. When we need the money in the future, we will liquidate the bonds and use the proceeds to cover the shortfall in the Social Security budget.

It sounds quite secure and straightforward: the money is in the account, and the investments are backed by the "full faith and credit of the United States government," which is not going to default on them. But is the reality as secure and straightforward as it seems?

When we ask whether the money in the trust fund will be sufficient to cover future obligations we do not merely count the money we've deposited; we also count the interest we will earn on that money. We, in fact, depend on that investment income to make the numbers work. But where does that income come from? The answer is: it comes from the federal treasury; interest paid on federal government bonds is an expense in the federal government budget. And, when the bonds are liquidated, the federal government will have three options for raising the extra money required to pay that expense: *cut the budget elsewhere, borrow money*, or *increase taxes*. Notice those are the same three options that were available for paying the Social Security shortfall directly in the first place.

Imagine that the bonds in the trust fund are held for an average of 30 years and return an average annual interest rate of 6.4% (the average in 2004 for all the assets in the trust fund according to the Social Security Administration web-site). When we liquidate those bonds, the accrued interest will amount to over 5 times the original principal. Thus, less than 20% of the money paid out on the bond represents the original money put in and more than 80% must come from the federal treasury and be financed by budget cuts or by borrowing or by taxes.

So what have we accomplished by carefully investing in the trust fund over all those years? We have succeeded in saving enough to cover about

20% of the Social Security shortfall and have replaced the other 80% of the cutting/borrowing/taxing needed to cover that shortfall with — *cutting/ borrowing/taxing to pay interest on the trust fund bonds*. It may be argued that taxing to cover bond interest is somehow different because it comes from the *income tax* rather than from the *payroll tax*; but ultimately it is the same money collected in a different form. Further, even that subtle difference is a matter of political will, not of principle: the form of taxation used to fund either is entirely at the discretion of the Congress and could be changed by them at any time. In the end, if the level of budget-cutting, borrowing, or taxation required to pay for the Social Security shortfall directly was untenable, then it is just as untenable when transformed into budget-cutting, borrowing, or taxation to pay interest on the trust fund bonds.

Of course the precise degree to which the value of the trust fund lies in interest income rather than principal depends on your assumptions about rates of return and how long the bonds are held, so 80% may not be the right number. And to the extent interest is accumulated in the account incrementally as accrued rather than as a lump sum at bond maturity — to the extent we pay the interest as we go along now rather than putting it off until later — the cost may at least be spread out over time. But in practice we can safely ignore those details, because the true situation is even worse.

So far, we've assumed that, even if we're not paying the interest as we go, we are at least accumulating the principal — that the money received from bond sales is put away somewhere to be returned in the future. In fact, it is not: we've been spending both that money and the interest accrued on it as fast as it's come in. The description of the trust fund as an IOU is more than just emotional rhetoric: it reflects the underlying reality. When we liquidate the bonds in the trust fund, the *entire* amount paid out will come from *contemporaneous* federal revenues, backed by some combination of taxes and loans and cuts in other parts of the budget.

In reality, the amount of money required from contemporaneous federal revenues to cover the Social Security shortfall will be *the entire amount of the shortfall — just as if the trust fund had never existed*. True, it won't come from the Social Security account (backed by the payroll tax); instead it will come from the general fund (backed by the income tax). Perhaps there is some advantage to one over the other, but it strikes me that the taxpayers and the economy of the future will not care overly about exactly which mechanism is used to extract that wealth from productive use.

Worse, in that regard the trust fund represents yet *another* kind of accounting fiction. By intent and by law the Social Security program is supposed to operate and fund itself independently of the rest of the government. But the trust fund, relying as it does on bond interest payments to meet its obligations, subverts that intention by building a dependence on general fund revenue into Social Security — by creating a backdoor mechanism for transferring money from the rest of the government into the Social Security program.

I am not an economist, but then this is not a matter of abstruse economic theory. It is a matter of simple cash-flow, and the flow in all cases is from taxpayers to retirees. Why, then, do some people who should know better seem to put such faith in the trust fund?

At least in part, that "faith" is really more a political calculation than a true belief. On paper, the Social Security Administration is, in fact, solvent. It has enough assets — government bonds in the Trust Fund — to allow it to cover its obligations. The administrators and trustees of the SSA can testify to congress, without lying, that they have been fiscally prudent and that the SSA can meet its obligations; and the politicians can duly report that reassurance to their constituents to keep them happy and calm.

The problem is not that the Social Security Administration doesn't have assets on its books to cover its obligations. The problem is that liquidating those assets in order to use them will create a fiscal crisis in the *rest* of the government as it is required to divert an enormous fraction of its resources into making payments on those bonds. That is, the Social Security Administration will maintain its solvency by pushing the rest of the federal government into *insolvency*.

One of the accusations leveled at President Bush and his supporters, when they attempted to reform the Social Security program, was that their real agenda was not to reform Social Security but to raze it. Although nothing they proposed came even close to that, it is true that the particular form of their primary proposal, the limited privatization of personal Social Security accounts, served the purpose of undermining the central tenet of Social Security in particular and of the welfare state in general: that personal welfare and security is the responsibility of the government rather than of the individual. Even if you give them the benefit of the doubt, if you grant that their primary concern was the solvency of the Social Security system, they also made no secret of their preference for individual responsibility over collective responsibility, for market activity over governmental activity. If they could ensure the continued viability of Social Security (a questionable proposition) and by the same measure rein-in the welfare state and undermine its philosophical foundation they would happily have done so.

What is never mentioned, but which I think is equally true, is that *those on the other side would just as happily do the opposite*, would *expand* the welfare state and *reinforce* its philosophical foundation. And the looming Social Security shortfall presents them with an opportunity to do so.

Once we begin liquidating bonds in the trust fund to cover obligations, the government has no choice — "full faith and credit" — but to honor those bond obligations by raising whatever revenue is necessary to pay for them. Realistically that means a dramatic increase in borrowing and in income taxes. To the Greenspan commission, thirty years ago, and to the current 'conservative' leadership now, such an increase is untenable; to the stalwart defenders of Social Security as-is, such an increase is not only tenable, *it is the very policy they've been advocating for decades*: the means to a comprehensive escalation of revenue to the federal government, the better to provide for the litany of public services and social regulation to which they aspire. *If that level of borrowing and taxation is not only acceptable but desirable, then there is indeed no crisis*; and if current policy forces us toward that desirable end then it rather constitutes an *anti*-crisis.

The beauty — to them — of the trust fund is that it takes the lid off. As borrowing and tax rates rise to cover bond payments, money pours into the general fund. If (inevitably, if we must avoid a shortfall) the rate is set a little too high — if the increased borrowing and taxation raises more money than Social Security actually needs — that money, as general revenue not earmarked for Social Security, is available for spending on other "urgent" forms of social welfare. And when, after several decades, the baby boom generation begins to die off and Social Security obligations recede, those borrowing and taxation policies remain, along with the habits of the social welfare mind-set that they feed. Thus is born a grander and more active social welfare state than we would ever have approved otherwise.

Is that an explicit agenda? Is there a conscious 'liberal' conspiracy to use Social Security as the launching pad to a grander and more benevolent federal government? Probably not — no more than there is a 'conservative' conspiracy to use Social Security as a stake to drive through the heart of the social safety net. But when a particular policy advances your long-term goals, then doubts about its short-term effect become much easier to dismiss.

Whatever you may think of the 'conservative' proposals for Social Security reform — and in particular the proposals for privatization deserve skepticism — the fundamental debate is over whether or not there is actually a crisis in the current system. To those who favor a general and large-scale expansion of the federal welfare state supported by a seemingly boundless capacity for "greedy corporations" and "the rich" to supply funding, the Social Security trust fund backed by that capacity is both solvent and adequate. To those who favor smaller and less obtrusive government with leaner claims both on individual liberty and on individual and societal wealth, the Social Security trust fund is an accounting sham that merely obscures the coming disaster.

Who is right? It depends on your view of the welfare state and of our capacity for sustaining it with loans and tax revenue. Which means neither side will be won over, even when one side eventually wins.

The argument over Social Security is at root a continuation of the more fundamental argument over social welfarism itself: *Is Not! Is So!*

Tort Reform

Civil litigation is eating us alive.

According to a 2010 report from the U.S. Chamber of Commerce, civil lawsuits in the United States cost small businesses over $100 billion per year.[1] In 2013, the Association of Trial Lawyers of America pegged total litigation costs to the overall economy at more than $230 billion annually,[2] on the order of 1½% of GDP. A 2010 study from by J. Mark Ramseyer and Eric B. Rasmusen at the Harvard Law School[3] characterized the American civil law environment this way:

> The U.S. is notorious not in the way it handles first-order law... but in the way it handles second-order law.... In the typical accident or contract claim, U.S. courts do reasonably well. They may face somewhat more litigation than other rich democracies, but not much. In the second-order cases, however, U.S. courts entertain claims that courts in other well-functioning economies would dismiss in short order. In the process, they necessarily create a drag on American business. Thus, we may say, as M.A. Petersen did in 1986...:
>
>> "Increasingly, the civil justice system seems like two different systems. One is a stable system that provides modest compensation for plaintiffs who claimed slight or moderate injuries in automobile and other accidents that have been the major source of litigation for 50 years. The second is an unstable system that provides continually increasing awards for claims for serious injuries in any type of lawsuit, and for all injuries, serious or not, in product liability, malpractice, street hazards, and workplace accidents."

1 *https://www.uschamber.com/press-release/lawsuits-cost-small-businesses-105-billion-study-shows*
2 *http://www.statisticbrain.com/civil-lawsuit-statistics*
3 "Comparative Litigation Rates," Discussion Paper No. 681, J. Mark Ramseyer and Erik B. Rasmusen, John. M Olin Center for Law, Economics, and Business, 11/2010

No doubt some of this can be attributed to the exploding complexity of our society and of our lives, and to the increasing degree to which our daily interactions — from business transactions to social engagements — involve strangers or casual acquaintances rather than friends and neighbors. In a world dominated by the remote and the impersonal, disputes become formalized; what long-term neighbors might iron out by compromise, mindful of their unavoidable future interactions and overlapping social networks, strangers will treat as war.

But that is not the whole story. American litigiousness has been exacerbated, and in many ways encouraged, by changes in the legal system and by evolving social attitudes. Our sense, and our legal definitions, about what constitute liability and moral responsibility is far less strict than it used to be. We place less emphasis on personal responsibility and more on the moral status of victimhood. And we have greatly expanded the degree to which we expect and demand government to regulate interpersonal interactions.

Added to this general trend toward litigiousness, we also have two new phenomena which intensify litigation itself: an increasing tendency for juries to use escalating punitive damages to express their general mistrust of, and contempt for, corporations; and a decreasing respect for the scientific method and the body of scientific knowledge in the evaluation of evidence. These are of particular concern as more and more litigation involves disputes over potentially widespread damage caused by technological activities: a notorious example is the Dow-Corning breast implant settlement, a $3.2 billion dollar award (enough to bankrupt the company involved) in a case for which the evidence of either actual damage or corporate malfeasance was essentially non-existent.[1]

Taken together, all these factors create a major problem for our civil tort system: the perception, frequently justified, that it amounts to little more than a complex and expensive lottery, a lottery for which the cost of a defendant's ticket is prohibitively high while the cost of a plaintiff's ticket is, due to contingency fee arrangements, nearly nothing. It is a lottery in two senses: first, in the increasing degree to which the ability of a defendant to pay, and the emotional susceptibility of a particular jury, have as much or more to do with a verdict than the behavior in question — the degree to which the outcome is a matter of chance, rather than reason; and second, in the increasingly arbitrary and exorbitant awards for punitive damages — in the potential for a blockbuster payoff that those exorbitant awards make possible.

---

1 "Panel Confirms No Major Illness Tied to Implants," G. Kolata, *New York Times*, 21 June 1999.

There have been many books written analyzing the various aspects of these changes to society and litigation — my favorites are *The Death of Common Sense*, by Philip K. Howard, *The Litigation Explosion*, by Walter K. Olson, and *Jurismania: The Madness of American Law*, by Paul F. Campos — and reading them could leave you feeling overwhelmed, convinced that there is no way out of the hole we've dug for ourselves. However, without resolving the underlying social and moral issues, I believe it is still possible, by focusing narrowly on the incentives created by the prospect of a legal lottery, to bring some semblance of sanity back to the civil tort system.

To the extent civil tort is perceived as a lottery, it attracts players — people with no real grievance but with a story plausible enough to buy them a ticket — and bookmakers — lawyers willing to help players into the game for a cut of the winnings. The high reward potential and relatively low entrance cost encourages a great deal of speculation and risk-taking, especially for lawyers who can spread their bets across many cases. And, unlike in a normal lottery, a winning strategy in one bet becomes precedent for the next, improving the odds over time for the winners.

To the extent civil tort is perceived as a lottery, it also elicits hedging — defendants buying out of the game early to avoid the risk of the play, regardless of the validity of the charge against them. It has become common advice to corporate defendants to "settle this out," often without even assessing the merits of the case; the potential for an enormous punitive award simply cannot be eliminated, even when the claims seem groundless or absurd.

Both of these practices are inefficient (in economic terms) and unjust (in moral terms), but tragically common. By themselves, changes that would remove the incentive toward such behavior would be a major step away from legal insanity. To that end, I propose the following plan for reforming the civil tort system:

Limit plaintiff awards to damages only.

The purpose of the civil tort system is the redress of actual damage, not the general transfer of wealth from defendants to plaintiffs. Compensation for the damage done serves the purpose of individual justice for the plaintiff, and no further compensation is required.

For the purposes of assessing damages, the following should be taken into consideration:

- actual out-of-pocket costs associated with repairs/replacement
- opportunity costs
- expenses (excluding legal fees) associated with bringing suit, such as court costs and days off from work for the trial.

These may be considered the 'actual' or accountable costs, because they are both measurable and beyond the control of the plaintiff. In addition, the following costs should be considered:

- aggravation costs (including pain and suffering)
- legal fees

These may be considered 'virtual,' or unaccountable costs because they are, to a large degree, within the plaintiff's control: they depend as much on his/her state of mind, his/her reaction to the injury, and his/her preferences for representation, as they do on external factors.

As a general principle, awards for unaccountable costs should be tightly correlated to the severity of the injury; for instance, it makes no sense to provide millions of dollars in legal fees to pursue thousands of dollars in actual damage. A reasonable approach would be to limit the size of awards for aggravation costs and legal fees to some fraction (perhaps 50%) of the actual damages awarded.

Note that this does not require — nor should it lead to — legal restrictions on what lawyers may charge their clients; it merely limits what the courts will extract from the defendant to pay for it.

There is one other category of cost that should be taken into consideration, solely at the discretion of the trial judge, when calculating awards:

- obfuscation and delay costs

These are legal costs incurred due solely to actions by the defendant or the plaintiff to obscure the facts of the case, unnecessarily delay the legal proceedings, or in any other way manipulate the legal system to prevent justice from being done. Obviously such things are hard to assess, but just as we trust judges with the authority to use their best judgment in issuing contempt citations, we should be willing to allow the same latitude in these cases. In the best scenario, awards to cover such costs would be paid not by the defendant or the plaintiff, but by the lawyers who created the costs in the first place.

Award punitive damages, if any, to the government for use as a benefit for the public at large, rather than to the individual plaintiff.

The purpose of punitive damages is to punish the defendant for reprehensible behavior, thus serving the purpose of social justice. The fact that the punishment also results in a benefit to someone is incidental, not primary. In the criminal justice system, we neither require nor expect the punishment of the criminal to benefit the victim; rather, we consider recompense and punishment to be completely unrelated, the former reflecting a moral obligation between the criminal and his/her victim, the latter reflecting a social covenant between the criminal and his/her society. Why should civil law be different?

Similarly, in the criminal justice system, juries assess culpability, but it is left to judges to determine the appropriate degree of punishment. This tends to promote consistency in punishment, making the system less a lottery and more a stable mechanism for enforcing accountability. The civil law should treat punishment decisions in the same way. To further facilitate consistency, legislatures should create guidelines for the size of punitive damages, based, as in criminal penalties, on the damage (both moral and economic) done; reasonable guidelines might take the form of specified cash awards, or a percentage (greater than 100%) of the benefit generated by the offending behavior, or perhaps, in the case of a corporation, a percentage of annual corporate profit.

A slight variation on the theme of using punitive damages to benefit the public interest broadens the scope of how that benefit is to be allocated. There are other organizations besides the government which exist primarily to serve the public good; perhaps these, rather than the government itself, could be the beneficiaries of such awards. It would be justice, indeed, if some coalition of environmental organizations received the punitive damages awarded in some high-profile environmental lawsuit; not only would the defendant be punished for damaging the environment, but the money paid out would actually pay to help defend the environment against future depredations.

Of course, such extra-governmental awards would need to be closely controlled to avoid conflicts-of-interest, in which organizations were both participants-in and beneficiaries-of a lawsuit -- just as government awards, for similar reasons, could not directly benefit the justice system which created them. But with proper safeguards this could be an efficient way to transform a net cost on society to a net benefit.

Restrict the basis for lawyer contingency-fee arrangements to plaintiff awards.
Legal fees are a private arrangement between a plaintiff and his/her lawyer, while punishment is a public arrangement between a miscreant and society. As lawyers are eager to point out whenever a disapproving public condemns some activity in defense of the indefensible, a lawyer's duty is to serve the interest of his/her client, not the interest of the public; if the public interest is served in the process, it is by accident, not by design. So be it. The interest of the client is limited to the compensation received; legal fees should follow suit.

Note that this does not limit the size of the contingency fee as a fraction of the plaintiff award; it merely states that, as a matter of law, the *punitive damages* may not be counted in calculating that fraction because they do not belong to the plaintiff.

As a purely practical matter, if, as suggested above, court-awarded legal fees were limited to some fraction of the actual damages, the market would largely enforce this even if the law did not — very few plaintiffs would be willing to cut seriously into their actual compensation to pay legal fees beyond those the court awarded. Nonetheless, as a statement of principle, to make unambiguous the nature of the relationship between the attorney, the plaintiff, and the court, this restriction would have great symbolic value.

It may be argued that these restrictions, enforced either by the law or by the market, would deny many the opportunity to pursue their grievances. This is undoubtedly true, but consider: is this really such a bad thing? If the damage done is so small that it is not worth a lawyer's time to pursue it, does it belong in civil court at all? Is this the best use of the limited resources of our legal system? I would say no. In such cases, small-claims court, or arbitration, or an appeal for regulatory relief would be much more efficient mechanisms for resolving disputes. A legal system which encouraged the use of these less expensive and less parsimonious routes to justice is to be desired.

Finally, as a further step toward reducing the random element of tort awards, particularly in technology-related cases, I propose the following process to restore confidence in the scientific method and scientific knowledge in deciding such cases:

Have the court provide independent experts to assist the judge and jury in assessing the facts of the case.

In cases for which 'expert' witnesses play a crucial role in elucidating underlying circumstances, liability, and/or actual damages, the interest of truth demands the availability of an impartial, intellectually-rigorous, and widely-accepted assessment of the facts at hand. The appearance of dueling experts, paid by the parties to the dispute and contradicting each other, cannot provide this. While it is not reasonable to prevent the litigants from presenting these experts, it would be prudent to supplement them with court-appointed experts, drawn from the ranks of mainstream academia or professional organizations to represent the court itself, not either of the litigants, and paid by the court from fees collected from both sides. As a matter of practice, these witnesses should be called to testify after all other 'expert' testimony is complete, so they could offer, in addition to an independent assessment of the facts, a critique of the methods and conclusions provided by the litigants' witnesses.

Overall, these measures restore a sense of predictability and stability to a legal system run amok. By aligning the legal processes with their underlying purposes, they eliminate the legal lottery, in which plaintiffs see even the most minor incidents as a shot a great wealth, lawyers pervert the most innocent of motives into nefarious evil in their bid to maximize fees, and defendants settle even baseless cases rather than risk open-ended exposure at the hands of an ignorant and emotional jury.

Immigration Policy

Imagine (I know it's hard at the moment) that the Red Sox have again won the pennant and are headed for the World Series. It's been an exciting year with an enthusiastic response from the fans, so there are an extraordinarily large number of people holding season- and pre-purchased tickets that will reserve seats for the series. The number of seats available to the general public is somewhat limited.

The Red Sox management carefully assesses the amount of room they have — they squeeze in some extra seats here and there — and the capacity of their restroom facilities and (under the careful scrutiny of the fire department) emergency egress paths, and decide on how many public tickets can be sold. They announce the number and, since it is clear there will be many more people desiring tickets than there are tickets available, they also announce a system for signing up to get tickets, part of which involves a lottery, part of which involves allocating blocks of tickets to fans of the opposing team, and part of which involves various demonstrations of particular team loyalty (and, let's face it, political importance within the environs of Boston). People sign up to get tickets, and tickets are distributed. Some get their tickets; many are disappointed. Those who are disappointed are told they can try again if the series goes past 4 games or, perhaps (the Gods of baseball permitting), next year.

Game day arrives, and the fortunate ticket-holders are allowed through the gates.

But there is a problem. The gates of Fenway had been left only carelessly guarded, and some people have snuck in. In fact, many people have snuck in. Some of them are vendors and service providers, let in legitimately ahead of time to deliver goods or perform a job but who never left when they were done. Some of them are people who tried and failed to get tickets, but many of them never even bothered — they figured sneaking in was an easier, cheaper, and more certain way of getting to see the game.

Some are sitting in seats, taking up space that ticket-holders were going to use. Many are sitting on the steps or standing in the walkways. They're even in the box seats. And in the skyboxes! As the game goes on, lines at the bathrooms back up. The hot-dog vendors start running low on food. It's hard to move through the stadium for the crowds. Everyone recognizes there is a problem. Something must be done!

But what?

Some people suggest that the ushers start asking people to show their tickets and expelling people who don't have one. That would seem reasonable. But others complain that they don't always carry their tickets around with them; and they declare (correctly) that it would be a fundamental violation of the spirit of "Red Sox Nation" — it would be the slippery slope to oppression and tyranny — to demand that they be required to produce a ticket wherever and whenever any stadium official might ask for one inside the ballpark. Giving ushers that kind of arbitrary authority and creating that kind of anxious atmosphere would be worse than putting up with the gate-crashers.

Moreover, there aren't enough ushers to ask everyone to show a ticket, and some naysayers point out that they are much more likely to focus their efforts on the poorly-dressed than on the well-dressed, since the season ticket holders are more likely to be wealthy and to dress better. How could that be fair? It would be sartorial profiling. In fact, some declare, the very suggestion that ushers check tickets is morally suspect: those who advocate it may *claim* that what concerns them is upholding the rules, but their real motive is classism, pure and simple. They are clearly bigots who would prefer not to have to mix with those in the bleacher seats, and certainly not with those who can't even afford the bleacher seats. We should feel free to dismiss them and their faux concerns.

And besides, do you know how much chaos would result from trying to track down and evict that many people from the stadium at this point in the game? Even if it were legitimate it would be thoroughly impractical.

And if we did, who would buy all the cheap beer? The low-end beer vendors would go out of business! Or they'd be forced to sell better beer at higher prices, and the legitimate-but-poor ticket holders would have no cheap beer to enjoy.

Some say that we should at least tighten up security on the gates now to keep out people still sneaking in and those who intend to sneak in for the next game. They say we should hire more ushers and gate guards, and perhaps put real turnstiles on the gates and a high fence all the way around the park. But contrarians say that such tight security would be too expensive, would waste resources that could be used for upgrading the seats in the bleachers; and that it would make it too hard for legitimate ticket-holders to get through the gates; and that it would signal that Sox Nation is elitist and xenophobic, would signal that the real problem is we don't want to let in the riff-raff; and that no acceptable level of security will keep people from sneaking in, anyway, because seeing the Sox play is just too attractive. Some even say that the only way to stop people from sneaking in is to crack down on concessionaires who sell programs and souvenirs and hot dogs and beer to people without first asking to see their tickets.

Others express great sympathy for those who snuck in. It's not their fault that they lost the ticket lottery. They have as much — perhaps more — team loyalty and desire to be at the game as the season ticket holders do. Who are we, the fortunate few, to tell them they shouldn't be here? Isn't it just luck that we got tickets? Wasn't their "cheating" really not a crime but just an artifact, a creation of an unjust system for distributing tickets? And wouldn't it be cruel to expel them from the game, especially if it meant splitting them from their friends and family who were still in the park watching, legitimately or not? And some of them brought their kids in with them. Do we throw out the kids, too? They didn't decide to sneak in — they just came with dad because he promised a day at the ballpark. Would you take that day away from them because of what their parents did?

Some go so far as to express the belief we should grant a general amnesty, that everyone who is already in the park because they snuck in should now be given a ticket to make their presence legitimate. Ignore the fact that they snuck in. If they've gotten away with it thus far, just let them stay and enjoy the game. Others propose a stricter version of amnesty that at least acknowledges there was an offense: all those who snuck in but turn themselves in now have to leave, but they will be guaranteed a ticket to the next game.

But what, say the detractors, does an amnesty say to the people who signed up for tickets but didn't get them and *didn't* sneak in? That they were suckers? That they'd have been better off sneaking in than following the rules? That good guys do, indeed, finish last? Is that fair? Is that just? And what incentive does it give tomorrow's fans to follow the rules next time? How can we expect to have social order if we consistently forgive social disorder? Doesn't that lead us right back to the chaos we have now when we win the pennant again next year?

Others go farther, and declare that the real problem is that the Red Sox management didn't provide enough tickets in the first place. Their solution is to increase the number of tickets to reduce the incentive to sneak in. In fact, some say perhaps we should do away with tickets entirely and just throw the gates open. To hell with the fire codes! To hell with limitations on seating and bathrooms! There's plenty of room for everyone. Just budge up and share your chair! In fact, didn't the Red Sox build their success on the support of all those fans out there? Don't we owe them a seat in the stadium? Isn't it wrong on its face to keep them out?

So what do you think? What is the right thing to do about people who sneak into the country — I mean into the ballpark?

Seatbelts (and Other Things Good and Bad for Us)

New Hampshire, with its libertarian-leaning political culture, is the last remaining state in America that does not require adults to use seatbelts while driving or riding in their cars. Periodically, a coalition of "public health" advocates, insurance lobbyists, generalized public nannies, and believers in national legal uniformity convince the legislature to propose such a requirement but, to date, their efforts have failed.

The gist of the argument in favor of seatbelt laws is twofold:

1. That the human cost — some number of extra deaths each year and the emotional trauma for friends and families that accompany them — dwarfs whatever (miniscule) price we would pay in liberty.
2. That the economic costs — for medical treatment — are borne by society, either through insurance costs (if paid by insurance companies) or through the social safety net (if, for whatever reason, no insurance company will pick up the tab); and that our financial participation gives society the right to enforce constraints on individual behavior that affect those economic costs.

Leaving aside the practical question of whether those 'extra' deaths really do impose financial costs (because injuries are more severe) or not (because we don't spend as much money burying the dead as we do healing the injured), both arguments lack any substantive moral foundation.

There are many personal behaviors — say smoking or drinking, or racing cars, or bicycling on the roads, or scuba diving, or playing a contact sport, or having unprotected sex with strangers — that increase our risk of disease, or injury, or even death. When accounted as statistics across the whole population, these all result in some amount of 'extra' misery and death each year; and at various times most of these have been the subject of more or less serious efforts by some compassionate souls to protect us from ourselves by prohibiting them.

But most of us value our freedom to choose such activities despite (or even because of) their risks, not just because they also offer benefits and pleasures that their detractors simply can't appreciate but, more fundamentally, because *the freedom to choose your own fate is the only true freedom.* Just as the freedom to say only what everyone else agrees is true is not "freedom of speech," the freedom to do only what everyone else agrees is good for you is not "freedom of action." If we grant society generally, and the government specifically, the authority to circumscribe our actions solely because they are potentially self-destructive, then we have sold our freedom for a false security.

The other argument — that our financial exposure gives us the right to dictate behavior that minimizes the exposure — is appealing, and might be legitimate if we had made a covenant with the recipients of our largesse rather than simply imposing our compassion as a policy. We might, for instance, have said up front that we would not pay their medical bills if their behavior contributed to their injuries, allowed them to make decisions based on that, and then enforced that policy even when compassion told us to do otherwise; or, alternatively, if recipients had explicitly and specifically asked for our help then we might have imposed our restrictions as a condition of providing it.

But we did not do either. As a matter of policy, we have promised, as a society, to cover the medical needs of the severely injured no matter how those injuries are sustained, either indirectly through the risk pool of insurance or directly through public and private subsidies for emergency medical care. In such circumstances we, in fact, take great pains to circumvent the normal mechanisms by which the costs of individual choices would be borne by the individual — we limit in various ways, for example, the ability of either insurance companies or the government to place restrictions on coverage based on the behavior of the insured. Such a policy is certainly compassionate and arguably pragmatic, and some would contend that doing anything else would be immoral.

But, however well-justified that policy may be, it is also *voluntary*: as a society we have *assumed* that burden by our own choice and for our own moral and practical purposes; and, having volunteered, for our own reasons, to take on that responsibility (and for all practical purposes denied all opportunities to refuse our generosity), we can have no moral claim on those we choose to help.

Imagine that your parents or in-laws, because they are both wealthy and care about the welfare of their children and their grandchildren, volunteer to cover all your family medical bills. You certainly appreciate their help but you didn't ask for it — perhaps, you even declined their offer but were rebuffed — and you didn't negotiate any conditions for its provision. They just arranged to pay for your insurance premiums and doctor's visits and didn't give you the realistic option of refusing.

Do they now have carte blanche to tell you how to run your life? Can they demand that you exercise for some number of hours per week? Can they dictate the menus for your meals? The hobbies you pursue? The model of car you drive? The vices you indulge or renounce? Does accepting help from someone who is adamant about giving it obligate you to indulge their notions of what is good for you? Does the fact that your choices determine the extent of their self-imposed obligation give them a moral authority over your behavior?

Most of us would say not. Yet that is the justification offered for imposing mandatory seat belt use on the drivers and passengers of New Hampshire.

If we grant the validity of the justifications for a policy of mandating behavior that is good for us or prohibiting behavior that is bad for us, what other similar policies might we see in the future? Will we prohibit smoking? Eating high-fat foods? Both are currently the subject of activism from particularly zealous advocates of public health. Will we again prohibit the drinking of alcoholic beverages? That certainly takes a personal and social toll. What about the bearing of children out of wedlock? That has been shown to be statistically and sensibly correlated with poverty, poor health, and low life opportunity for both mothers and children, and it costs society a bundle. Should we mandate the use of condoms during sexual intercourse? That would decrease the risk of contracting AIDS. Perhaps we should outlaw SUVs because we all pay for the incremental pollution and depletion of energy reserves that they cause. Perhaps we should ban guns — that argument has been made for decades.

If these seem impossible, they shouldn't. The principle that government can and should prohibit behavior solely because it might, under some circumstance, create personal harm and social cost can be easily applied to any one of those scenarios, and to hundreds more besides. If we grant the principle, then the only thing preventing extending it in those and other ways is fickle political will.

The fact is, we should all wear seat belts. We really should, and the excuses people make for not doing so are pretty pathetic and the costs of doing so are vanishingly small. We also all should refrain from smoking (either tobacco or marijuana), and should never drink alcohol (but should drink red wine to protect our hearts), and should eat vegetables fourteen times a week, and should avoid fatty foods, and should exercise regularly, and should watch our weights. According to some people, we should all attend church regularly for the good of our souls; others claim soul health requires, rather, a life of asceticism and servitude. I'm sure I'd be better off if I got enough sleep instead of using those nocturnal hours to broaden my horizons by reading — or perhaps not if you consider my intellectual and spiritual well-being of importance equal to my material well-being. My father has always insisted that bicycles and cars cannot coexist safely, and that people, therefore, should refrain from riding bicycles on the public thoroughfares; the empirical evidence to support his position is overwhelming. Or, perhaps, they should refrain from driving cars, instead, because bicycles give us more exercise and generate less pollution. If we disagree over which it is, does the fact that 50.1% of the people agree with you make you more right than if only 49.9% of them did?

There are things we all could do to improve one or another aspect of our lives. Perhaps there are even things we *should* do. Sometimes those things are inexpensive; sometimes they are not, and have deleterious consequences for other aspects of our lives; sometimes those consequences are things that only we, individually, can fully and truly appreciate, things that would seem petty or inconsequential to others. And sometimes such improvement would benefit society by making us healthier or by making us better citizens (or more pliant subjects) or by making us friendlier to our neighbors or by making us more attentive to the needs of humanity.

But is that enough to justify mandating them? By what tenet of our founding political philosophy, and under what article of our Constitution, is the government granted authority to enforce such things? And should we really trust it with that authority?

I'm sure I do not. Do you?

What is true for seatbelts, and other matters of "public health," is equally true for myriad other troubling bits of human social and economic conduct that have been, or have been proposed to be, the subject of regulation and law. The fact that you don't like some behavior, that it is insulting or unfair or risky or self-destructive or self-indulgent or repulsive or uncivilized or blasphemous or socially or economically corrosive — or that it simply has consequences you find uncomfortable — does not lead inexorably to the conclusion that it should be regulated by the government, even if you feel your preference to be particularly enlightened and even if you find yourself aligned with a voting majority. Proponents of free choice over abortion advocate for their position in the name of a woman's individual autonomy and liberty, social conscience and democratic preference be damned. What is true in that context is true generally — that the liberty to choose only what is good for you or enlightened, only what is morally or spiritually or physically uplifting, only what is socially and culturally tolerable or is in synchrony with the majority viewpoint, is no liberty at all. The autonomy to choose only what others would choose for you is not autonomy but supplication.

Benjamin Franklin famously proclaimed, "Those who would give up essential Liberty, to purchase a little temporary Safety, deserve neither Liberty nor Safety."[1] Freedom is messy. Free people will sometimes do things you don't like, things that make you uncomfortable, things that you find outrageous or despicable or even intolerable. Risk of offense, or even of harm, is the price of liberty. And tyranny is the price we would pay for eliminating that risk.

As a rule, coercion — the application of violence or the threat of violence to impose some standard of behavior (and no one should doubt that a threat of arrest and imprisonment or impoverishment, which ultimately lies behind enforcement even of civil regulation, is a threat of violence) — should be reserved for regulation of behavior that actually threatens the liberty and autonomy of others. It should not be unleashed indiscriminately and merely in defense of good taste or of personal health or of egalitarian ideals or of social harmony or of moral rectitude.

But the notion that not all bad behavior should be regulated *politically* doesn't imply that it should not be regulated *socially*. Quite the opposite: the fact that someone is at liberty to behave abominably does not transform abominable behavior into something desirable or even acceptable. That you have the *right* to do something does not mean that you *ought* to do it, and certainly does not grant it an automatic and indisputable patina of respectability.

Rather, the absence of political sanction for bad behavior makes social condemnation of such behavior in defense of social or moral concordance all the more important. "Tolerance" does not mean never passing judgment, nor does it mean never expressing that judgment. Despite the common protestations of those who have misconstrued and commandeered the term, tolerance doesn't demand that you not disapprove or criticize; it merely demands that you not forcibly interfere.

What irony, then, that so many, in the name of tolerance, will decry and proscribe social judgment and social criticism of behaviors that they happen

---

1 *Reply to the Governor* from the Pennsylvania Assembly, 11 Nov 1755.

to find comfortable (or at least not too uncomfortable); and yet just as often, in defense of some vague sense of goodness or fairness or indignation, will demand political interference with behaviors that they happen to find harmful or inconvenient or offensive. Tolerance, indeed...

Alas, notwithstanding the differences of opinion between 'liberals' and 'conservatives' about what is and isn't disagreeable, the urge to regulate anything and everything disagreeable appears to be wholly bipartisan. But in this regard, at least, social conservatives are consistent even if they are wrong: they unambiguously want behavior regulated and the mechanism is merely a matter of convenience.

By contrast, social liberals appear to believe, on the one hand, that any *social* regulation of personal conduct — any intellectual or moral or spiritual or emotional defense of social mores or cultural norms, any expression of outrage or any imposition of social consequences — is mean-spirited and ignorant and oppressive and to be abhorred; while, on the other hand, *political* regulation of personal conduct — speech codes and sensitivity police, prohibitions on smoking or on the eating of trans-fats or foie gras or salt or raw milk or on the possession of firearms, seat-belt and helmet laws, restriction and regulation of wage scales and insurance terms and interest rates and price "gouging" and other rights of contract, and the like — is redeeming and enlightened and to be encouraged.

They seem to believe that a democratic political process can somehow transform that which they find morally offensive — individual reproach expressed through social "intolerance" — into something morally uplifting — collective reproach expressed through political coercion.

And they seem to believe that, unlike social sanction, which can vary from community to community and therefore leave some small room for dissent even against broad-based social judgment, the most appropriate scope for their political regulatory aspirations is universal, crafted and imposed as a uniform standard everywhere once a barest majority can be mustered in their favor.

Violence and Social Disorder

Another week. Another killing spree. Or so it seems. Although the statistics say otherwise, our emotions — egged on by the daily, or even hourly, news updates that keep it fresh and immediate in our minds — tell us it has become almost that routine.

As has the aftermath: "Who was he?" "Why did he do it?" "What were his grievances?" "Was he also a victim?" "How could we have prevented this?"

And: "It was the guns; no, in the victim's hands they would have helped." "It was righteous anger; no, it was mental illness." "It was right-wing hate; no, it was left-wing disdain." "It was social breakdown; no it was social inequity."

And through it all, the murmuring and desperate refrain: "What do we do now?"

In the early 1970s, when the world seemed rushing toward catastrophe and the latest manifestation of the enveloping contagion was an epidemic of politically-inspired airline hijackings, my father announced one day a simple and effective countermeasure: as soon as a hijacking was discovered and before it was known who the hijackers were or what they wanted, before their message or their cause could be validated by constant repetition on the evening news, dispatch an interceptor to blast the airliner out of the sky. Hard on the first one or two groups of passengers, no doubt, but the hijackings would stop.

It was, in its martial simplicity and clarity, an elegant solution, a rational trade of short-term pain for long-term security born of a political culture increasingly willing, on both the right and the left, to sacrifice individuals to "the good of society."

It was also, of course, inhumane to the point of absurdity — the equivalent of "destroying the village in order to save it" — but it did recognize a fundamental truth: excepting the few truly deranged, who act out a reality only they can perceive, predators hunt for profit. The profit may be financial or political or emotional or spiritual, may be grand or petty, may accrue to an individual or to a clan or to an ideological movement, may be obvious or may be inscrutable even to themselves. But it is profit that drives them, and the most effective way to minimize the toll of their victims is to remove the potential for gain.

These modern villains are no exception. They hunt because it brings them attention that otherwise seems to elude them. They hunt because it brings them power when they feel otherwise powerless, power not only over their victims but over an entire society suddenly helpless before their strength of will. They hunt because — well, because we've promised *we will notice*. And, worse, we've promised *we will make them immortal*.

Their atrocities are acts of vanity, ego unrestrained by ethics, and they mystify us. Greed, we understand, and grievance. We condemn their consequences but we understand their genesis and understand how to tame them. But how do we understand this arrogant disregard for *us*? How do we tame an ego that denies significance to anything outside itself, that treats other human beings as mere toys for its own amusement or tools for its own aggrandizement? How do we tame evil?

And these acts *are* evil, if not as an actual metaphysical force then at least as a moral classification — chaos not as a side-effect, not as a means, but as its own end. Not a breakdown in civility but its utter absence, a vacuum into which reason, compassion, order, civility, community — humanity itself — are sucked and dissipated.

How do we tame evil?

To *name* it is a start. To perceive it as it is: as unredeemable and alien, not merely a radical extrapolation from ordinary anger or frustration but sundered from them by an unfathomable abyss. To resist attempts to humanize it or rationalize it or comprehend and classify and contain it. And, most importantly, to deny it the power it seeks over us, the benefit it craves above all else: self-justification.

For just as greed demands payment and grievance demands change, so evil demands attention. Good acts stand alone in silence, but evil must be heard. To deny it voice is to make it irrelevant.

But we *don't* deny it voice. Indeed, in our quest for answers, in our quest for understanding — in our insistence on taking comfort in its explicable banality — we provide a rapt and credulous audience for its narcissistic rant. We demand motives, biography, grievances, failings, warning signs, missed opportunities that will make us safe next time if only we are more attentive. We demand regulations on the tools they chose to use. We demand better surveillance and treatment of their mental or emotional turmoil. We demand more guards and more metal detectors. We demand official omniscience. We demand to see where the fault was in ourselves.

What we never seem to demand, or offer, is simple, inarguable, condemnation. What we never seem to accept is that there really are bad people who do bad things, and that the fault can be — and is — entirely within them.

Ultimately we must confront how we got here, what we have done to ourselves, to our culture, to our children, that inculcates — that *permits* — a vanity and selfishness of such depth and force that it disconnects its bearer from every vestige of humanity. It is our mistake and our hubris to think that we *create* bad people. We don't need to: they create themselves. But it is within our power to create a society that either guides more people out of that path or does not. If our current society does not, then we must understand why and strive to turn it around. That is our only hope in the long-term.

But in the short-term, here and now, the best we can do is to deny evil its relevance, not by *ignoring* it but by *dismissing* it as beneath contempt. Shut off the publicity engines of the press. Refuse to read the interviews with the perpetrators. Condemn the professional apologists. Recognize and *insist* that the story is not about the villain, but about the victims. *Their* names should be the names we remember; *their* stories should be *the* story; what happened to *them* should be *what happened*.

Focus our attention there and mourn for what we have lost. Let the villain rot in hell, forgotten and alone:

Who did it? "That cowardly asshole!"
Why did he do it? "Because he's a cowardly asshole!"
Finis.

And accept that there is no explanation for evil beyond solipsism. No more explanation is required, or even desirable, because there is no circumstance, no narrative, no grievance that could possibly provide even a modicum of justification. If there are insights into the human condition or into how to protect ourselves to be gleaned from examination of the perpetrators — and there may well be — they can and should be anonymous ones, deciphered by the psychologists and sociologists and criminologists quietly, thoughtfully, and far, far from public view.

Guns

These are tough times for anyone who believes in a right to bear arms. The headlines are relentless: neighborhoods in Chicago and Boston and New York and LA where schoolchildren are gunned down while riding their bikes or playing basketball or doing their homework; reporters shot on live television; random shootings in schools and shopping malls and clinics; policemen killed at traffic stops or executed while they are pumping gas; whole families murdered in their beds by disgruntled boyfriends or depressed fathers or alienated children; lone-wolf terrorists who execute scores of non-believers in the name of some political or religious agenda.

Our society is seemingly awash in violence. Our culture appears sick. And at the center of almost all these stories of depravity and anguish are guns and a "gun culture" that appears uniquely American and uniquely pathological.

What is wrong with us? And what should we do about it?

Notwithstanding the statistics, which say violence has actually been decreasing in America over the last few decades,[1] people are understandably and reasonably terrified. Doing anything we can to eliminate the tools used in such mayhem seems not only rational but necessary. Why would anyone disagree with that? What is behind the resistance to "reasonable" controls on guns?

The 2nd amendment to the American Constitution specifies that "A well-regulated militia being necessary to the security of a free state, the right of the people to keep and bear arms shall not be infringed."[2] That is the elemental *legal* basis for the defense of "gun rights" in the United States. There has been a great deal of debate over whether the first phrase of that statement does or does not imply a limitation on the second, whether the second phrase applies to people as individuals or only as members of a militia, and over whether any of the quirks and vagaries of punctuation accompanying those phrases in the various written versions change that implication. Recent Supreme Court rulings have settled that for the moment, favoring the interpretation that the amendment identifies a right of individual citizens[3] and enforcing that right at the state level and not just at the federal level.[4] But those rulings have come recently enough, and from a court that is perceived as sufficiently politicized, that the issue is still contentious.

At least one of the amendment's meanings is, however, completely clear.

The 2nd Amendment is one of the ten comprising the "Bill of Rights" that was added to the Constitution immediately after its initial ratification. Their purpose was specifically to address a popular worry about the new form of government we had just created: that the various powers granted to the federal government would be used by future politicians as justifications for undermining the separate, complementary powers of the sovereign state governments and the rights of individual citizens.

That is, the Bill of Rights was a reminder that the reach of the federal government was intended to be limited; that many aspects of governance and of daily life were supposed to be beyond its authority and its purview. The first nine amendments addressed specific subjects that were of particular

---

1 *America's Faulty Perception of Crime Rates*, Lauren-Brooke Eisen and Oliver Roeder, Brennan Center for Justice, 16 March 2015 (*https://www.brennancenter. org/blog/americas-faulty-perception-crime-rates*)

2 That is the version officially authenticated by then Secretary of State Thomas Jefferson after ratification by the states. The version originally passed by Congress and available in the National Archive uses the same words but somewhat different punctuation.

3 *District of Columbia v. Heller*, 2008

4 *McDonald v. Chicago*, 2010

concern as a result of recent experiences with British colonial rule, including the right to bear arms; the tenth was a final and open-ended warning:

> "The powers not delegated to the United States by the Constitution, nor prohibited by it to the States, are reserved to the States respectively, or to the people."

The "United States," the federal political entity, was identified as distinct from the individual "States," independent political and cultural entities which reserved to themselves any powers they had not specifically delegated away. In the context of the time, that might have been stated more boldly and directly as: "*We don't completely trust the federal government and we will resist if it ever tries to overstep the authority we have agreed to grant it!*"

In that context, it was understood that the "well-regulated militias" mentioned in the 2ⁿᵈ amendment were instruments of the individual states, not of the federal government; and that the reason for maintaining those militias was, not wholly but at least in part, to protect "the security of a free state" — meaning the state government and the rights of its citizens — not from foreign powers but from an encroachment on its sovereignty by the federal government.

Today, that notion seems quaint and anachronistic to a great many Americans who, having never experienced anything close to real despotism within their own lifetimes or the lifetimes of their parents or grandparents, and not being able even to imagine it, have come to trust in the fundamental goodness of the American government and in its ability and its desire to make the world better for everyone. To them, the idea we might need to retain a right to bear arms as a protection against a creeping federal despotism seems paranoid and extreme. And, in large measure, they are right: the American government is still generally bound by its Constitutional limitations and does generally operate as if protection of the rights guaranteed by the Bill of Rights was a sacred trust.

But many people are not so sanguine about any government, even the American one. They may or may not have experienced despotism directly, but they have observed it in many places around the world, have read about it in many times throughout history, and can easily imagine it taking root here at some time in the future. That attitude is most often these days attributed to the political right, but it is not unique to them: the Weather underground and the Black Panthers, not to mention #Black Lives Matter, all assumed that despotism had already prevailed; and remember that Margaret Atwood's *The Handmaid's Tale*, which imagines an America transformed into a Christian fundamentalist theocracy, was, at the time of its publication, considered a frighteningly plausible cautionary tale by many on the political left, a vision of what could easily happen if the self-proclaimed Moral Majority were allowed to gain the power it sought. Those fears, of the federal government and of governments generally, are reinforced by a litany of contemporary stories featuring attempts at government overreach, from the NSA data mining efforts and various CIA misadventures, to instances of police brutality and arrogance, to unconscionably unfair applications of eminent domain and civil asset forfeiture, to federal intransigence over legalization of marijuana, to countless failed and successful attempts at regulating various aspects of our lives.

There is a long, honorable, and rational American tradition, tracing back to the founding of the country, of a fundamental mistrust toward government power; there are plenty of very good historical reasons for that mistrust; and we must admit that the slow and steady usurpation of both State and individual prerogative by an ever-expanding federal government, against which the writers of the 10th Amendment tried to warn us, has been the overarching reality of the last 100 years in the American political evolution. To people with clear vision and historical perspective, yes, one purpose for having access to guns is as it was intended to be: a hedge against the possibility that government may, some day, overstep its bounds in such a way and to such an extent that armed resistance becomes necessary — just as it did once before some 240 or so years ago.

Notwithstanding the fears of those who do *not* harbor such reservations about government power, the vast majority of people who contemplate the remote possibility of armed rebellion neither desire nor advocate for insurrection. They are not revolutionaries, ready to man the barricades. They are not planning or hoping for a *coup d'état* in any foreseeable future. They are people who fear insurrection, just as any sensible person would, but who want, nonetheless, to be prepared for the necessity if it were to arise. To think that we are even close to that necessity today is, indeed, a sign of rampant paranoia; to deny that the necessity *could* arise at some point in the future is to ignore thousands of years of political history and human failings. And to prohibit our children and their children, in the name of some short term sense of security for ourselves, access to the tools they would need in the event of such a necessity would be both selfish and foolhardy.

To be clear, the fundamental *moral* basis for a right to bear arms — and for the *desire* to bear arms, either individually or in the communal form of a militia — comes down to autonomy. What is a weapon? What, in particular, is a gun? It is a tool that extends an individual's personal power over the world around him.[1]

---

1 Or, of course, "her." The limitations of the English language create an unfortunate choice of being either fair or concise...

There are, to be sure, many sportsmen who use guns not as an assertion of autonomy but merely for recreation. Both hunters and sport shooters depend on access to guns in order to pursue their passion, and incidents of such sportsmen harming anyone in the process are exceedingly rare. The traditional use of guns in sports and recreation is often cited in arguments defending gun rights, and the general principle of governmental non-interference with harmless personal pass-times — not to mention non-interference with ancient cultural traditions — would argue that such sportsmen should be left alone. But, if that were the limit of the passion for gun rights, it would not be nearly the all-consuming national issue it is.

The premise and moral justification for the American uprising against British rule — the very basis of our founding political philosophy — was that human beings are and should be free to live their lives, free to choose their own fates, free to pursue happiness in their own ways and on their own terms; that human beings are morally autonomous and that their autonomy should not be subject to arbitrary and capricious restraint. In a world in which size and strength and quickness and coordination determined who ate and who starved, determined who commanded and who served, determined who prevailed and who cowered, determined who lived and who died, a weapon was a leveler: an armed man is no longer smaller or weaker or slower or less coordinated than other people or than his natural predators; he is, or at least can be, their equal.

An armed man is not dependent on anyone else for his livelihood because he can hunt his own food, can keep predators from his flocks and vermin from his crops. An armed man is not dependent on anyone else to protect him from harm because he can protect himself. An armed man is not subject to the depredations of his enemies or to the mandates of his peers because his fortitude is a match for theirs. He is sovereign. He is self-determined and self-fulfilled. He is free to exercise his autonomy not only in theory but in practice, not only because justice demands it but because no one has the power to prevent it.

Of course, according to our founding document, the very reason for establishing a government is because that premise can never be as true in practice as we might like it to be in theory. Arms may be a leveler, but they don't necessarily make everything level; and a society in which one is only as secure as his individual strength can guarantee is little better than the jungle. Arms are not enough, nor are they the ideal: we need a civil society that treats the weak and the strong alike with dignity; and it must be buttressed by laws and institutions that act on our behalf when the depredations of our enemies and the mandates of our peers threaten to overwhelm us.

We like to think, in modern America, that we have achieved such a paradise, that we no longer live in the jungle. We like to think that size and strength and quickness and coordination no longer determine our place either in nature or in society. We like to think that, having established an enlightened government to protect us, we no longer have the need to depend upon ourselves. We like to think that we, and all those we encounter, are civilized, that we have progressed together beyond that medieval mindset. Perhaps most of us have, at least most of the time.

But not all of us have, and not all the time. Crime may have receded since the bad old days of the 1970s and 1980s and 1990s, but it hasn't gone away entirely. There are still predators out there and the police can't be everywhere. For those who live in rural areas — and there are still many of us — help may be more than mere minutes away, assuming we even have either the time or the opportunity to call for it. Inner cities are notoriously dangerous, and would be so even if their gangster classes relied on knives and clubs and fists instead of on guns. And the whole point of terrorism is to make us all feel vulnerable.

Asking people to rely solely on society to protect them from thugs and predators, asking them to rely solely on the police and the courts and the legislature, is asking people to swallow their dignity, to surrender their autonomy, to willingly risk playing the victim in the hope and faith that someone will see to it they come out whole on the far side. It is asking people to put their fates entirely and quixotically into the hands of strangers.

Some people — many people — have no desire to play the victim. Some people are not willing to be so passive. To a certain segment of the population — perhaps a large segment — a certain degree of sovereignty and self-reliance is not merely a preference but a primary psychological need.

Yet, in our modern society, in which people largely work for impersonal corporations and live by laws imposed from thousands of miles away by people someone else voted for, in which cultural ideals increasingly disparage individual striving and glorify communal action, in which people are all too often isolated from their families and ciphers to their neighbors, in which social norms are mass-produced in Hollywood and distributed over the airwaves and the internet, in which most of the daily interactions through which we manage our lives are performed anonymously and with strangers, opportunities to claim and exercise sovereignty are precious and rare.

In that environment, a gun is actually more than merely a tool. It is a symbol of self-reliance, a declaration of independence and of self-determination. To be told one cannot be trusted with a weapon is to be infantilized and denigrated. To be told one is not permitted to protect oneself from those who intend harm is to be reduced to the status of ward and supplicant, to be made wholly dependent on the state and necessarily subservient to it. The first of those is an insult; the second, a condescension.

To be denied access to a gun, then, is to be denied both dignity and agency; and "gun control" is both a practical expression of and a metaphor for the triumph of the communal over the individual, of and for the exaltation of the human hive.

There are many people who, like myself, don't own any guns and don't intend to but who, nonetheless, value the right to do so. Most people, being more or less content with their lives and not inclined to make things difficult for themselves, will also never bump up against the limits of free speech. For them, whether or not they may speak their minds is irrelevant in practice because what they have to say is neither controversial nor troublesome. Yet they may, nonetheless, value their right to speak out. They want the right to speak freely to be available to them, even if they never need or choose to use it.

So it is with gun rights. I want the option to depend on myself even if I choose, for the most part, to put my faith in others. For many people, the right to bear arms is something to hold in reserve, not something to exercise, not necessarily something with any immediate effect on their daily lives. But that does not make it less precious.

I have often commented on the parallels between Guns and Abortion as contemporary political issues. If you took a typical argument about abortion and substituted the word "gun" — or vice versa — the conversation would not appear significantly different, other than that the advocates on either side would have switched places. Both revolve around the fundamental question of how far the government may and should go in regulating personal behavior in the name of some "social good." Both inspire extreme emotion because both are intertwined with a need and a desire for personal autonomy, with the right to control one's own fate, to act for oneself rather than being forced to rely on others, to decide for yourself what is in your best interest rather than being coerced into what others decide.

Defenders and supporters of both guns and abortion agree they are debating matters of life and death; they merely disagree over whose lives and whose deaths are at stake.

Defenders of both guns and abortion go over the top any time any kind of restriction is proposed, even a "modest" and "reasonable" one — not because they are neither modest nor reasonable but because they fear that the modesty and reason of their opponents are only for show, that their opponents' goal is not, and never has been, moderate regulation but outright prohibition. For sound reason, and based on long experience, they believe that the real purpose of any "modest" or "reasonable" proposal is merely to advance the starting line for something more extreme.

Defenders of both guns and abortion cling to the Supreme Court like a lifeline because they know they might well lose if a democratic majority were allowed to impose its tyranny upon them.

Defenders of guns and abortion should be natural allies if it were only a question of consistent political philosophy. That they are not illustrates a conundrum: despite the fact that the arguments are phrased in philosophical terms, these are not philosophical contests. They are emotional battles over what people want, not moral battles over what people believe is right. Hence, at the very least, defenders of both guns and abortions should be able to understand each other, to empathize with each other, to identify with the intensity of emotion behind each other's arguments, even if they can't agree with each other's goals.

Yet, anyone who believes in a right to bear arms must also acknowledge one fundamental and indisputable difference between guns and abortion: setting aside the contested moral status of the fetus, a woman seeking an abortion is causing no harm to anyone else, is not dragging others unwillingly into the consequences of her choice; whereas, those who exercise their right to own guns far too often abuse that right by turning those guns on others.

Let's face it. Gun rights are under assault because a few gun owners behave irresponsibly and because the consequences of that irresponsibility are disastrous. It's that simple. Some people use guns to kill other people. And any rational assessment of a hierarchy of rights would say those other people have more right to their lives than anyone has to their guns.

My wife, in her rare cynical moments, is fond of saying that we get the government and the society that other people deserve. We have restrictive speed limits because a reckless few can't or won't tell the difference between prudence and excess. We all put up with anti-virus utilities and SPAM filters on our computers because a few jerks try to infect them with malware and dump hundreds of worthless come-ons into our mailboxes. We risk condemnation by our neighbors and assault by Child Protective Services when we allow our children normal freedoms that used to be commonplace because there are a few perverts on the streets who might kidnap them. We can't carry pocket-knives onto airplanes or into a courthouse because a few nihilists would use them as weapons. We have police and a military because there really are people, both among us and out there in the wider world, who mean us harm.

By most accounts, there are nearly as many guns in America as there are Americans. And yet, despite that and despite all the headlines, the chance that nearly any individual American will be killed, or even threatened, by someone wielding a gun is still negligibly small.[1] What does that tell us about people who own guns? We can only conclude that the vast majority of them use their guns responsibly and sensibly. We can only conclude that gun owners, as a class, are neither villains nor sociopaths. We can only conclude that gun ownership, in and of itself, is no threat to society. We can only conclude it is an irresponsible and malicious few that cause all the mayhem we fear.

But, of course, that's all it takes. We all learned in childhood that it only requires a few behaving badly to ruin something good for everyone. And collective punishment, however much we may loathe it, is a natural human response to bad behavior, if for no other reason than that it is so often far easier and far more efficient to implement than individualized alternatives.

And, just to be clear, the more restrictive varieties of gun control, not to mention an outright ban on gun ownership, *are* forms of collective punishment. People who advocate for such things like to point out that we place restrictions on driving for people who drive irresponsibly, and use that to generalize about placing restrictions on access to guns. It is true we take driving licenses away from people who are caught driving drunk, or who are caught driving particularly or repeatedly in a reckless manner. We do not, however, deny driving licenses to people *generally* because of those few malefactors; and we do not pre-emptively deny driver's licenses to people with subscriptions to *Hot Rod* magazine, or who shop at liquor stores, or who own smart phones simply because we suspect they might, some day, speed or drive drunk or send a text from their car.

---

1 Statistics about gun violence are hotly contested, but the general consensus is there are on the order of 11,000 murders committed each year using firearms. In a population of 310M, that would imply an average of about 1 chance in 28,000 of someone being murdered by a firearm in any given year, or about a 1 in 370 chance over a 76 year life-span.

One certain thing, however, is that statistics which average across the entire population overstate the risk for most Americans because most gun violence is isolated in a few particularly dangerous areas, typically within certain inner-city neighborhoods that have high concentrations of desperate poverty and gang activity ("60 percent of U.S. firearm homicides occur in the 62 cities of the country's 50 largest metros"; *URBAN NATION: Narrowing the Gun Violence Map*, by Harry Munoz @NextCity.org, 26 November 2012) and is concentrated within a particular age group (late adolescence to early adulthood: *Deaths: Final Data for 2013*, Centers for Disease Control).

For people who do not frequent those dangerous areas, and particularly for those who are not connected, either directly or indirectly, to gang activity, the chance of being killed by gunfire is orders of magnitude less than those averages imply. Further, there is no real way of knowing how many of those murders-by-gun would have been prevented, rather than merely becoming murders-by-some-other-means, if a gun had not been available.

Yet, that is exactly what is often proposed for guns: restrictions that would apply not merely to those who have proven themselves irresponsible but to everyone, across the board, or to broad categories of people whose lifestyles or personalities make them, for some reason, "suspect." People resist "reasonable" controls on guns for the same reason people resist "reasonable" restrictions on abortion and "reasonable" censorship of speech: because the line between "reasonable" and "extreme" depends overwhelmingly on emotion, on how much you despise or treasure what is to be restricted. Common proposals for "reasonable" gun controls, if applied to the automobile, would be the equivalent of prohibiting most people from buying, or even *possessing*, a car, never mind having the audacity to drive one.

Certainly, there would be good justification for such a prohibition. Based purely on the statistical record, and strictly as a matter of public safety, cars are far more dangerous to most Americans than guns: a typical American is *at least* three times more (and probably 30 to 300 times more) likely to die in a car accident than they are to die as the result of a gun homicide.[1] In fact, though the statistics in this regard are harder to come by, it's a safe bet that a typical American is far more likely to be killed by someone else *wielding* a car, either irresponsibly or maliciously, than they are to be killed by someone else wielding a gun.

Yet, no one ever seriously proposes outlawing the automobile.[2] What is the difference?

The difference is that everyone appreciates the value of a car but a large fraction of the American public cannot comprehend the value of a gun. And,

---

1 Selected entries from *Detailed Tables for the National Vital Statistics Report (NVSR): "Deaths: Final Data for 2013*, Centers for Disease Control:

Cause of Death	Number of Deaths
Heart Disease	611,105
Poisoning	38,851
Car Accidents	35,369
Children (0-14yrs)	1,345
Pedestrians/bicyclists	5,612
Guns	32,888
Accidents	505
Suicide	21,175
Murder	11,208
Murder (non-gun)	4,913
Suicide (non-gun)	19,974

2 At least for reasons of public safety; environmental zealots are another matter...

because they don't value it themselves, they cannot find sense in anyone else's valuing of it and cannot, therefore, see any reason why they should not apply their prejudice to everyone else as a matter of public policy.

Is that not the same argument applied by those who would outlaw abortion and censor speech?

Yes, gun violence is a problem in America. Set aside the statistics: *any* murder,[1] by gun or otherwise, is a tragedy and an outrage. Whether or not you think the solution to that problem is more gun control, you should certainly be able to agree that there is an urgent need to find *some* solution.

But it would be as accurate to make that statement more broadly: *violence is a problem in America.* Advocates for gun control frequently contrast the murder rate in the United States with that in Europe and other places to make the case it is our obsession with guns that makes the difference. And the contrast is real: the American murder rate was nearly 6 times higher than that of Europe in 2013.[2] But, consider that only about $^2/_3$ of murders in the United States are generally committed with guns. If we were to assume — implausibly — that *none* of those murders would have occurred but for the availability of guns, that would *still* leave the murder rate in America nearly *twice* as high as that of Europe. An obsession with guns cannot explain that difference.

Quite aside, then, from the arguments about liberty and autonomy, or the legal arguments over the 2nd Amendment, fixing the problem of violence by prohibiting access to guns merely treats the symptom without treating the disease. It may give us some relief, and it may be a convenient and humane short-term palliative, but it doesn't solve the problem; and, to the extent it makes us feel better, it may actually allow us to ignore the underlying cancer rather than do something about it.

---

1 I have purposely left the question of gun-related suicides out of this discussion, for three reasons.

(1) The first is, the statistics show that almost as many people commit suicide without guns as with them, which implies that people without access to a gun have plenty of other effective options available to them. Hence, it is not clear that removing access to guns would put a serious dent in the suicide rate.

(2) The second is that suicide is, both morally and practically, a very different issue than violence. Using statistics about violence to justify a policy about suicide, or statistics about suicide to justify a policy about violence, is simply misguided.

(3) The third is that, if we think justifying restrictions on everyone's liberty based on the potential for someone harming others is a problem, how much more a problem would it be to justify restrictions on everyone's liberty based on the potential for someone harming himself? "I'm sorry: you can't buy rope because someone else might use rope to hang themselves...."

2 *Global Study on Homicide, 2013*, UN Office on Drugs and Crime

The irony is that 'conservatives' generally — and that means the bulk of people who would defend gun rights — believe that the root of the problem of violence lies largely in the general dissolution of social concordance that has occurred over the last few generations. And they largely blame 'liberals' — which means the bulk of people who oppose gun rights — for that social breakdown. Hence, they feel doubly aggrieved: they feel, on the one hand, that the problem was created by policies and social trends that they not only opposed but were castigated *for* opposing; yet, now that the problems they predicted have come to pass, it is *their* liberty that is to be curtailed in order to solve those problems that others created. Even if they are not entirely correct in their assessment, is it any wonder they are angry?

Notwithstanding what the Supreme Court has said about the individual right to bear arms, and notwithstanding the need to address the myriad historical and sociological issues that contribute to America's violence-prone culture, it seems likely that some more restrictive forms of gun control will become a part of the political landscape over the next few years in response to the wave of gun violence that is plaguing us. Those who cherish the right to bear arms will bear some additional burden for solving the problems that arms are creating. And that is not entirely unfair.

Historically, we have expected and demanded that communities police their own. Whenever some self-identified Christian zealot bombs an abortion clinic, mainstream Christian churches see it as their duty to denounce the act, not because they had anything to do with it but because the claim that it was done in the name of *their* God implies a connection that requires a response. Many people have a similar reaction when terrorism is committed in the name if Islam: fairly or not, a silence from the mainstream Muslim community appears as a tacit acceptance of the terrorists' claims to piety. Whenever a candidate for a political party — and, particularly, whenever a Republican candidate — utters something outrageous or merely stupid, we demand that other candidates from the same party weigh in to denounce them. Why? Because the party tie is presumed to be more than a mere label; it is presumed to imply a community of interest and, so, the community as a whole is tarnished by the action of the one.

Whether we like it or not, the same is true of those who misuse guns to cause misery for others. The NRA likes to distinguish between "law-abiding gun owners" and "criminals," but that is not the way most people see things. If you want to defend the proposition that *anyone* should be able to acquire a gun, then you have claimed anyone who does so as part of your community. And, so, we expect you to take responsibility for them. If responsible gun owners want to preserve their gun rights, it falls on them to propose practical and concrete ways to minimize the irresponsible use of guns and to minimize the ill-effects of such irresponsible use on the rest of us. If they fear the gun control proposals that are pushed by their opponents, they should propose and support realistic alternatives to achieve the same ends.

Short of an outright prohibition on gun ownership, the greatest dream of gun control advocates, and the greatest fear of gun rights supporters, is some kind of official "gun registry" which would allow the government to identify every gun owner and to locate every gun in the country. The putative use for such a registry is benign: it would, in theory, provide police with a way of tracking each gun crime back to a person, making it much more difficult to get away with using a gun irresponsibly or maliciously. People who say that the problem is those who misuse guns should rejoice: it would allow the government's focus to be aimed precisely at those criminals and not at everyone else.

However, such a registry would also, inevitably, place much more stringent restrictions on how guns could be purchased and sold, since any such transactions would need to flow through the registry in order to keep it up to date. And, worse, it would mean some future government, operating in a time when both support for gun rights and the legal barriers that protect them had eroded significantly, could use the information from the database to help it achieve its greater desire, to track down and confiscate all those guns. People who propose such a registry treat that notion with disdain, but the fear is in no way irrational, or even far-fetched. Outright prohibition is and will remain the dream of the gun control visionaries; and once the tool exists to make such a power grab easy and quick, using the tool always seems much more reasonable and justifiable than it ever would have before the tool was created.

Nonetheless, if the current epidemic of random violence continues, it seems nearly inevitable that some kind of gun registry is eventually going to exist. And, in that case, it would seem prudent that those who care about preserving their right to bear arms take the lead in defining what such a registry might look like.

To that end, here is a proposal that might — and I emphasize *might* — create an acceptable middle ground between those who would ban guns outright and those who would countenance no restrictions at all on gun ownership. I like to think of it as a "quasi-anonymous" registry implemented as a public/private partnership between a government interested in minimizing gun violence and a community interested in preserving their rights to own and use guns responsibly.

The basic premise of the quasi-anonymous registry is that it be operated not by the government but by a private entity whose charter is to protect the rights of gun owners. Just as the government chartered an independent operating agent — ICANN — to manage the assignment of URLs on the internet, so we might charter an independent agent to manage the registration and tracking of guns. The registration agent would serve as a firewall between the government and gun owners. As an initial proposal, I would nominate the NRA to fill that role, since there is no doubt that they take gun owners' interests seriously and their public position is that we should encourage *responsible* gun ownership. It is appealing to think that they might take the opportunity to become *part* of a solution rather than merely an impediment to finding one.

Rather than requiring a permit for each gun purchased, along with a discrete background check for each purchase, I would propose allowing an individual, including anyone operating as a gun dealer, to register with the registry *independent* of any particular gun purchase and be assigned a personal registration number. I hesitate to call it a "license"; it would, rather, be a tracking identifier to which responsibility for individual guns could be assigned. Obtaining the registration number, rather than the purchase of a gun, would be what triggers the things currently associated with a gun purchase, including any required background checks; and background checks would be routinely updated at some regular interval to keep the information current. It is, in all likelihood, necessary that the government conduct the background check because it has access to information that would not be available to a private group. However, *information about registrants would be maintained by the private registrar, not by the government.*

The registrar would also maintain records of every individual gun which entered the system, including its serial number and a record of its ballistic signature. Each gun would be assigned to a valid registered individual by associating it with that individual's registration number; and, once the gun was registered to an individual, they would become legally responsible for it: under law, there would be a presumption that the registered owner of a gun — the one whose registration number is associated with it — *is responsible for any and all uses of that gun.* That means there would be a *strong* incentive for owners to update the registry when a gun was sold to someone else, or if a gun was stolen or lost, because, until that happened, the original owner would still be legally responsible for its use. As with the information about registrants, *information about individual guns and, the assignment of responsibility for them to registrants, would be maintained by the registrar, not by the government.*

Any transfer of a gun, either from a dealer to an individual or from one individual to another, would require re-assignment of responsibility for that gun within the registry from one registered user to another. That would create a continuous chain of traceable responsibility for the gun, from manufacturer to dealer to each individual that subsequently buys (or inherits) it. Upon such a transfer, both users would be notified of the change of responsibility and both would need to acknowledge it; if one user did not acknowledge the transfer, a red flag would be set in the system and an automatic investigation would be triggered to resolve the apparent discrepancy. Similarly, any attempt to use a fraudulent registration number would trigger an automatic investigation.

Under law, the registrar would be neither required *nor permitted* to transfer data about a particular gun, or about the assignment of responsibility for that gun, to the government unless the information was requested through a valid warrant, identifying a specific investigation of a specific crime in which the gun was identified to have been used. Such requests would typically identify the gun either by serial number or by ballistic signature; the registrar would be required to provide the capability of searching their database for a specific gun using either method of identification.

Under law, the registrar would be neither required *nor permitted* to transfer data about an individual registrant except upon receipt of a subsequent valid warrant identifying a specific investigation of a specific crime in which a specific gun, verified to have been their responsibility, was confirmed to have been used.

Except as retained in the records of a specific investigation that led to an actual criminal charge, government agencies would not be allowed to retain the information about individual guns and/or registrants obtained from the registry for more than 3 months after it was obtained.

The general intent of this quasi-anonymous registry is to give law enforcement the tools it needs to investigate and prosecute genuine criminal behavior that threatens both individuals and society, while minimizing the potential for abuse of individual rights. It acknowledges that guns are, indeed, uniquely dangerous tools and places a high legal burden on gun owners to take responsibility for how their guns are used, either by themselves or by others. It documents a chain of responsibility for those tools that can only be broken by explicitly illegal activity. And it protects the privacy of gun owners, and limits the ability of the government to persecute them, by building a double wall between them and their government interrogators: a private entity, chartered to protect gun owners' rights, to stand as the gatekeeper between the government and information about individuals; and a two-step process of obtaining and presenting warrants in order for the government to acquire information from the registrar.

In a perfect world, the right to keep and bear arms would not be controversial because no one would misuse their arms to prey upon others. Of course, in a perfect world, and for the same reason, no one would have much of a need to keep and bear arms in the first place.

Alas, we do not live in that perfect world. In the world we live in, our collective propensity toward violence makes the underlying desire for the autonomy those rights provide seem even more urgent; and, yet, that propensity also makes the widespread exercise of those rights seem ever more dangerous. That danger will continue to feed the urge to make ourselves safer by curtailing those rights at every opportunity.

But, imagine if those defending their rights, instead of asserting the authority of the 2nd Amendment, instead of asserting their natural right to self-protection, took the position that this was their problem to solve. What if the NRA, rather than merely obstructing any attempt to limit the use of guns, took on the responsibility for making all gun use responsible gun use? What if gun owners and would-be gun owners stood up and said, "*This is on us. We want the freedom; we have to accept the responsibility that goes with it.*"

How would that change the debate?

The Death Penalty

Ten years ago, as the Governor of Massachusetts, Mitt Romney submitted a bill to the state legislature to reintroduce the death penalty after a hiatus of over 120 years. Sensitive to recent death row exonerations that had led, among other actions, to a moratorium on executions in Illinois and to a broad national discussion about the reliability of convictions in capital murder cases, the proposed bill was intended to protect against the possibility that the innocent would be inadvertently executed. As reported by The *Boston Globe* at the time, the bill required extraordinary levels of "verifiable scientific evidence" (like identifiable DNA that linked the accused to the crime scene) and a "no doubt" standard of guilt before the death penalty could be imposed.

The flurry of activity surrounding the death penalty in recent years has come at a policy conjunction. On the one hand, a generally 'conservative' attitude toward crime and punishment has been ascendant, engendered in part by legitimate anxiety, by a sense that *acts* of violence — both domestic and foreign — are becoming more random and by a sense that the *perpetrators* of violence are becoming less civil and less humane, are at times not even recognizably human. That makes the death penalty generally more popular among politicians and the electorate. On the other hand, death penalty opponents have shifted their focus away from the basic morality of the death sentence itself and toward the inherent fallibility of the justice system, toward the very real moral risk of an unjust execution.

Those two trends correspond to two divergent moral themes: a socially moral desire that justice be adequate to the harm caused by a callous disregard for life — that we acknowledge and signify the depth of moral depravity in the act of murder by imposing a sanction of equal moral gravity — and the politically moral mandate that justice be deferential to the harm created by the potential for error or malice, to the injustice of a misguided prosecution of the innocent by the organs of political power.

In responding to those themes, Governor Romney was attempting to give us the moral benefit of a death penalty without the moral hazard. Thus the proposal was carefully structured to be "virtually foolproof," with extraordinarily high evidentiary thresholds and a standard of guilt that seems to leave no room for doubt.

But, despite the care taken to eliminate error, even Romney admitted that it could not provide a guarantee against mistakes under some "extreme circumstances." Even if it made the problem of wrongful execution less severe it did not eliminate it entirely.

That is a fundamental problem, for that and for the death penalty statutes in other states and at the federal level. For, in truth, even if you believe in the inherent justice of a death penalty for crimes against life, the prospect of making a mistake in a capital case — the prospect of executing an innocent human being — is not a minor consideration that may be brushed casually aside by resort to some statistical assurance. That it "hardly ever happens" is not a good enough standard. If innocent human life is, indeed, so sacred that justice demands execution for those who would obliterate it, then the injustice of a single wrongful execution must weigh more heavily than the injustice of a few, or even a few hundred or a few million, murderers escaping their rightful fates — especially if an approximately just alternative like imprisonment is available for them.

Even the utilitarian argument that the death penalty will deter more innocent deaths by murder than it will create by wrongful execution — and even assuming that such an argument is supported by solid evidence — cannot negate the moral affront created by the execution of someone convicted wrongly. To presume that it does is to fall into the trap of socialistic idealism (either of the left or of the right): that in the name of some greater and prophesied social good we may and should sacrifice the individual with impunity.

Of course, any punishment imposes a cost on the punished, so one might make the same argument against lesser penalties or against the very notion of a penal system. But society must have a way to deal with harmful and predatory behavior, and realistically that must involve some form of penalty for the predators — and some risk that those penalties will be mistakenly applied to the innocent.

The difference, in contemplating the death penalty, is that death is irrevocable and incompensable. If we find we have wrongfully imprisoned someone we cannot give them back the years we have taken, but we can at least restore their freedom and award them something of value to compensate — to "make up" for those years. But we cannot restore life to the wrongly executed and there is neither anything of sufficient value, nor any meaningful mechanism by which to award it, that could compensate for the life we have taken.

If a residual potential for error is enough to undermine Governor Romney's proposal — or any similar proposal — on grounds of harm to the innocent, the mechanisms provided to minimize that potential undermine it in a more fundamental way: they make it so difficult to impose the penalty that it utterly fails to provide the primary justice for which it is intended.

That failure manifests in two ways. First, if justice truly demands a death penalty for certain crimes, then a death penalty rarely applied to those crimes must deny justice in the cases for which it cannot be imposed. In a sense that is worse than having no death penalty at all: where we ought consistently to emphasize the moral severity of crimes that would merit the death penalty, we, instead, symbolically devalue both the crimes and the victims in those cases for which the death penalty may not be applied by contrasting them with those few cases in which it is. A death penalty that cannot be consistently applied is, thus, morally counter-productive.

Worse, in the name of emphasizing the moral repugnance of murder, such a death penalty instead, through its restrictive rules, does exactly the opposite: it makes punishment contingent on the quality of the evidence available for prosecution rather than on the nature of the crime itself. In effect, death becomes the penalty not for the crime of murder but for the crime of sloppiness and/or stupidity — for leaving sufficient incriminating evidence in your wake. That not only subverts the moral connection between punishment and culpability, but it ensures that application of the death penalty would be both rare and capricious, and therefore in the sense of "equal treatment under the law," unjust and unfair.

Thus, while the intent of Mitt Romney and those like him may be honorable, in practice such proposals give us the worst possible outcome: a death penalty that would be so sparsely and unevenly imposed that it could not but fail to serve justice; and, yet, the lingering (if remote) prospect that this fallible human institution would, nonetheless, fail to protect the innocent from its irrevocable judgment.

It would seem this contradiction is too fundamental to resolve. Human institutions are prone to error; and attempts to eliminate errors tend to render them inert. Does this mean there is no way to serve the interests of justice on both counts? No. There is an alternative.

To come to that alternative, we must recognize that the moral purpose of a death penalty is symbolic, not practical. Execution is no more effective at protecting society from murderous recidivism than is indefinite incarceration. And, notwithstanding the arguments of some death penalty proponents, justified concerns with wrongful execution increasingly preclude any significant deterrent benefit from the death penalty: even in Texas, which notoriously and by far leads the nation in executions, practical constraints on application of the death sentence ensured that only about one in 50 murders were punished by execution over the last 5 years; the Illinois and Massachusetts examples show that nationwide and in the future that number can only decrease even as the death penalty gains support. If the chance of actually being executed for committing murder is less than two percent (and falling) — and if the "lenient" alternative is a lifetime in prison — then how much deterrence can execution realistically offer?

But the fact that the death penalty is fundamentally symbolic does not make it either inappropriate or futile. Symbols matter, and the psychological and social and cultural effects of moral symbols can transform the human world. A burning cross rarely does much physical damage, nor does a burning American flag; a swastika scrawled on a door or a wall is easily removed; neither the Confederate battle flag nor the Hammer and Sickle stir more than a bit of air in any immediate practical sense. Significance is not to be found in the symbols themselves or in their immediate and incidental effects, but in the memes that they embody and in their ability to arouse passions around those memes.

The meme coded into the death penalty is the moral principle of proportionality in both retribution and contrition — the principle that moral justice demands penalties morally commensurate with the sins for which they are imposed. That is distinct from the political requirement for justice — that the justice system and the penalties it imposes be sufficient to promote individual safety and communal order, either by deterring criminal behavior or by separating the criminal from society. In the political sense, a sentence of a lifetime in prison for committing murder adequately serves society's need for justice; in the moral sense, it is disproportionate and therefore unjust, demeaning both of the victim's loss and of the perpetrator's corruption.

That moral principle is, of course, at the root of the dispute over the need for a death penalty: death penalty opponents simply reject the moral imperative. For them, the requirements of political justice are not only necessary but sufficient and, in the absence of moral imperative, execution in the name of justice is merely another form of murder. For proponents of the death penalty, the imperative to moral proportionality demands death for death; and moral culpability transforms execution from murder into a just reckoning. It is neither my intent nor within my grasp to resolve that dispute here. But if we presume, as Romney and others have, that the death penalty is morally desirable, it is so as a symbol of proportionality not as a practical policy of political justice.

Given that the moral purpose of the death penalty is its symbolic import, we can formulate an alternative death penalty that both preserves that purpose and protects the innocent from unjust execution. The key is to separate the sentence of death from the implementation of that sentence. The imposition of a death sentence communicates our moral intent; the execution of the condemned merely closes the account.

To that end, I propose the following implementation of the death penalty:

- Prescribe a sentence of death for appropriate crimes against innocent life. Such sentences attach to the nature of the crime, not in any way to the evidence at hand or to the sympathy with which we view the defendant.
- Impose the death sentence in the same manner and under the same rules as any other punishment — upon conviction for certain crimes under normal rules of evidence and beyond a reasonable doubt.
- Place those who have been so condemned, as we do now, on "death row," where they sit indefinitely awaiting our final act of judgment.
- As a matter of policy — and as a reflection of our own need for surety in our judgment, not as a form of mercy — prescribe as our method of execution to *let nature take its course*. In other words, instead of, "death by lethal injection," or "death by hanging," let the sentence be, "death by old age."

This rather obviously ensures there would be no unjust executions of the innocent, inasmuch as there would be no executions of anyone. The immediate objection to this is, of course, that a death penalty without an execution is no death penalty at all — it is merely "life in prison" dressed up in a rhetorical flourish. What would be the point? But this scheme offers both moral and practical advantages over the alternative of a life sentence.

First and foremost, it allows us the luxury of moral clarity: it allows us to put the focus of justice on the crime rather than on the process of the prosecution; it allows us to pass honest moral judgment on the crime without inciting a conflict over the potential failings of our legal institutions; relieved of the responsibility for avoiding irrevocable errors, it allows us to focus on what constitutes appropriate retribution for unforgivable crimes — and to proclaim our moral revulsion without reservation; and it allows us to reserve our moral right to impose such sanctions even if we choose not to do so. In other words, it allows us the moral benefit of a symbolic execution even if the practical limits of a fallible human justice system preclude a tangible one.

Further, because the sentence imposed is death rather than incarceration — incarceration is merely the incidental effect of awaiting execution — there can be no question of parole or of time off or of furlough or of privileges for behaving civilly while in prison. Death row is not the destination from which one may be given relief; it is merely an interminable stop along the way.

As a practical matter, the routine nature of the rules of evidence and standards of guilt under which this death sentence may be imposed also allows us to apply the death penalty in a manner truly equitable and just — or at least as equitable and just as for any other facet of our system of justice. And it reduces the compulsion to litigate death sentences for decades over due process minutiae, because the proximate practical result is not irrevocable. Hence it is not only just, it is efficient.

One final practical advantage to this scheme — one that may be included or omitted without affecting its basic structure — is that it allows a potential disciplinary lever over those on death row. Although the scheme prescribes old age as the standard executioner of choice, it would be a simple matter to define special circumstances under which a more immediate execution method could be applied. In particular, the presumption that a life sentence satisfies the political needs of justice is based, in part, on an assumption that those serving such a sentence cannot constitute an ongoing threat to society. It would be perfectly reasonable to accelerate execution for those who, despite their imprisonment, demonstrate that they represent an ongoing risk — those who, for instance, attack their guards or other inmates while in prison, or perhaps those who remove themselves from supervision by escaping. If the punishment for such threatening acts was the activation of an otherwise deferred death sentence, the incentive for good behavior would be severe. And, under those circumstances, there would be no mistaken executions of the innocent: the penalties would accrue specifically to the crimes committed within the prison environment and, given the high level of supervision and the small community of potential suspects, there could be no meaningful doubt about guilt or innocence in such cases.

By focusing on the symbolic import of a death sentence, rather than on the practical exigencies of execution, we can take a moral stand against the most heinous of crimes and still protect the innocent against the vagaries of mistaken executions. Those who favor the death penalty could have the moral import of the death sentence, but without the act of execution; those who oppose the death penalty could abolish executions, but without eliminating that moral statement of proportionality.

Perhaps that is a compromise both can agree — uncomfortably — to support.

WHAT NOW?

In Defense of Moderation

If a man goes into the street to mug another man at gun-point, that is robbery. If a group of such people get together and systematically rob those they encounter that is a gang, and we call it banditry. If the group, having grown to encompass over half the population of the town, moves *en masse* through the streets looting houses and demanding money of whomever it encounters, that is a mob or a riot.

But if that group, instead, goes into the voting booth and passes a law authorizing the government to take the money on their behalf — in the form of taxes and under threat of violence to be applied by the police as arrest and imprisonment — that is modern 'liberalism.'

That is also dramatic overstatement. It sounds like a rhetorical coda to some right-wing manifesto. But it is precisely the failure of many, if not most, modern 'liberals' either to acknowledge any philosophical limits on the authority of government to tax in the name of the "public good" or to acknowledge the fundamental fairness and morality of demanding such limits, that makes this brand of 'liberalism' a threat to liberty.

Daniel Webster famously said that the power to tax is the power to destroy.[1] For many decades it has been the philosophy and policy of the American Left to

---

1 The actual quotation, from Daniel Webster's argument before the Supreme Court in *McCullogh v. Maryland* (1819), is: "An unlimited power to tax involves, necessarily, a power to destroy." Chief Justice John Marshall concurred in the written decision for the case, stating "That the power to tax involves the power to destroy...[is] not to be denied."

deny that maxim, to assume economic liberty is distinct from and of lesser substance than — and, therefore, less important than — political liberty. They presume that political liberty is defined by a sacred right to conscience, while economic liberty derives from the merest craving for grubby and inconsequential desire. They presume that any objection to infringing economic liberty in the name of the public good must arise from the basest of motives and need not be taken seriously. They presume that any call for limits on that infringement may be simply dismissed as morally hollow and socially repellant.

But in practical terms, without such limits what is democratic government but a collective mechanism for unfettered economic coercion — a formalized mob, what P.J. O'Rourke called a "Parliament of Whores"?[1] And what is the U.S. Bill of Rights — and all the more modern extensions and customizations which we call collectively "civil rights" law — if not a statement and celebration of precisely those limits in all areas *not* economic? We often forget — most people probably never knew — that Robin Hood was not stealing from the rich to give to the poor; he was stealing back from the government what it had illegitimately taken. Robin Hood was a tax protester, a crusader against government rapacity.

If you had to simplify and summarize the entirety of 'conservatism' in a single precept it would probably be the recognition of the need for boundaries and limits: boundaries between good and bad, between right and wrong, between acceptable and unacceptable; limits on human understanding and human virtue; boundaries between reason and emotion, between knowledge and ignorance; limits on human control over nature and over other humans; boundaries between private and public; limits on personal behavior and on the rate of social change; boundaries between civil and political, between society and government; limits on government authority and on government spending. 'Conservatives' intuitively understand that boundaries, both conceptual and practical, are what separate the good from the extreme. 'Conservatives' intuitively understand that limits, both moral and institutional, are what stop our good intentions from becoming paving stones on a road that leads us, inadvertently but inevitably, into hell.

Modern 'conservatism' — despite the evidence of its many ignorant, closed-minded, and clamorous devotees — is fundamentally an intellectual philosophy. Modern liberalism is, by contrast and notwithstanding its academic sheen, fundamentally an emotional one.

'Liberalism' observes that it is not "fair" that some people have a lot while others have only a little and proposes, since there are a lot of us (with

---

1 In his eponymously-named book.

less than we want) and not many of them (with more than they "need" or "deserve"), that we should just take their stuff and distribute it to ourselves to make us all equal. 'Liberalism' observes that certain people are mean and make other people feel bad by what they say, so it proposes to outlaw meanness by prohibiting mean speech. 'Liberalism' observes that people are less healthy if they eat certain foods, so it proposes to make us all healthy by prohibiting the sale of those foods. 'Liberalism' observes that people fall into conflict when they misunderstand or disrespect one another and conclude that conflict is the result of misunderstanding and disrespect; so they focus their attempts at diplomacy on the conversation, rather than on the result, downplaying real and irreconcilable differences in goals and interests. 'Liberalism' observes that moral and cultural choices far from the moral and cultural norm lead to marginalization and distress, so it proposes curing that distress by eliminating norms entirely and declaring all choices to be morally and culturally equal.

In other words, 'liberalism' is about making people feel better, right now and in the simplest, most direct manner. It is dominated by "all things being equal" thinking: all things being equal, if I do this then I will get that. It appears much less concerned with — sometimes seemingly oblivious to — what happens later as the inevitable unintended side-effects and consequences pile up.

'Conservatism,' on the other hand, acknowledges that all things are never equal — that when I do this I probably won't get that because I will also change something else in between; and, at any rate, doing this is going to cost us something. 'Conservatism' looks at the proposal to redistribute from the rich to the poor and concludes not only that it is an abridgement of liberty but that it is the rich who are, in general, most productive, that, if you remove their reward, they will have no incentive to continue to be productive and we will all be poorer. 'Conservatism' looks at the proposal to prohibit mean speech and foresees a time when the definition of what is "mean" comes to include anything and everything the censors disagree with, that my "mean" will, at some point, be your "sincere." 'Conservatism' looks at proposals to ban certain products that have been deemed to be "bad for us" and wonders whether the liberty to do only those things approved as "good for us" is any kind of liberty at all. 'Conservatism' looks at "confidence building" exercises and the "peace process" and observes that none of those will get past the fundamental problem that one side believes the other side should utterly cease to exist. 'Conservatism' looks at moral relativism, at the destruction of mores and cultural norms, and sees not a society without conflict but a society that is headed toward balkanization and disintegration.

In other words, 'conservatism' is about "what happens next?," about thinking through the secondary and tertiary consequences of changes, the ripples they will make throughout society as they alter the ways people relate to each other and the ways in which they are encouraged in or discouraged from pursuing their interests.

When you think about it, it's rather amazing that 'conservatives' can ever win any election. 'Liberals' are offering to give you something for nothing and to make you feel good; 'conservatives' are trying to rain on your parade. Why *would* you vote for them?

If we are honest with ourselves, we have to acknowledge it is not because 'conservatives' convince a large number of voters to think through the likely consequences of 'liberal' proposals. Deep thought has not been a prominent feature of recent elections. It is more likely 'conservatives' win, when they win, because what 'liberals' propose is as frightening as it is enticing, frightening because it demands changing things in some dramatic and disruptive way. Security is as much a primal motivator as aspiration, and the accusation that 'conservatism' is an ideology of fear is, perhaps, closer to truth than many 'conservatives' care to admit. If 'conservatism' is not an ideology of fear then it is, at least, an ideology of caution and prudence.

But the modern guises of 'conservatism' and of 'liberalism' are often, despite contrary accusations, less ideological than practical. Opposing abortion is not an ideological position; it is an agenda. Opponents know abortion — and contraception and sexuality — is wrong largely because God said so: what they are asserting is not so much a fetus' "right to life" as God's jurisdiction over life; the language of "rights" has been grafted onto that as a convenient way to frame the political debate. Similarly, proponents of a "right to choose" rarely think of that right in abstract terms: they often *oppose* the right to choose other equally personal things, like how much you may charge for your labor and pay for someone else's, or whether or not you may say something mean to someone else, or whether or not you may take a particular medicine, or whether or not you will wear a seatbelt, or whether or not you may smoke a cigarette or overdose on sugary soda. Rather, they want abortion to be an available option for smoothing out a particular rough patch in their lives and have identified some ideological language to justify that desire.

'Liberals' defend offensive speech right up to the point that speech offends them. 'Conservatives' defend welfare for business but not for people. 'Liberals' espouse "tolerance" until they find something intolerable. 'Conservatives' espouse "family values" but only for families whose values mimic their own. 'Liberals' condemn sexual harassment unless Bill Clinton is the harasser. 'Conservatives' defend deference to presidential authority until Barack Obama exercises that authority.

A great part of the reason for this springs from the foundational modern 'liberal' ideal now embedded firmly in our culture: that government should be in the business of redistributing resources and controlling people's behavior. For, if the government is taking and giving, if the government is choosing sides and enforcing belief systems, rather than merely refereeing the contest, rather than merely stopping us from bullying each other, then it is no longer enough, in defending your interests, to *influence* the government. You must *control* it because, otherwise, it will control you. Politics is no longer about organizing principles. It is about protecting your own and grabbing as much as you can.

For the last 30 years or more, the primary electoral message, the primary appeal to voters, from both of our major political parties has been, "If you vote for me, I will give you something and make someone else pay for it!" That something, and the cost, could be economic or cultural, visceral or intellectual, physical or spiritual but, whatever it is, it is wrapped in both a promise and a threat. For the accompanying warning, implied by that appeal, is, "If you vote for my opponent, he will give *someone else* something and make *you* pay for it!" Someone will win and someone else will lose. There is no draw, and there is no way for everyone to win at least a little.

That is the corrupting effect of a political philosophy that sees government as society's caretaker and disciplinarian: elections must, inevitably, become contests over who gets which part of the pie and who gets told what to do; people must be classified and categorized so we can distinguish between those who will receive and those who will give, between those who get to command and those who must obey; and positions must become ever more polarized and rigid because the winners get not only to govern, but to rule.

Where are those who remember that a democracy is supposed to be about consensus, not about compulsion, that we elect a President, not a King?

And, when I vote, why must I choose between someone who favors social Darwinism and someone who thinks the Law of Supply and Demand can be repealed? Why must I choose between someone who favors a global Manifest Destiny and someone who thinks that the primary goal of collective security is "the collective" rather than "security"? Why must I choose between someone who wants to use the government to impose his personal moral code on the rest of us and someone who wants to deny that there is any such thing as objective morality? Why must I choose between someone who thinks profit is the primary measure of good and someone who thinks profit is morally repugnant? If I want to respect traditions and institutions, why must I vote for religious fundamentalism? If I want to provide a social safety net for the downtrodden, why must I vote to demolish Capitalism? If I acknowledge that there are things that could be better about America, why must I vote for those who refuse to see anything good? If I want to praise and defend America's virtues, why must I vote for those are utterly and willfully blind to its flaws?

In other words, where is the middle?

There is an axiom in computing, written into the earliest networking specifications,[1] called the "Robustness Principle," otherwise known as "Postel's Law" after its author, Jon Postel. Although it was formulated for a narrow technical purpose, its message offers a surprisingly good rule of thumb for most things in life:

> "Be conservative in what you do, be liberal in what you accept."

Be conservative in what you do: In your speech, in your behavior, in your requests, strive to understand what others need, want, and expect; try to accommodate them if they are being reasonable.

Be liberal in what you will accept: Be tolerant in evaluating others' speech, others' behavior, others' requests; try to accommodate them even if they don't perfectly match your needs, wants, and expectations.

That doesn't mean ascetic restraint and heroic tolerance. That doesn't mean you should accede to *unreasonable* demands or countenance *unreasonable* behavior and speech. Society, like the internet, breaks down and fragments when too many people fail to follow its standards and abide by its rules. And no one wants to be the good guy who always finishes last.

But it means you should do your best to be reasonable. It means you should keep an open mind. Be cooperative. Neither take offense nor give it. Be flexible. Give the other guy the benefit of the doubt. Don't ask for too much or give too little. Do your best, but pardon others if their best is less than you wanted. Don't judge a man until you've walked a mile in his shoes. Forgive us our trespasses, as we forgive those who trespass against us....

In all things, moderation.

Moderation used to be a conservative virtue. Moderates recoil at tyranny, even at a tyranny of the majority. Moderates refuse to use a slim electoral victory as an opportunity and excuse for imposing their view of the world and their program for salvation upon everyone. Moderates remember when "bipartisan" meant "work it out," not "agree to my demands." Moderates understand that compromise is an act of equalization, of acknowledging opponents not merely as intellectual or material or moral *adversaries* but also

---

1 "TCP implementations should follow a general principle of robustness: be conservative in what you do, be liberal in what you accept from others," from section 2.10 of RFC793, *Transmission Control Protocol*, September 1981   .

as people with moral worth, as people with legitimate interests, viewpoints, and desires.

Of course principle is principle, and compromise can reasonably go only so far. But it can go *somewhere*. Even if you have the strength of conviction, even if you believe you are right, both doubting your own infallibility and accommodating alternate viewpoints are valuable, legitimate, and honorable approaches to political affairs — and essential to the functioning of democratic government. In a constitutional democracy, elections are not supposed to be about determining who will get to impose their will on us for the next term of office. They are supposed to be about choosing who will lead, who will speak for our beliefs; and they are supposed to be about measuring both the width and depth of those beliefs, about telling our leaders how enthusiastically we choose to follow.

In our current political climate, "moderate" has become an epithet and an insult. But indecisive panderers are not moderate and moderates — either 'conservative' or 'liberal' — are not indecisive panderers. Moderates are those who remember that Republicans were originally republican and Democrats were originally democratic. They are those who believe that the duty of one who would govern is to represent the interests of his or her constituents — of *all* constituents — and not merely to accede, untroubled by conscience, to the dictate of the majority. They are those who remember that government *"derive[s] its just powers from the consent of the governed,"* from the consent of *all* the governed and not merely from those who voted for the winning side in the last election.

One of the biggest problems we face at this moment in the American political saga is that we act and debate as if there were only one, monolithic 'conservatism' and only one, monolithic 'liberalism,' and that those two monoliths are striving for a final victory in some kind of political death-match. Our political parties, the mainstream media, and our fractured online communities-of-interest encourage and reinforce that view until we can no longer tell, by what they say or with whom they associate or even by what they might have done in the past, what *kind* of 'conservative' or what *kind* of 'liberal' stands before us bribing us for our vote. We are asked to vote for and against caricatures, not candidates.

Most people have 'veto' issues — issues they use to disqualify candidates — even if they are not strictly single-issue voters. Thus, feminists tend to disqualify candidates who oppose abortion rights; fiscal 'conservatives' tend to disqualify candidates who propose new spending; African Americans tend to disqualify candidates who are hostile to affirmative-action or friendly to policies perceived as racially tainted; Hispanic voters tend to disqualify candidates who want tighter controls on immigration; and so on. If you can't tell which part of 'liberalism' or 'conservatism' a candidate really represents, you don't know with certainty where he or she stands on your veto issues — so you must either assume the worst or risk the worst. Even if you agree with most of what a candidate seems to stand for, if you disagree on your veto issue — or if you are afraid, because he is one of "them," that he is lying about your veto issue as an electoral stratagem — your vote goes elsewhere.

That is why it is so important to see both 'liberalism' and 'conservatism' for what they are: fractious aggregations of disparate values, beliefs, traditions, ambitions, and desires; evolving coalitions of disparate groups with overlapping but divergent interests. They are not monoliths. They are not even consistent. Mitt Romney, whatever he really is, is not Sarah Palin. John Boehner is not Ted Cruz. George Bush is not Adolph Hitler. And no, Barack Obama is not Karl Marx.

If we want the kind of government that can once again solve problems, if we want the kind of culture that feels like an integrated whole instead of a fractious collection of tribes, we must look beyond 'conservative' and 'liberal' to their components. We must find the things we have in common, the things we can use as points of agreement and as bases for negotiating accords. There are many things on which 'conservatives' and 'liberals' could agree, or on which they could at least do some serious horse-trading, if they would look honestly and fairly both at others' beliefs and at their own.

That is my charge, to both 'conservatives' and 'liberals': think about what you really believe. I doubt there are many 'conservatives' who agree with every item in my list of 'conservative' principles with equal vigor; and I'll bet there are many 'liberals' who find things in that list they find agreeable to one degree or another. So, which of the things — and which things in some equivalent list of 'liberal' principles — do you agree with? Which ones do you dispute? And, just as importantly, why? What kind of 'conservative' or 'liberal' are you?

And what can you agree on? Let's start a conversation there.

BIBLIOGRAPHY

Atwood, Margaret. *The Handmaid's Tale*. Boston: Houghton Mifflin, 1986

Boaz, David. *Libertarianism: A Primer*. New York: The Free Press, 1998

Burke, Edmund. *A Vindication of Natural Society: A View of the Miseries and Evils Arising To Mankind*. London: M. Cooper, 1756

Burke, Edmund. *A Philosophical Enquiry Into the Origin of Our Ideas of the Sublime and Beautiful*. 3rd Ed. London: R. & J. Dodsley, 1761

Campos, Paul F. *Jurismania: the Madness of American Law*. Oxford: Oxford University Press, 1998

Constitution of the United States. Philadelphia, PA: the Philadelphia Convention, 17 Sep 1787

Dalrymple, Theodore. *Life at the Bottom: The Worldview That Makes the Underclass*. Chicago: Ivan R. Dee, 2001

Dunne, Finley Peter. *Observations by Mr. Dooley*. New York: Harper & Brothers, 1902

Eisen, Lauren-Brooke and Oliver Roeder. "America's Faulty Perception of Crime." *Brennan Center for Justice*, 16 March 2015

Eisenhower, Dwight D. *Farewell Address*. Televised 17 January 1961.

Emery, Noemie. "Greed, Oppression, Patriarchy." *The Weekly Standard*, 20 January 2003, Vol. 8 No. 18.

Figgis, J.N. and R.V. Laurence, eds. "Letter to Bishop Mandell Creighton from Lord Acton". *Historical Essays and Studies*. New York: Macmillan, 1907.

Frank, Thomas. *What's the Matter with Kansas? How Conservatives Won the Heart of America.* New York: Owl Books, 2005

Friedman, Milton. *Capitalism and Freedom.* Chicago: University of Chicago Press, 1962

Friedman, Milton and Rose Friedman. *Free to Choose: A Personal Statement,* New York: Harvest - Harcourt, 1990

Golding, William. *Lord of the Flies.* London: Faber and Faber, 1954

Goldwater, Barry. *The Conscience of a Conservative.* Shepherdsville, KY: Victor Publishing Co., 1960

Haidt, Jonathan. *The Righteous Mind: Why Good People are Divided By Politics and Religion.* New York: Vintage Books, 2012

Hardin, Garret. "The Tragedy of the Commons." *Science,* 13 December 1968, vol. 162. Issue 3859: pp. 1243-1248

Hayek, F.A. *The Road to Serfdom.* Chicago: The University of Chicago Press, 1944

Hayek, F.A. *The Fatal Conceit: The Errors of Socialism.* Chicago: The University of Chicago Press, 1989

Hirsch, E.D. *Cultural Literacy: What Every American Needs To Know.* New York: Vintage Books, 1988

Howard, Philip K. *The Death of Common Sense: How Law is Suffocating America.* New York: Random House, 1995

Jefferson, Thomas. *Notes on the State of Virginia.* London: John Stockdale, 1787

Knight, Douglas A. and Amy-Jill Levine. *The Meaning of the Bible: What the Jewish Scriptures and Christian Old Testament Can Teach Us.* New York: HarperOne, 2011

Kresge, Stephen and Leif Wenar, eds. *Hayek on Hayek: An Autobiographical Dialogue.* Chicago: University of Chicago Press, 1994

Locke, John. *A Letter Concerning Toleration.* London: Awnsham Churchill, 1689

Locke, John. *Two Treatises of Government.* London: Awnsham Churchill, 1690

Marx, Karl and Friedrich Engels. *The Communist Manifesto.* New York: Washington Square Press, 1964

Official Report, The House Of Commons (5th Series), 11 November 1947, vol. 444; speech by Winston Churchill

Olson, Walter K. *The Litigation Explosion: What Happened When America Unleashed The Lawsuit.* New York: Truman Talley Books - Dutton, 1991

O'Rourke, P.J. *Parliament of Whores: A Lone Humorist Attempts to Explain the Entire U.S. Government.* New York: The Atlantic Monthly Press, 1991

Orwell, George. *Animal Farm*. London: Secker & Warburg, 1945

Orwell, George. *Nineteen Eighty-Four*. London: Secker & Warburg, 1949

Postol, Jon, ed. *RFC793, Transmission Control Protocol*. Arlington, VA: Defense Advanced Research Projects Agency (DARPA), 1981.

Publius. *The Federalist: A Collection of Essays, Written In Favor of the New Constitution, as Agreed by the Federal Convention, September 17, 1787*. New York: J. & A. McLean, 1788

Remseyer, J. Mark and Erik B. Rasmusen. "Comparative Litigation Rates", *Discussion Paper No. 681*, John. M Olin Center for Law, Economics, and Business, 11/2010

Rand, Ayn. *The Virtue of Selfishness*. New York: The New American Library, 1964

Rawls, John. *Justice as Fairness: A Restatement*. Cambridge, MA: The Belknap Press, 2001

Shaw, Bernard. *Pygmalion*. New York: Penguin Books, 1951. Reprint, New York: Penguin Books, 1979.

Sowell, Thomas. *The Vision of the Anointed: Self-Congratulation as a Basis for Social Policy*. New York: Basic Books, 1995

Smith, Adam. *The Theory of Moral Sentiments*. 2nd ed. London & Edinburgh: A. Millar, A. Kincaid & J. Bell, 1759

Smith, Adam. *An Inquiry Into the Nature and Causes of the Wealth of Nations*. London: W.Strahan & T. Cadell, 1776

Storing, Herbert and Murray Dry, Eds. *The Complete Anti-Federalist*. Chicago: University of Chicago Press, 1981

Will, George F. *The Woven Figure: Conservatism and America's Fabric*. New York: Touchstone, 1998

Unanimous Declaration of the Thirteen United States of America. Philadelphia, PA: The American Continental Congress, 4 July, 1776

Index

S

Same-Sex Marriage, 196, 197
Scarcity, 19, 35, 36, 124, 136, 158
Seatbelts, 205, 230, 233
Self-Interest, 15, 16, 21, 31, 40, 50, 64, 66, 76, 81, 95, 120, 125, 137, 139, 143-145, 158, 175
Smith, Adam, 18, 136
Social Norms, 21, 35, 52, 57, 243
Social Responsibility, 50, 88, 152, 170, 183, 184
Social Security, 18, 99, 116, 170, 173, 216-221
Socialism, 10, 84, 98, 100, 101, 107, 108, 114, 116, 118, 205
Society, 1, 4, 14-18, 20-25, 31, 33, 35-40, 42-44, 49-55, 57, 60-62, 67-70, 73-76, 80-84, 88, 90, 94, 95, 98-103, 105, 108, 109, 111-119, 122, 127, 129, 130, 134, 135, 137, 145, 146, 149, 151-153, 157, 162, 163, 171, 173, 179-181, 183-185, 188-190, 192-194, 199, 200, 203-206, 214, 222, 223, 225, 230-233, 236-238, 242, 243, 245, 246, 252, 255, 256, 258, 262-266

Sovereignty, 24, 70, 78-80, 92, 112, 128, 240, 243
Stability, 2, 13, 14, 16, 25, 28-30, 62, 81, 84-86, 100, 109, 110, 113, 115, 118, 139, 151, 182-184, 191, 227
Strict Construction, 206, 208-210
Supply-Side, 120, 145, 146
Supreme Court, 55, 90, 91, 197, 202, 203, 206-209, 214, 239, 245, 249, 261

T

Truth, 10, 15, 17, 19, 20, 33, 34, 36-39, 65, 100, 105, 186, 196, 215, 226, 236, 254, 264

V

Values, 26, 34, 37, 47, 52, 53, 84, 89, 95, 97, 100, 101, 105-107, 110-112, 117, 118, 124, 134, 152-154, 158, 184, 201, 213, 215, 216, 264, 268

Printed in the United States
By Bookmasters